QUOTOONS®

QUOTOONS®

A Speaker's Dictionary
by O. A. Battista

A PERIGEE BOOK

Perigee Books
are published by
G. P. Putnam's Sons
200 Madison Avenue
New York, New York 10016

Library of Congress Cataloging in Publication Data

Battista, Orlando A
    Quotoons: a speaker's dictionary.

    Reprint of the ed. published by Research Services
Corp., Book Pub. Division under title: O. A. Battista's
Quotoons.
    Includes index.
    1. Epigrams. I. Title.
[PN6281.B38 1981]   818′. 5402   80-39716
ISBN 0-399-50514-8 (pbk.)

First Perigee Printing, 1981
Printed in the United States of America

To:

My wife, Helen, and my two children —
William and Elizabeth Ann — who provided
many of the ideas and much of the inspiration
for the best of the original *Quotoons* in this book.

ABILITY

1. Nothing is hard work if you have the ability to get others to do it for you.

ABNORMAL

2. An abnormal person is any one who behaves differently from you.

ABSENCE

3. Absence does not always make you fonder of the absent one — it may only increase one's fondness for the present one.

ACCIDENTS

4. There would be fewer accidents if the law required motorists to own their cars before they could drive them.

5. Some of the most heated highway arguments are started by accident.

ACCORDIAN PLAYER

6. The only fellow who gets anywhere playing both ends against the middle is an accordian player.

ACHIEVEMENT

7. Some men achieve distinction by the kind of car they drive — others by the kind of wife that is driving them.

ACID-TEST

8. The acid-test of a happy marriage is . . . time.

ACTING

9. One time a woman really enjoys acting is when she doesn't let on that she knows what is in the package her husband has hidden from her.

ACTION

10. One sure thing that will make a lazy person "get up and go" is — an urgent call from nature.

11. Sometimes a man of action is one who suddenly gets a severe attack of diarrhea.

12. Sometimes the man of action is a fellow who just got both of his feet in hot water.

13. Nothing turns out to be more satisfying at the end of a day than doing the hardest tasks ahead of you first thing in the morning.

14. Nothing is more contagious than action . . . when it is the boss who shows it.

15. Nothing incites some persons to action like the opportunity to do something wrong.

ADDICTION

16. The most serious habit-forming drug of all is self-esteem!

ADDRESSES

17. One way to discover what a fast moving world we're living in is to notice how many addresses you have to change each time you write Christmas Cards.

ADMIRATION

18. Nothing increases your admiration for a person than

watching him keep his cool while he is being taunted by someone trying hard to heat him up.

19. When it comes to getting into a bathing suit, you have to admire a woman who goes to two pieces.

20. A woman always admires a man standing on his own two feet after he gets up and lets her have his seat.

ADMISSION

21. The surest way to prevent an error from becoming a mistake is to admit it.

22. One nice thing about admitting that you are wrong is it just might be the more accurate thing to do!

ADOLESCENCE

23. Adolescence is that period when a young man would never believe that someday he will become bald.

24. Adolescence is that period when a young man can show you the best crop of hair that he'll ever own.

25. Adolescense is the time of life when a pretty young girl should be afraid of the dark . . . and handsome.

ADULT

26. An adult may see human wisdom manifested in its highest form by watching a child's boundless capacity for ignoring celebrities.

27. An adult is a person who runs the risk of losing his balance when he stands up straight.

28. An adult is a person who has stopped growing at both ends and starts growing in the middle.

29. An adult is a person who starts thinning on the top and thickening in the middle.

30. You can tell when a young man has become an adult —
he starts complaining about taxes.

31. An adult is a person who seldom realizes how lucky he is
not to be an adolescent or senile.

ADULT EDUCATION

32. Most of the wisdom I have I learned not at my mother's
knee — but from my children at my own knee.

ADULTERY

33. Nobody encourages adultery more than a wife who
consistently refuses her own husband's advances.

ADULTS

34. One of the troubles with many adults today is that even
though they don't believe in Santa Claus, they are sitting
around waiting for him to come.

35. The trouble with Santa Claus today is that the adults act
as though he is real, and the children act as though he isn't!

ADVANTAGE

36. The disadvantage of always following the straight and
narrow path in life is that it is the surest way to antagonize
your neighbor.

37. One advantage of being a man is that you don't run the
risk of catching cold in evening clothes.

38. The only time an advantage is a truly enjoyable pleasure is when you know you have it, but choose NOT to use it.

39. The most important advantage that anybody can have in life is freedom from illness.

40. The greatest advantage a man of mediocre talent can have over one of great genius is the ability to make decisions.

41. Beware of being seduced by temporary advantages or successes — they have put 99 percent of the prisoners behind bars.

ADVERSITY

42. The world is filled with people who can take adversity lightly — the other fellow's, that is.

43. Adversity can work wonders in shaping a man's future if it hits him hard enough and early enough in life.

44. There is no more protective umbrella against adversity than knowledge.

ADVICE

45. You can learn a lot of confidential information about a man — by flattering his wife.

46. The trouble with advice is that it is as widely distributed as the air we breathe . . . and usually just as polluted.

47. Trying to give advice to some persons is like giving medicine to children; badly as they need it, they would rather go without it.

48. Never give advice to a woman until she asks for it. By then, she will have made up her mind to reject it anyway.

49. You can learn a lot of confidential information about a man simply by asking him for some advice.

50. To get some people to follow the straight and narrow path, stop giving them advice and start leading the way.

51. If you're wondering what is on another person's mind, just ask him for some advice about a problem of your own.

52. When I give someone a piece of advice and he takes it, I know I have told him exactly what he wanted to hear.

53. Good advice is anything that doesn't stop you from making valuable mistakes.

54. The main reason that advice is cheap is that its supply is always greater than the demand.

AFFECTION

55. Affection may add flavor to a marriage, but it's the cooking that makes it last.

AFTER-DINNER SPEAKER

56. The recipe for being a successful after-dinner speaker includes using plenty of shortening.

AGE

57. Age is so deceiving. It is amazing how much faster 60 comes after 50 compared to 50 after 40!

58. A man is getting old as soon as he decides that it is a lot easier to run a lawnmower over the backyard than it is to plant a garden in it.

59. Nothing makes you resent birthdays like passing life's halfway mark.

60. A man is getting old when he waits in line to take the escalator to the basement floor.

61. A man is getting old when he encourages a woman to go out so that he can have the house to himself.

62. The droop of a man's shoulders is proportional to the weight of the chip he carries on them.

63. A man is getting old when he starts to ring for the elevator to the second floor.

64. A man is as old as he feels on a beautiful weekend.

65. All too often the only thing time does to the human head is to make it whiter and smoother.

66. When it comes to lengthening your life, it's hard to beat slowing up the gait at which you take it.

67. A man is as old as he feels when he gets up from his knees after weeding his garden.

68. People are like plants — some go to seed with age, others to pot.

69. One of the greatest pleasures from growing old is the freedom you enjoy from life insurance salesmen.

70. How old you really are depends on how many birthdays you're still looking forward to.

71. Nobody is harder on a woman's age than another woman guessing it.

AGE OF REASON

72. Most persons fail to reach the age of reason until they have lost all of their money and their health.

AGING

73. Some women who refuse to grow old do a mighty good job of working hard at trying to stay young.

74. A man knows that age is creeping up on him when he gets all upset because he cannot find his glasses — and all he did was rest them on his forehead.

75. I pity any person of 90 who reaches it with nothing more to show than how pleased he is to have reached it.

AGING RESEARCH

76. The best justification I can think of for supporting aging research is that I can't think of a better way to overcome the profit-motives of undertakers.

AGREEMENT

77. As soon as you observe that everyone agrees with you, you can be sure they don't really mean it.

78. As soon as you notice that everyone has started to agree with you, you had better amend your dictatorial ways.

AIM

79. All through life, it is better to have a good aim than to be loaded down with ammunition.

AIRPLANE

80. An airplane is a place where you can open your soul to the person next to you and forget who it was by the time you collect your baggage.

AIR TRAVEL

81. One of the most satisfying sights during air travel is the one when you arrive at the baggage claim location and spot your luggage.

ALARM

82. When a man becomes alarmed at what his wife is wearing it usually is because she is wearing too little, or something he doesn't know how much she paid for it.

83. No one is more prone to view things with alarm than those who enjoy viewing things with alarm.

ALARM CLOCK

84. A day isn't long enough for some persons to get rid of the dirty look they gave their alarm clock on getting up.

85. Too many people lose an argument with an alarm clock because they take it lying down.

ALCOHOL

86. Alcohol is an extremely stable chemical — until you drink it.

87. Nothing is more soluble in alcohol than a man's conscience.

AMAZEMENT

88. It amazes me how women who detested arithmetic in high school can get so much pleasure out of counting calories.

AMBITION

89. A cemetery is a place where a lot of over-ambitious young men come to a dead stop.

90. Too many people in this world sit back and expect the grass to grow under their feet even though they didn't plant any seeds.

91. How long a shadow that is cast by ambition is far more significant than what one's track record is to date.

92. People who do things because they have to are a dime a dozen; the ones who get ahead are those who do things because they don't have to.

AMERICA

93. America is the only country in the world where a man can afford to build a four-bedroom house by the time all of his children are old enough to go to college.

94. There are two things in America that are growing bigger together-garbage cans and taxes.

95. What America really needs is more young people who will carry to their jobs the same enthusiasm for getting ahead that they display in traffic.

96. America is the only country in the world where a man can build a three car garage and fill it with cars he doesn't own.

97. Some of the most impressive cars driven in America are really owned by finance companies.

98. The most accurate fortune tellers in America are full-time employees of the Internal Revenue Service.

99. In America when something becomes "popularly priced," it simply means that millions who can't afford it are buying it.

100. America is an enigma in that its people can exhibit such extremes of thoughtfulness and thoughtlessness.

101. America is the only country in the world where the people who can think and the people who can't think pay about the same amount of taxes.

102. Anybody can become a success in America if he's willing to work while nearly everybody else is killing time.

103. Anyone can become wealthy in America by inventing something useful that has a short use-expectancy.

104. America is the only country in the world where so much is printed and said about exercise and so much effort is expended to make it as easy as possible to avoid.

105. America is still the land of opportunity for any young man who can invent a new way for people to do nothing.

106. If America is to survive, union labor leaders must remember that it cannot do so without plenty of hard work by their members.

107. A badly needed invention in America today is some kind of dough that really sticks to your fingers.

108. America is the only country in the world where a gang of people will congregate at a water cooler and get paid handsomely while they're doing it.

AMERICANS

109. An American is a person who will work his head off just to buy something that will make him work even harder to pay for it.

110. Americans will pay a big price for any invention that will help them to save time they won't know what to do with.

111. Many modern Americans have forgotten that Uncle Sam owes most of his success to wearing overalls.

112. You never realize how speed-conscious Americans are until you see a crowd of them trying to go through a revolving door.

113. Nothing makes an American feel rich like being loaded down with time payments on the installment plan.

114. America is the only nation in history that has shed so many of the lives of its young people to help others who kept telling them to go home!

115. In America there are thousands of dictators--if you count all those under one year of age.

AMOUR

116. The most dangerous phase every young girl goes through is the one during which she gets delusions of amour.

ANATOMY

117. The one part of the human anatomy that continues to grow after 21 is the wishbone.

ANCESTRY

118. There is an obvious reason why it is so hard to trace one's ancestry — most of us try our level best NOT to!

ANGER

119. The only time I like to see a person get mad is when he gets mad enough to do something really worthwhile.

ANNIVERSARY

120. A happily married man is one who never remembers his wedding anniversary and never gets into trouble because he doesn't.

ANNOUNCEMENT

121. One way a man can cheer up his wife is to come home from the office and announce that his pretty secretary got married.

ANNOYANCE

122. How big the other man's annoyances are depends on how easily you are annoyed by them.

ANTIFREEZE

123. An average person is one who waits for the first snow before putting antifreeze in his radiator.

ANTIQUES

124. There are two kinds of antique furniture — the kind that is too uncomfortable to sit on, and the kind that's too comfortable to get up out of.

APARTMENTS

125. Sounds that come from apartments without babies are even less musical.

APPEARANCE

126. The way people picture you behind your back is the way you look in front of them.

APPETITE

127. Many persons complain that they lack an appetite when the truth of the matter is they can't do enough to develop one.

APPLAUSE

128.   A good speaker is one who gets more applause when he is finished than when he is introduced.

APPLIANCES

129.   If you have any doubt that material things are only temporary on this planet, you haven't bought any household appliances.

APPRECIATE

130.   The best way to appreciate gravity is as a law of physics.

131.   People who appreciate a good speaker the most usually are program chairmen.

132.   Some wives appreciate their husbands the most while they are away at work . . . and he's at home doing the housework.

133.   One of the best ways to appreciate your loved ones and your home is to make a trip halfway around the world without them.

APRIL

134.   April is the month when most taxpayers wonder why they worked as hard as they did to give away so much money.

ARGUMENT

135.   Argument with a woman is like getting caught in a rainstorm; the best thing to do is to take shelter somewhere until the storm passes.

136. Once you are able to see both sides of an argument, you are sure to win it because then it is obvious how to get around it.

137. When it comes to generating a lot of heat its hard to beat an argument over cold cash.

138. Nothing helps to keep an argument going like two people who speak the same language.

139. Too many people lose an argument with an alarm clock because they take it lying down.

140. One time you can't believe everything you hear is soon after the sweet young couple you met move into the apartment next to you.

141. A phony salesman's arguments resemble a sieve; they won't hold water, but they sometimes pan gold.

142. The fellow who claims his arguments are sound might be admitting the truth.

ARITHMETIC

143. Arithmetic is something you should use to correct hearsay; always multiply a woman's age by two and divide a man's reputed wealth by ten.

144. A girl's arithmetic is usually at its best when she's counting on her figure.

145. A truly good person is one whose arithmetic is at its best when he's counting his blessings.

146. People who can count all their money these days don't have to be very good at arithmetic.

147. Some persons have such a command of arithmetic that they think they can figure out what the other fellow is worth.

148. A lady is a woman who can hold a man in her grip without ever letting him come within an arm's length of her.

ARTISTS

149. I have always thought that a social deviant is an artist who can sit and paint a nude model from a distance.

ASSET

150. A married man's greatest asset is a wife who is madly in love with him.

151. Nobody helps a man to increase his assets like a wife who is a penny-pincher.

152. The best way to increase your assets is by hiring the brains of others.

ASSISTANTS

153. Nothing adds to an executive's leisure time like having a group of capable assistants around him.

ASTONISHMENT

154. The amount of work done by some people is astonishing, especially when you add it all up and discover how little it really is.

155. You can always astonish your wife by doing something that proves you are smarter than she thinks you are.

ASTRONAUT

156. A budding astronaut is a young man who is determined to go far.

ATHEROSCLEROSIS

157. Nothing will make one's blood pressure rise to dangerous levels quite like hardening of the hearteries.

THE ATOM

158. It is becoming increasingly evident that when God said what I have joined together let no man put asunder, he also meant the atom.

ATTENTION

159. Always try to be like the locomotive in life - more people wave at the engineer than at the man in the caboose.

160. A smart wife is one who handles her husband with all the attention and tenderness he deserves as her most valuable asset.

161. It is easy to spot the fellow who is carrying his own weight around by the way it requires his undivided attention.

162. Troubles and weeds thrive on lack of attention.

163. Whether or not a woman will pay any attention to what her husband is saying depends on how pretty the woman is that he is talking to.

164. From the passing attention some motorists give traffic signals, you can't help wondering why they're called stop lights.

165. If you want your wife to pay close attention to what you're saying, talk to her about buying some new clothes.

166. The ability to win people over depends not so much in paying close attention to what they say as it does in expressing approval of it.

167. All a man has to do to get special attention from his wife is offer her his portion of the bedroom closet.

ATTITUDE

168. It is easy to spot a fellow who is really up on things . . . he's never down on people.

169. Attitudes are so much like mirrors - some can make you look and feel so much better than others.

ATTRACTIVENESS

170. Some women who aim to please first make attractive targets of themselves.

AUDIENCE

171. Nothing encourages your audience to clap like a cold auditorium.

172. An accomplished speaker is one who can gauge exactly how much his audience can take from him.

AUTHORITY

173. Nothing intoxicates some people like a sip of authority.

174. Some men who speak with authority at work know enough to bow to a higher authority at home.

175. Authority that rules for long without having its power challenged invariably ends up ruling with injustice.

AUTOGRAPHS

176. Sometimes it is a short interval between giving autographs and getting fingerprinted.

AUTO INSURANCE

177. Auto insurance is the only kind of insurance for which the premiums get higher the younger you are.

AVERAGE

178. The average person is just as close to failure as he is to success.

179. By the time the average man finds he is finally getting out of the fiscal woods he's bushed!

AWAKENING

180. Nothing helps you to get up in the world like getting up ahead of everybody else.

BABIES

181. Babies may not be able to lift much, but they're strong enough to hold most marriages together.

182. The stork is a very charitable bird. Note how much more frequently it visits the poor than the rich.

183. Doctors say that having a new baby in the home makes the days brighter. They could also include the nights.

184. There is no flower in the world that breathes a sweeter fragrance than a freshly bathed baby.

185. A new father never realizes how deeply indebted to society he is until he receives the obstetrician's bill.

186. A happy parent is one who believes in waking up a new baby just to see it smile.

BABY SITTER

187. The most economical time to hire a baby sitter is when the refrigerator is about empty.

188. Many a grandmother would be accused of spoiling her grandchildren if she weren't a perfect baby-sitter.

BACHELORS

189. Most bachelors who fall in love at first sight enjoy looking in mirrors.

190. A bachelor is a man who can still choose the time and place to get into hot water.

191. When a bachelor has to eat his own words it may only mean that his meals are now being prepared by the girl he would never marry.

192. A bachelor is a man who believes that opportunity is meant to be embraced, but not engaged.

193. A bachelor is a man who doesn't know what it feels like to wear a darned stocking.

194. Any man who can take a nap or a hot water shower whenever he feels like it is still a bachelor.

195. A bachelor is a man who refuses to play second-mate.

BACKBONE

196. Some women with a lot of backbone are just dressed up in evening clothes.

BAD ACTOR

197. A child is accused of being a bad actor sometimes when all it is doing is imitating its parents.

BAD COLD

198.   Every time my friend insists on coming to work with a bad cold we know it's because his wife has too much work lined up for him if he stays home.

BADNESS

199.   Our young people aren't nearly as bad as they might be - most of them aren't even half-trying.

200.   All a father has to do to knock the badness out of his son is beat the tar out of him on a tennis court.

BALANCE

201.   Nothing upsets the average man's balance like a wife who likes to write checks.

202.   When a man starts throwing his weight around he's bound to knock himself off balance.

BALANCE OF PAYMENTS

203.   With taxes the way they are, even a computer would have difficulty in calculating what profit a man would make if he gained the whole world.

BALDNESS

204.   The trouble with being bald is not so much in combing your hair as in knowing where to draw the line when you wash your face.

205.   Sometimes a man who does a lot of reflecting isn't bright; he's just bald.

BALL GAME

206. Nothing can put flavor into a hot dog like a good ball game.

BANK ACCOUNTS

207. Persons in a hospital seldom boast about their bank accounts.

BANKING

208. A bachelor is a man who can keep both a savings account and a checking account.

BANKRUPTCY

209. There would seem to be a lesson of some kind to be learned from the fact that of all the businesses in the United States the one having the lowest bankruptcy rate is that of morticians!

BARBERS

210. As far as barbers are concerned, they can prove that two heads are always better than one.

211. When a barber cuts your hair without talking to you he's probably just as interested in the magazine article you're reading as you are.

BARGAINS

212. A woman's arithmetic is never more dangerous than when she's calculating how much she can save by shopping for bargains.

213. Temptations are like bargains. You never know how badly you're being stung until after you've fallen for them.

214. A happy marriage is the world's best bargain.

BASE OF OPERATIONS

215. A girl's idea of expanding her base of operations is to acquire a bigger diamond.

BATHING SUIT

216. A woman who looks good in a bathing suit usually looks even better in an evening gown.

217. You know a woman is in love with her husband if she isn't ashamed of him even in a bathing suit.

218. Nothing makes a woman resolve to diet like the arrival of summer weather.

219. From the size of modern bathing suits, one would think that the people who design them are more interested in selling suntan lotion.

BATHTUB

220. All you have to do to get a telephone call is step into a bathtub.

BEACH

221. Some women who go to the beach to find a husband succeed in getting what they bask for.

BEATNIKS

222. Stocks in companies who produce stainless steel razor blades have a great future -- just think of the market when all the beatniks decide they would look better without the beards?

BEAUTICIANS

223. Beauticians are making serious inroads into the income of physicians - clients come to them every week for hair-raising treatments.

BEAUTY

224. America is the only country in the world where beauty is more celebrated than talent.

225. Nobody can add poise to a successful husband like a beautiful wife standing beside him.

226. Judging from the way some men chase after it, there can be no doubt that beauty is fleeting.

227. Next to falling in love with a beautiful woman the most satisfying experience in life comes from falling in love with your work.

228. Beauty in a woman is a great hazard - more so to her than to the men she impresses.

BEDROOM SLIPPERS

229. One of the hardest things for a man to understand is how his bedroom slippers manage to move so far away from him during the night.

BEGINNING

230. God loves beginnings — that is why He's so good to people who get things started.

231. The most important part of every beginning is an intense enough urge to get it started.

BEHAVIOR

232. Nothing holds a modern family together like good behavior on the part of the children.

233. A person's behavior whether for bad or good has little to do with heredity or environment — it has most to do with the true state of a person's health.

BELIEF

234. Nothing drives a man to reach unprecedented heights more than an unyielding belief that he can.

BELITTLE

235. At no time do you feel better for not having said something than when you thought of saying something to belittle a person.

BELLYACHERS

236. The trouble with so many people who bellyache is that usually their digestion is just fine.

BEST FOOT FORWARD

237. Nothing makes a man put his best foot forward quicker than to have his other one in hot water.

BEST OF LIFE

238. The surest way to lose the best in life is to fail to recognize it when you already have it.

BEST SELLERS

239. The authors of some of the best sellers that will never be written are employed by the Internal Revenue Service.

BEAUTY

240. Nothing dispels the beauty normally evident in a pretty nurse like a hypodermic needle in her hand.

BICENTENNIAL (U.S.A.)

241. Americans, on their 200th anniversary of freedom, still were so intent on preserving the freedom of others that they're willing to kill themselves trying to do it.

BICYCLE

242. The bicycle has taught me the secret of getting ahead; you've got to keep peddling to get anywhere.

BIGNESS

243. Bigness in a man is not measured in feet . . . but in feats.

BIG GUN

244. Sometimes a man who acts like a big gun at the office isn't even a pop at home.

245. Nothing prompts you to pay a bill like the arrival of a reminder with the discount added.

246. Just as soon as we get all of our bills paid, one of the neighbors buys something we haven't got, and we have to start budgeting all over again.

247. Today the only way some people can face bills . . . is with pills!

248. A considerate doctor is one who never mails his bills until he's sure the patients are well enough to receive them.

249. Usually a man can tell how much his wife really cares for him by the size of the bills that arrive each month.

250. Nothing leaves a man colder in winter than adding up the fuel bill.

BIRTH CONTROL

251. It has been my experience that you never hear a person who was the tenth child promoting birth control.

BIRTHDAY

252. A man who is very hard of hearing is one who forgets his wife's birthday.

253. Nothing hits a man harder below the belt than his half-hearted celebration of his 50th birthday.

BITTER TREAT

254. The most expensive treat you can give yourself is to tell the other fellow exactly what you think of him.

BLAME

255. The fellow who isn't afraid to take a little more than his share of the blame usually gets more than his share of the credit.

BLANK CHECK

256. An optimist is a borrower who brings along a blank check.

BLESSINGS

257. The trouble with many people who stop to count their blessings is their arithmetic is so poor.

BLONDE

258. Some men discover that there's fool's gold in a head of blonde hair.

259. The subjects that give a lot of college students the most trouble are usually blondes.

BLOOD PRESSURE

260. There is nothing wrong with a man's blood pressure as long as a smile from a pretty girl will bring color to his cheeks.

BOAST

261. The trouble with some people who boast that they have reached the top of the ladder is that there are so few rungs in it.

262. When a fellow starts blowing his own horn ... you can be sure he's alarmed about something.

263. There is a thin line that marks the difference between people who talk about themselves and people who talk to themselves.

264. Before most people start boasting about their family tree, they already have done a good pruning job on it.

BONERS

265. Before swallowing food-for-thought it often pays to check it for boners.

BOOK

266. Tact is the ability to ask a person for a book you loaned him and succeed in getting back the other half dozen he borrowed from you.

267. A wife doesn't mind her husband saying he can read her like a book as long as he doesn't put her on the shelf.

BORE

268. A bore is a person whose conversation never runs out of gas.

269. A bore is the kind of a man who never knows how badly he feels until you ask him.

BORROWER

270. A borrower is a man who tries to live within your means.

BOSS

271. Usually the man who gets to work ahead of everybody else — is the boss.

272.   Nothing encourages a man to quit work early like a boss who just did.

273.   A good employee always keeps one jump behind his boss.

274.   When it comes to getting ahead in the world, you don't have to be the boss' son . . . marrying his daughter will do just as well.

275.   These days nothing gives the boss a shot in the arm like sneaking up on his help and finding them hard at work.

276.   Reality consists in discovering that your boss knew all the time that you were loafing on the job.

277.   A man can always surprise his boss by picking up flowers for her on his way home from the office.

278.   Nowadays a patient man is often the boss waiting for his employees to show up for work.

BOTHER

279.   The easiest way to stop your children from bothering you is to have a neighbor they prefer to.

BOY

280.   It's easy to believe that a little boy is telling the truth as long as he's telling you something about one of your neighbors.

281.   One of the nicest things about a little boy is the way he hates you when you wash his face and worships you when you fill it for him.

282.   A little boy's arithmetic is at its best when he's counting the minutes before school's out.

283. A lucky farmer is one who raised a bumper crop of boys.

284. Most little boys feel that they can get along without father's helping hand, until they are old enough to start college.

285. A father of five boys will hardly agree that there is safety in numbers.

BRAINS

286. Some men have more brains than money, but they can't prove it.

BREAD

287. I am sure if you were to butter both sides of a slice of bread it would never fall on the floor because it could not make up its mind which side to fall on.

BREAKFAST

288. A happy person is anyone who can approach his breakfast humming a tune.

289. You know a woman is still very much in love with her husband if she gets all dressed up for breakfast with him.

290. A good joke is one that can make you laugh . . . before breakfast.

BREATH

291. Most people get out of breath these days, installment by installment.

BREATH MINTS

292.   A person who offers you a breath mint seldom realizes that he could use one himself.

BREVITY

293.   The best way for a man to be brief these days is never to put into his conversation more than his two cents' worth.

BRIDES

294.   A man sometimes forgets that he can't carry his bride over the threshold without letting her put her foot down.

BRIDGE

295.   A man has reached middle age when all it takes to exhaust him is an evening of bridge.

BRILLIANCE

296.   A brilliant person is one who never misses an opportunity to give you a compliment.

BRILLIANT CHILD

297.   A brilliant child is one who asks the guests questions that they can answer.

BRILLIANT MAN

298.   A brilliant man is one who is shrewd enough to recognize that you are a GENIUS.

BRUTE FORCE

299. The only time I have ever seen brute force accomplish anything is when I have watched excavaters at work.

BUDGET

300. A budget is a good idea as long as you don't try to budge it.

301. Nothing helps to stabilize the family budget like an economy drive by your closest neighbor.

BULL

302. Sometimes a sporting bull is just a golfer who shoots it.

BURDEN

303. The best way to lighten life's load is by lifting a weight off of somebody else's back.

304. The best way to make your weight felt is by lifting a burden off of somebody else's back.

BUSES

305. When it comes to picking up speed from a stop-position, you can't beat a bus you've just missed.

BUSINESS

306. In the business world the cash register frequently speaks louder than honesty.

307. Most people find running a business is no trouble at all - as long as it is the other fellow's.

BUSY

308. The difference between being busy and busy busy is that the busy busy person doesn't have enough time to tell you he's busy.

309. A really busy woman is one who is finishing off somebody's reputation.

BUTCHER

310. The only time overweight is a healthy sign is when it means the butcher really likes you.

CAMOUFLAGE

311. Humility is either a sign of greatness or a handy means of camouflaging one's imperfections.

CANOE

312. The nice things about paddling your own canoe is that it permits you to do the steering.

CAR POOL

313. The conversation of a car pool usually concerns the dangerous driving of the person that is missing.

CAR

314. You know a man really loves his wife if he invites her to break in his brand new car.

315. Nothing will rattle a person like hearing one in his brand new automobile.

316. One of the surest ways to get your son to follow in your footsteps is to refuse to put any gas in the family car.

317. These are days when nothing encourages a young man to burn the midnight oil like a tank full of gas in his father's car.

318. If you want to discover how easily a man's character can be dented, see what happens when you accidentally bump his car.

319. Nothing depreciates a car faster than a neighbor buying a new one.

320. Some men achieve distinction by the kind of car they drive — others by the kind of wife that is driving them.

CARE

321. Many people who are extra careful behind the wheel of their car don't do nearly as careful a job driving their bodies.

CAREER

322. Sometimes the biggest stumbling block in a man's career is the chip of wood on his shoulder.

CAREFUL DRIVER

323. A careful driver is one who is following a traffic cop.

CAREFULNESS

324. If motorists would only learn to drive carefully, our hospitals would probably have room to spare.

CAR KEYS

325. The sensible thing for a father of a teenager to do is to look for his car before he starts searching for his car keys.

326. Before the father of a teen-ager looks for his car keys, he should look for his son or daughter.

CARS

327. A man always finds a car has fewer rattles when his wife is at home.

328. Credit keeps more cars running than gasoline.

329. The only reason some people lose control of their car is they can't keep up with the payments.

330. Our young men have their problems these days — just as soon as they convince a girl the engine is giving them trouble they can't find a place to park.

331. There are too many middle-of-the-roaders in America, and a good many of them drive cars.

332. When the modern youngster asks his father for his key to success he's really thinking of his car keys.

333. One of the biggest safety features of the new cars is the way the drivers have gotten themselves strapped down by finance companies.

CASTLES

334. The trouble with building castles in the air doesn't start until you try to take possession of them.

335. The trouble with most people who like to build castles in the air is they have no experience as architects.

336. These are days when most people aren't interested in building castles in the air — they can't even afford a lot to build one on the ground.

CATSUP

337. A person with a good aim is one who can hit the target the first time with a bottle of catsup.

338. A lazy person is one who decides to do without catsup because none came out on the first couple of shakes.

339. A patient man is one who likes catsup.

CEILINGS

340. Sometimes the fellow who keeps hitting the ceiling may only be trying to quiet the people in the apartment above him.

CELEBRITIES

341. An adult may see human wisdom manifested in its highest form by watching a child's boundless capacity for ignoring celebrities.

342. Many persons who don't know celebrities well enough to speak to them think they know them well enough to talk about them.

CENTENARIANS

343. Any person who lives to be 100 has at least one good reason to be famous.

CHANCE

344. You can always interest a woman in taking a chance as long as it is a slim one.

345. Most people are never more irresponsible at taking chances than when they make chance remarks.

CHANGE

346. Those changes which may cause us the most immediate discomfort often do us the most good in the long run.

347. Nothing is more certain than death, taxes — and change.

CHARACTER

348. Character is the ability to win an argument by keeping your mouth shut.

349. The true test of a man's character is not so much how he accepts things, but how he behaves when he has to return them.

350. A man's true character is determined when his will is read for the first time.

351. People who aim to lower your character make an especially good target of themselves.

352. Some persons think they are hammering another's character when all they're doing is nailing down their own.

353. Character is what it takes to destroy your enemies by praising them.

354. A man's true character is determined by whether it wears out or rusts out in the face of life's elements.

355. Character is the ability to win an argument by letting the other person think he's having the last word.

356. The true character of some people doesn't become an open book until you throw it at them.

357. When vigilance and resoluteness are combined, you have the best pillars for building outstanding character.

CHARGE ACCOUNT

358. Far from being discouraged by an empty pocketbook, some women charge straight ahead.

CHARITY

359. The kind of charity that does you the most good is the giving-in kind.

360. True charity consists of helping those you have every reason to believe would NOT help you.

361. Everytime I give something away for a charitable purpose at the front door, I find that God sneaks more in by the back door.

362. Some persons never give a thought to charity until they sit down and fill out their tax return.

363. The best kind of charity is the kind that helps others to eliminate any further need of it.

364. Charity of thought, word, or deed always leads to the most lasting honors man can attain.

365. The trouble with some of the most charitable people I know is that they are deeply in debt.

CHECKBOOK

366. A woman likes to read a man like an open book . . . especially his check book.

367. Nothing encourages a woman to take a pen in hand like a checkbook in front of her.

368. When a woman turns the other cheek, she's probably just interested in getting a better look at the woman her husband is talking to.

CHEERFULNESS

369. Next to Godliness, cheerfulness can do more to make this world a better place to live in than anything else.

CHEMIST

370. Sometimes when a chemist appreciates the value of hard work, he's got an able assistant to be thankful for.

371. A successful chemist usually is one who has succeeded in mastering the art of getting along with molecules and people.

372. Nothing makes a chemist prouder of his profession than an unexpected increase in salary.

373. A chemist who doesn't let any grass grow under his feet may just be experimenting with a new weed killer.

374. Many chemists enjoy a good game of bridge, especially if they can squeeze it into a lunch hour.

375. A good chemist is one who never argues with the experimental facts . . . until after he has gone to the trouble of checking them out himself!

376. Most of the chemists I know are patient men . . . especially those that are married, and punctual.

377. About the only time some chemists feel that they have come face to face with a stone wall is when they're asked to sit down and write a report.

CHEMOLOGY

378. Someday it will be proven that our personalities and our emotions are controlled entirely by body chemistry.

CHILD RAISING

379. The secret of raising a child properly is in knowing when to give it a hand — and where.

380. The child who is always two jumps ahead of his class is probably the only one who can read the clock.

381. The best compliment a child can pay his parents is to set a good example for them.

382. Training a child to follow the straight and narrow path is easy for parents . . . all they have to do is lead the way.

383. A child with big ideas is one who is working on upping his allowance.

384. When a child marches off to school smiling, the chances are his mother didn't believe him when he said he had the day off.

385. A sick boy is one who comes down with a bug on a Saturday morning.

386. A spoiled child is one who isn't content with only imitating his parents' faults — he insists on acquiring a few of his own.

387. A brilliant child is one who asks the guests questions they can answer.

388. A smart child knows how to throw a tantrum and when!

389. Discipline may help to train a child, but only love will make him come running into your arms when you come home from work empty handed.

390. It is a wise child that knows who his next treat is coming from.

391. You can make a child do a lot of things by spending money lavishly on him, except run into your arms when you come into your house.

392. Nothing curbs a child's appetite like forcing him to sit down at the dinnertable.

393. One of the hardest things to do is make a child eat his words after you cook the egg he asked for.

CHILDISH QUESTIONS

394. When I close my eyes does an electric light switch turn off inside of me?

395. Does the grass feel hurt when people tramp on it?

396. Why don't you spank the dog when HE sticks his tongue out at you?

397. When I say my prayers tonight can I ask God to put butter and grape jelly on our daily bread?

398. Are psychiatrists doctors who tell people why they sigh?

399. Does God fire a shooting star from a gun?

400. Did YOUR daddy ever make YOU eat turnips?

401. Why can't I be thinkative when I don't feel like being talkative?

402. Does the man in the moon have any children?

403. If I put some hot mustard on the dog's tail, will that make him stop shivering?

404. Is Michael called the Archangel because maybe he was Noah's son?

405. Must I say my prayers tonight even though I can't think of anything I want to ask God for?

406. Do all dogs have to walk in their bare feet?

407. They have a Mother's Day and a Father's Day. Why don't they also have Children's Day?

408. Why is spinach always so much better for me than for you?

409. Who disciplines the policemen when they're bad?

410. Must I be a little gentleman even if it means I won't have a good time at the party?

411. May I eat my cereal bare this morning?

412. Why must I wash my face before I even get it dirty again?

413. How can God keep a close watch over me at night when you insist on turning out all the lights?

414. Is the man in the moon the sun's father?

415. Why do we ask God for bread? Isn't that what bad people get in jails?

416. Dad, does your boss ever make you sit in a "Thinking Chair" for being bad at work?

417. Why don't poisonous snakes poison themselves?

418. If Eve was the first lady, who was the second?

419. If dogs have to wear collars, why don't they have to wear ties too?

420. Who spanks policemen when they are bad?

421. Do birds ever wear sweaters?

422. Don't you think that a tree without leaves looks like a chicken without feathers?

423. When my teacher asks me to read, why does one of my knees keep shaking even though I don't tell it to?

424. May I listen to the heartbeat of your wristwatch?

425. If I do stop crying will you tell me what the good reason is?

426. Should I kiss the boys at school everytime they ask me?

427. When are you going to start paying me for keeping the baby-sitter awake?

428. Why do you keep saying that you are running out of patience, and you're not a doctor?

429. Now will you go back and read the 2 stories that you skipped?

430. Why doesn't Santa Claus use the front door instead of the chimney?

431. Why don't we move to the North Pole so we can have Santa Claus as our neighbor every day of the year?

432. Is Santa Claus so fat because he eats goodies at every house he visits?

433. When can I take showers instead of baths, because they are so much quicklier?

434. Why don't we take a shade-bath like Ranger is doing?

435. Are mommy's shoes really going to kill her?

436. Now that the doctor said that I can get up out of bed, am I really sickless?

437. Is it all right to tell people that my little Sister is really only three and two quarters instead of three and a half?

438. Now that I have grown so big, Mommy, will I start growing littler?

439. Who makes Aunt Nan not smoke?

440. Why do they call them square dances? All I've ever seen people do is dance in circles!

441. When the sun goes away at night, does God turn a switch to turn it off like a giant searchlight?

442. How big is the television set that God uses to watch all of us all of the time?

443. Will you please take me to a ball game, Dad, so that I can see it in natural television?

444. Why don't you ever ask me what I would like to do before you tell me what I must do?

445. Why can't you see a person's thinking cap?

446. May I leave the room to do clergyman's dust?

447. Why is it that only little girls have a trade-in value?

448. Why don't you ask Daddy to put some turnips on his plate before he passes them on to me?

449. Do you think Mother could get a stomach ulcer from over-happiness?

450. Didn't you know that the newspaper boy fired himself from that job?

451. Don't you think a museum looks like a cemetary for dead animals that should have been buried?

452. What comes first . . . the little lambs or the blankets that God wraps them in?

453. Why do you tell the neighbors you are so proud of me one minute, and then spank me when we come home?

454. Will God be on vacation the same time we are?

455. If God listens to everybody's prayer, are his ears even bigger than an elephant's?

456. Do clouds that park up in the sky have to worry about parking meters?

457. Do little boys get badder as they grow older because they're getting to be more like grown-ups?

458. Do robins ever speak to the blackbirds?

459. Can all fat women get thin again just by having a baby?

460. When I grow up, Mommy, how many babies can I have in one litter?

461. Do squirrels do anything else but collect nuts?

462. How long must you wait before you decide whether or not you want to trade the new baby in for another one?

463. Will you please breathe this balloon up for me?

464. What do beavers do when they aren't busy?

465. Shouldn't there be a law that every home must also have a bird-house?

466. Are blackbirds colored people in the world of birds?

467. Will the angels think enough of Jesus to bake Him a cake on His birthday?

468. How does Daddy's boss cover the hole that Daddy keeps saying he has in his head?

469. How can Daddy's boss be a slave driver when there aren't any more slaves?

470. What did Daddy mean when he says his boss was a stinker today?

471. Are bosses like policemen at work?

472. Must I say 'excuse me, please' every time my tummy goes over a burp?

473. I sunburn easily so when I die, will you bury me in the shade of a tree?

474. Why didn't God make those bad men tie His Son to the cross with Scotch Tape instead of nails?

475. Please God, will you make sure that Santa brings me the new sleigh I asked him for. And will you please cooperate Yourself and send me a good heavy snowstorm for Christmas morning?

476., Must I promise you that I have to stop being badder?

477. Do they have 'Excuse me, please' rooms in churches?

478. Don't clocks ever get tired of clicking to themselves?

479. Why do you make me wear all these clothes just because you're cold?

480. Do those puzzles that Nanna likes to do in the newspaper really have cross words in them?

481. When I say my prayers tonight do you think God would mind if I ask Him to put peanut butter and grape jelly on my daily bread?

482. When people dance do they really trot like foxes do?

483. Do people ever live again after their funeral is all over?

484. Did the dishwasher spill all those suds over the floor because it had an upset stomach?

485. If the world is really like a giant orange, is it seedless?

486. May I have 2 fried eggs with their eyes wide open?

487. When you write to Santa Claus for me next year will you please ask him to bring me some fourtle track?

488. Why can't I pick up both of my feet at the same time?

489. Don't you know I'm allergic to food from somebody else's plate?

490. Can men really catch girls just by whistling at them?

491. Why didn't God make my hair out of nylon so that it would dry faster after you wash it?

492. If God doesn't ever sleep, doesn't He get cranky sometimes?

493. If Jesus is God and the Son of God, too, should He have two faces instead of only one?

494. Why do grown-ups say "God bless you!" to me when I haven't even sneezed at them?

495. Dad, why don't you wait until we eat our food and see how it tastes before you thank God for it?

496. Why doesn't the juice from a pink grapefruit look pink when it is in my spoon?

497. Why did you tell Daddy to "grow up" when you know he can't grow anymore?

498. Do you think Joe the Barber was here to give those hedges a crew-cut?

499. Can't you see that I smell hungry?

500. How can you stop me from telling automatic lies?

501. Does God send rain to put out the lightning?

502. Why is it that I'm supposed to listen to you when you tell me something, and you turn your ears off when I want you to listen to me?

503. Daddy, why don't you like the kind of mischief that I like?

504. Daddy, when God put the moon up in the sky did He use a stepladder?

505. Why doesn't God paint the sky with pretty rainbows more often?

506. Who turns the switch that makes the moon go off and on?

507. Do you know what the most naughty word I said was? I told Johnny's father that Johnny's little sister had pooh-pants!

508. Who fills the ocean up for us each morning?

509. Do olives grow on trees with their little red hearts showing?

510. Do you mind if I get myself a pencil sharpener that works autoelectrically?

511. What do grown-ups say when somebody makes them take piano lessons?

512. What's the difference between borrowing money from my piggy-bank and stealing it?

513. Do my night prayers get to God just as fast as my morning prayers?

514. Does a man become a preacher just so he can have lots of fun counting all that money in the collections?

515. God made the moon, the sun, and the stars; why can't he wipe away sickness and funerals?

516. Does the postman really have to read all the mail he delivers?

517. How can a fish drink so much water without choking?

518. Mommy, is it all right if I fall in love with my kindergarten teacher . . . extra to you?

519. Why can't you see a person's thinking cap?

520. Does daddy's boss ever spank him?

521. When people dance do they REALLY trot like foxes?

522. Are people who smoke really trying to kill themselves?

523. Are people ODD because they can't get EVEN with somebody?

524. How did I breathe, Mommy, when you carried me around in your inside pocket?

525. Do oranges get their peelings because they got sunburned?

526. Does my guardian angel run away each time you spank me?

527. Does God keep his little angels as busy as you do yours?

CHILDREN

528. One of the reasons some children sound so grown up is they're usually just quoting adults.

529. An adult may see human wisdom manifested in its highest form by watching a child's boundless capacity for making the most of today.

530. Judging from the way some children succeed in imitating their parents, you certainly can't accuse them of being bad actors.

531. The easiest way to get some children to school is to drive them there.

532. The secret of raising a child properly is in knowing when to give it a hand — and where.

533. Too many parents think they can raise children by their voices.

534. The childish things that trip most adults are usually left strewn around the house.

535. The reason a mother can get so much done in a day is that the children give her so much to do.

536. The easiest way to clean out the refrigerator is to leave several growing boys all alone in the kitchen.

537. The most foolhardy thing to put off until tomorrow is having children.

538. Too many times the chip off the old block is made of even denser wood.

539. What most little boys save for a Saturday morning is the urge to get up with the birds.

540. Children may not always listen to what their parents say to them, but there isn't a thing they won't copy if they see their parents doing it.

541. Youth gives children a great advantage, especially when you chase after them.

542. One of the surest ways to get your son to step into your shoes is to buy yourself a new pair that fits him.

543. A father knows he's doing right by his children when he finds himself trying to live up to their good example.

544. Children always prefer the straight and narrow path . . . across your lawn.

545. A well-trained child is one who knows how to behave, especially when he's being watched.

546. There are many things I admire in children, but the one that impresses me the most is the way they can get the thrill of a lifetime out of the little things that we adults usually can't be bothered with.

547. Children are the most wonderful furnishings in a house, even if they don't last as long as you would like them to.

548. The number of virtues a child possesses increases as the distance of his home from yours.

549. These days children not only learn to talk early, they learn to talk back.

550. One of the easiest ways to acquire a bigger house is to marry off some of the children.

551. If you are in doubt as to whether or not your house needs redecorating, the children will usually do all they can to help you decide.

552. The best security a parent can give his children is an insatiable thirst for hard work.

553. Parents should remember that a few fingerprints on the wallpaper is better than having them on a police record later.

554. The other fellow's backyard always looks greener until after your children are through playing in it.

555. One of the worst ways to bring up a child is affluently.

556. All the average parent needs to recover any lost love for his children is a good night's sleep.

557. Children seldom misquote you . . . they repeat what you shouldn't have said word for word.

558. Children talk much earlier nowadays, even before you're ready to get awake.

559. Children seldom misquote you because their hearing is still perfect.

560. Class hatred in the United States could be dealt an almost fatal blow simply by allowing children to skip grade school.

561. Every child should receive an introduction to a literary background — preferably by the proper application of a book, now and then, hard enough and low enough.

562. It really pays to get an education and if you want to know how much ask the man who has some children in college.

563. Middle age is the time of life when a father wishes he could have taught his six year old daughter how to drive a two-wheel bicycle ten years earlier.

564. No father has really tasted the thrill of fatherhood until his six-year old daughter starts waiting on him hand-and-foot.

565. Nothing gives a parent a shot in the arm like the sight of his children heading for a neighbor's backyard.

566. One of the greatest pleasures a parent can experience is to gaze upon the children when they're fast asleep.

567. Watching children playing happily together is an almost unbelievable sight, especially if they all happen to be your own.

568. Children have wonderful memories. They can repeat word for word everything a parent wishes he hadn't said.

569. It's easy to get children to follow the straight and narrow path — all you have to do is live in a corner house and grow a nice lawn in front of it.

570. One thing you've got to admire children for is that the world would be drugged with antique furniture without them.

571. Some modern parents are willing to pay a terrible price for obeying their children.

572. Sometimes you can't read the handwriting on the wall because the youngster who wrote it hasn't been to school yet.

573. The best inheritance that a parent can leave his children is a will to work and the wisdom to enjoy it.

574. The best way to test the guarantee on a new house is to let the children loose in it.

575. Algebra always seems like simple mathematics, until the time comes when you have a daughter taking the course and she asks you for help.

576. The other evening my son and I spent more than an hour having all kinds of fun blowing bubbles with what amounted to a penny's worth of soap solution. And then it occurred to me that the cost of a child's toys means little or nothing to him in comparison with having his dad as a playmate.

577. The best things to get out of marriage are children.

578. An adult may see human wisdom manifested in its highest form by watching a child's boundless capacity for ignoring celebrities.

CHILD'S PLAY

579. A man knows that his age is creeping up on him when a little bit of child's play makes him exhausted.

580. The average father is willing to admit that the most exhausting form of exercise is child's play.

CHINA

581. A smart husband gets out of having to do a lot of chores around the house by dropping a piece of prized china on the floor now and then.

CHIP

582. When it comes to starting a fiery argument, its hard to beat two persons with chips on their shoulders rubbing each other the wrong way.

583. A fellow with a chip on his shoulder is most likely to get splintered.

584. All a man has to do to take the chip off his wife's shoulder is put a new hat on her head.

585. Everytime I run across a man with a chip on his shoulder I look for wood higher up.

586. Any man who likes to shoulder his responsibilities never has any room left for a chip.

587. The heaviest chip on a man's shoulder is a mistake he refuses to correct.

588. The heaviest piece of wood in the world is the chip a man carries on his shoulder.

589. The trouble with some people who carry a chip on their shoulder is they are mostly all bark and have little bite.

590. People who have a chip on their shoulder are easy to knock off balance.

591. People who like to stir up trouble usually do it with the chip on their shoulder.

CHISELERS

592. The only people who are successful chiselers are in the tombstone business.

593. People in the tombstone business don't mind being accused of chiseling for a living.

CHIVALRY

594. Chivalry is all but dead, and with its demise has gone honesty and courtesy.

CHRISTMAS

595. An average person is one who waits until Christmas Eve to do his Christmas shopping.

596. A woman is a person who can get a big thrill thinking about a fur coat in July that she's going to get her husband to buy her before Christmas.

597. Christmas is the one time of the year when a man's wife believes in giving him all the credit she can get in his name.

598. When it comes to decorating the home for Christmas you can't beat a family that is all wrapped up in itself.

599. Some manufacturers spend all year manufacturing Christmas toys that Santa Claus will break before he can complete putting them together.

600. A discouraged Christmas shopper is a woman who has just lost her charge plate.

601. A smart wife is one who knows how to retie the Christmas package her husband has hidden from her.

CHRISTMAS CARDS

602. A person with a good memory is one who can remember where he placed last year's list of people who sent Christmas cards.

603. One way to discover what a fast-moving age we're living in is to notice how many addresses you have to change each time you write Christmas cards.

CHRISTMAS EVE

604. Christmas Eve is about the only time of the year a woman knows for sure where her husband is . . . out shopping.

605. Christmas Eve is the time of the year when you resolve to do your Christmas shopping earlier next year.

CHRISTMASTIME

606. The trouble with most persons is that the only time they worry about the present is at Christmastime.

607. One of the reasons that goodwill is so appropriate at Christmastime is that often that is when it is needed most.

CHURCH

608. A really good golfer is one who goes to church on Sunday . . . first.

609. One time a man can expect his date to be on time is when he's waiting for her at the church door.

610. The value of a nickel frequently depends on how much more you would have to put in the collection plate if you didn't have it.

CIGARETTES

611. Of all the breath-taking inventions of man, the cigarette is by far the most successful . . . and the most deadly!

CIRCLES

612. About all a fellow gets, sometimes, from going around in certain circles is rings around his eyes.

CIRCULATION

613. When it comes to stopping a man's circulation the best tourniquet of all is alimony.

614. When it comes to stopping a man's circulation you can't beat a jail sentence.

615. When it comes to stopping a young man's circulation you can't beat a young girl who can tie him in a knot.

616. When it comes to stopping a man's circulation you can't beat a cemetary.

617. When it comes to stopping a man's circulation, the best tourniquet of all is a wedding ring.

CIRCUMSTANTIAL EVIDENCE

618. Some circumstantial evidence is irrefutable — like a fly in the ointment.

CIVILIZATION

619. Not until man can control himself as dutifully as he does his animals can he be considered civilized.

CLAIM

620. One claim that a modern woman seldom hesitates to prove is that she has little or nothing to wear.

CLASS HATRED

621. Nothing makes a child develop class hatred like being forced to repeat a year in one.

CLASS REUNION

622. Nothing ruins a class reunion like a stranger hitting you on the back and mistaking you for somebody else.

CLERICAL ERRORS

623. Some of the most serious clerical errors are those made by clergymen.

CLEVER WOMAN

624. A clever woman knows that she can get more out of a man by making him feel like a genius than by making him feel like a fool.

625. When it comes to clock-watching, it is hard to beat a little boy just a few minutes before school's out.

CLOTHES

626. The latest thing in clothes is usually the woman you are waiting for.

627. A husband knows his wife dresses to please him when she makes all of her own clothes.

628. A sure sign that one of your daughters is growing up is when she becomes particular about how you're dressed when she invites her friends in.

629. Middle age has set in when a man is more interested in how much his wife's clothes cost than he is in how they fit her.

630. The easiest way to win an argument with your wife is to buy her the outfit she started the argument about in the first place.

631. When some women get all dressed up to please a man, they obviously know where to draw the neckline.

632. From the looks of things you would think designers of women's clothes were in show business.

633. When it comes to dressing up the bare facts, some women get a little careless.

634. A woman is impressed by lovely clothes, especially if they are worn by a woman she doesn't like.

CLOTHESLINE

635. An old timer is one who remembers when giving a women some more rope meant she would string up another length of clothesline.

COCKTAIL PARTIES

636. As a rule more handsome men attend cocktail parties than women because the hostess writes the invitations.

637. Most people will agree that any cocktail party that leaves them breathless is a failure.

COFFEE BREAK

638. We seem to be headed for a four-hour work-week and a four-coffee-break work-day.

COLD

639. Sometimes the woman who is out to land a man catches a cold.

COLD CASH

640. Nowadays when it comes to things getting out of hand, it is hard to beat money in your pocket.

641., The trouble with silver linings is they're no substitute for cold cash.

COLD FEET

642. The fellow who displays cold feet before marriage is sure to find himself in hot water afterwards.

COLD WATER

643. How good a red hot idea is usually depends on how much heat it loses when somebody throws cold water on it.

COLLEGE

644. You can lead some people to college these days, but you can't force them to think.

645. Most little boys feel that they can get along without father's helping hand — until they're old enough to start college.

COLLEGE DEGREES

646. There is too much attention today paid to the importance of an advanced college degree; we are forgetting that some of the greatest scientific and industrial successes of all times started in the minds of men who never finished grade school.

COLLEGE EDUCATION

647. Most young girls are interested in a college education — and the sooner they can help their boyfriend get one the better.

648. A lot of people with a college education have to take off their hat to a boss who doesn't have one.

COLLEGE STUDENT

649. An enterprising college student is one who selects a father-in-law who can guarantee him a job.

650. An enterprising college student is one who studies while he waits for his date to get ready.

651.   Most college students insist on their independence on all matters but financial support.

652.   Nobody helps a student get through college like a father who is a professor.

653.   The subjects that give a lot of college students the most trouble live in sorority houses.

654.   The first thing a college student does with a letter from home is hold it to the light to see if there is a check in it.

655.   When it comes to taxing a family's future inheritance, it is hard to beat a couple of youngsters in college.

656.   The subjects that give some college students the most trouble are blondes.

COMFORT

657.   The most comfortable feeling in the world comes from having plenty of hard work behind you.

658.   A woman will go to almost any extreme to put a man back on his feet if he's comfortable, and her husband.

COMMITTEE

659.   A committee consists of three or more persons each of whom thinks the others talk a lot of nonsense.

COMMONSENSE

660.   Commonsense is seldom exercised by anyone but the common people.

COMMUTING

661.   One of the greatest discoveries you can make while driving a car back and forth to work is a push-button

combination between stations that permits you to completely by-pass the commercials.

COMPANY

662. A company is best known by the activity of its public relations department.

663. A company is known by the men it keeps losing.

664. A company is best known by the competition it creates.

COMPETITION

665. The man who does things without worrying who is going to get the credit never has to worry about competition.

666. Competition between father and son is extremely healthy, especially when it is demonstrated on a tennis court.

COMPETITOR

667. It pays always to remember that a competitor does give a damn about getting ahead of you!

COMPLAINERS

668. The same persons who complain that they cannot see their way in life frequently make spectacles of themselves.

669. In almost any large organization, those who complain the most usually have the least to show for their work.

COMPLAINTS

670. A contented man is one who never has anything to complain about except the weather.

COMPLEXION

671. Nobody can do more for a young girl's complexion than a handsome young man who has fallen in love with her.

672. A man is not old as long as the presence of a beautiful woman improves his complexion.

COMPLIMENTS

673. Nothing is better for the other person's digestion than at least one compliment a day.

674. Compliments can be as dangerous as bones in a fish if you try to swallow them all.

675. People who get high on compliments soon decline on their laurels.

676. Breathes there a man with soul so dead that a compliment from a fan doesn't go to his head.

677. The best way to give a person a bouquet of words is to cut them short.

678. The most treasured of all compliments that I can ever remember was one expressed by a person who had been my most severe critic.

679. The value of the dollar has deteriorated so much that even when people pay you a compliment these days it sounds cheap.

680. Never overestimate the compliments of your friends and relatives; it is when perfect strangers take the time to praise you that you should coddle your ego a little.

681. The best compliment you can give a man is to praise him for some wonderful quality he didn't realize he had.

682. People who live on compliments should diet.

683. Some folks pay a compliment with as much enthusiasm as they pay their income tax.

CONCEIT

684. Conceit in a man is a sure sign that he still hopes to become successful some day.

685. Conceit is an obvious illness to everyone but the person who suffers from it.

686. Conceit may lift you up and suspend you in midair, but it makes no provision to catch you when you fall.

CONCENTRATION

687. Concentration is the secret of all success — concentration on one idea, one goal, one dream.

CONCLUSION

688. The trouble with some people who reach a logical conclusion is that they behave illogically.

689. Conclusions are an important part of every speech, especially when they come as close as possible to the beginning.

690. Speed is so characteristic of our day and age that people are now even jumping to wrong conclusions.

CONFESSION

691. Confession is good for the soul . . . and it sure is a bonanza for the Internal Revenue Service.

CONFIDENCE

692. Beware what you disclose to a friend in strict

confidence — it may give him just the information he needs to convert him into your worst enemy.

693. No misfortune can befall a man that will prove more disastrous than his loss of self-confidence.

CONSCIENCE

694. When a person says he has a well-trained conscience, he usually means that it obeys him!

695. There is a spark of conscience in each one of us, but most of us don't clean our spark-plugs often enough.

696. A good conscience is one that can be heard — and listened to.

697. About the only time a man can get a strangle hold on his conscience is when his wife is with him.

698. When your conscience is your guide, it will take you over some rough terrain.

699. Conscience is that still small voice that tells you a traffic cop has beaten you back to an expired parking meter.

700. When a man no longer can hear his conscience, it's high time he improved his living habits.

701. Nothing is more soluble in alcohol than a woman's conscience.

702. Conscience is something you know you have when you say something about the other fellow, and you feel it could apply equally well to yourself.

703. Anybody with a good conscience can get along without worrying about ghosts in the past reappearing.

704. The surest sign of fatigue from an overworked conscience is its sudden loss of hearing.

705. Conscience is that inner voice that warns that the man in the unmarked car trailing you is a State Trooper.

706. No matter how weak one's conscience may be, it still is capable of whittling you to size.

CONSCIENTIOUSNESS

707. There are two types of conscientious taxpayers — those who are conscientious about paying their taxes and those who are equally conscientious about evading them.

708. When it comes to describing how much work the other fellow should do, everybody's over-conscientious.

CONSCIENTIOUS OBJECTOR

709. A smart girl is one who believes in being a conscientious objector — until he asks her to marry him.

CONSERVATIVE

710. A conservative person is one who realizes that he's talking to a close friend of one of his neighbors.

711. The most conservative man on earth is an internal revenue agent listening to your story.

CONTENTMENT

712. A contented man is one who never runs anything down except the weather.

713. Nothing adds to a married woman's contentment like her husband's pretty secretary getting married.

714. When you see a man with a contented look on his face, the chances are that he knows his wife has finished the dinner dishes.

715.. A truly contented husband enjoys his wife's cooking whether it is burnt or not.

CONTRADICTION

716. It seems like a mathematical contradiction, but it is true that the fellow who says the most is the one who speaks the least.

717. One of the most contradictory things I know of in the English language is calling a viewing a wake.

CONVALESCENCE

718. Convalescence is a phase of every illness; the more enjoyable part which cautions a person from getting better too quickly.

CONVENTION

719. You know a man is still very much in love with his wife if he uses all of his free time at a convention to catch up on his sleep.

CONVERSATION

720. The hardest part of thinking before you speak comes when you try to edge into an on-going conversation.

721. The dullest conversationalist is one who says only what he thinks the other person would like to hear.

722. A housewife's idea of talking shop is to keep the conversation going while her husband does the dishes for her.

723. If you must wag your tongue, always make it sound friendly.

724. The conversation of some persons reminds me of a road under construction — it is fraught with detours.

725. Some conversation is like hash-house soup; a lot of broth from a very small soupbone.

726. Nothing brightens up your conversation like mispronouncing a word or two so your listener can correct you.

727. Making conversation is no trouble for a pretty girl at a cocktail party — all she has to do is listen to the men making passes at her.

728. Nothing adds spice to your conversation like sprinkling it with compliments about your listener.

729. Nothing brightens up a conversation like a pause to catch your breath.

CONVICTION

730. Conviction is what some people never have until after the judge has pronounced sentence.

731. Logic is any line of reasoning that confirms your conviction.

732. A person with the strongest convictions will either be a tremendous success or end up in jail.

733. The trouble with too many personal convictions is they're mostly family hand-me-downs.

734. Always remember that those people who hold the strongest convictions are behind bars.

735. When a man has the courage of his convictions he'll never lose his temper trying to defend them.

736. Nothing confirms a man's convictions like being handed one.

COOK

737. A woman who is an expert cook seldom has much trouble getting her husband to eat out of her hand.

COOKBOOK

738. Most modern women get their husbands to eat out of their hands with the help of a cookbook.

COOPERATION

739. A father knows the real value of cooperation as soon as his son starts cutting the lawn for him.

740. A man learns the real value of cooperation as soon as his wife starts helping him do the daily dishes.

741. A cooperative young man is one who wants to help you marry off your daughter.

742. A man learns the real value of cooperation when his wife sticks to her diet, too.

743. One of the most cooperative young men a man can find is one who is courting his daughter.

CORDIAL

744. How cordial some people are frequently depends on how many cordials they've had.

CORPORATION

745. The bigger a corporation the longer it takes to get a little job done.

746. When it comes to getting ahead in a large corporation, it never pays to beat your boss — at anything.

COUNTRY MUSIC

747. I can never understand why country music almost always is about poverty, infidelity, or the sadness of city life.

COURAGE

748. Courage is what it takes to turn down an undeserved compliment.

749. A woman of courage is one who insists on using the correct number of candles on her birthday cake.

750. Courage is what it takes for a woman to show friends the family album containing her birth certificate.

751. Courage is what it takes to pass a State Trooper even when you can keep within the speed limit.

752. It takes courage to climb to the top but intelligence and wisdom to stay there.

753. Courage is what it takes for a woman to show friends the family album containing her birth certificate.

754. The most remarkable form of courage is not to face an enemy in war; it is to be able to muster the strength to do what is right when you know nobody would be able to tell the difference.

755. Courage is what the average person needs to get to know himself better.

756. A brave man is one who has the courage to watch his wife park the brand new family car.

757. People who have never snuffed a candle with their

fingers may credit a man who does it with more courage than he deserves.

758. The courage that is most admired in a man is the courage to do what makes him happiest.

759. There is often a thin line between courage and cowardice — and it often depends on whether or not even a single avenue for retreat exists.

COURTESY

760. Courtesy consists in letting your guests talk your ears off.

761. Courtesy consists in giving the other fellow every chance to prove that you're wrong . . . when you're certain that you're right.

COURTSHIP

762. The advantage of a long courtship is that it prolongs the period during which a girl will never receive so much attention again.

763. A smart woman is one who can keep a man pursuing her even after she lets him catch her.

764. A girl will wait for the right man to come along as long as the one she's going with doesn't try to make a get-away.

765. Courtship often turns out to be a period during which a man pursues a woman who is pursuing him.

COWARD

766. A coward is a man who says "yes" when his honest opinion about the subject is "no".

767.   A coward sometimes is a man who boasts that he is a pacifist because he knows his opponent could trim the pants off him.

CRACKPOT

768.   This much should be said for the crackpot — every now and then, he hits the jackpot.

CREATIVITY

769.   Creativity is bound to stir up controversy because its ultimate impact always is to change the status quo.

770.   The two handcuffs of a creative man are custom and tradition.

771.   The common nexus of creativity that transcends the whole lifespan is the preservation of childish curiosity.

772.   A truly creative person who embarks on a career into the land of research should realize from the start that he will reach a dead end but his research never will.

773.   Creativity is not always favored by an environment of tranquility . . . to get the paste out of the tube you still must squeeze a little.

774.   Of all the enemies of creativity, success is by far the most insidious.

775.   The shortest route to true creativity is a straight line between the eye and the brain.

776.   It always amazes me how a handful of innovative people have kept the rest of the world busy doing things with the ideas they started.

777.   No one thing separates man more clearly from all other

forms of life than his ability to make his wildest dreams come true.

778. Most men are endowed with an inexhaustible flare for creativity — the trouble is, however, that most people think they are creating problems at first.

779. You cannot plan creativity — you can only prepare the environment for it.

780. Two marks of a creative mind are: (1) An ability to look at facts tangentially, and (2) An open lack of fear at being dead wrong occasionally.

781. The creative man is very much like a hunter seeking a prey he hasn't seen yet — but he keeps his gun constantly ready for the unexpected.

782. Most men are endowed with an inexhaustible flare for creativity — the trouble, however, it is for creating problems.

783. The key to creativity invariably requires unlocking the secret of combining a smooth interplay of the mind, the heart, and the hand.

CREDIBILITY GAP

784. Credibility gap — what happens to the same news between the morning telecast and the evening paper.

785. A husband learns the true meaning of a "credibility gap" by the amount of chit-chat he must listen to before his wife admits that she smashed the car up.

CREDIT

786. You can tell a lot about a man by how willingly he gives another fellow credit when you're sure he doesn't have to.

787. A man's credit standing is determined by how comfortably the bank is sitting on the loan they made him.

788. Most men ultimately learn that it pays them to be cautious about giving credit to women.

789. People who think they can charge their sins up to experience are going to be shocked when they discover how poor their credit is with God.

790. A good executive is a man who believes in sharing the credit for the work somebody else does.

791. Christmas is the one time of the year when a man's wife believes in giving him all the credit he can get.

792. Credit is something a man gets in one department store which enables him to buy something else in another.

793. Credit keeps more cars running than gasoline.

CREMATION

794. One reason why I believe in cremation is that it is a sure way to undermine the undertakers' racket.

795. The re-creation of the human body after cremation is no more difficult a job for God than its re-creation from the end result of bacterial destruction in a coffin below the ground.

CRISES

796. The surest way to prevent any family crisis from coming to a head is to take a sleeping pill.

CRITICISMS

797. Criticisms are like stones you throw into the air; on their way down they are liable to knock you out.

798. There are two kinds of criticism — the kind that hits you in the heart and the kind that hits you in the butt.

799. Criticism, like good medicine, can do a lot for you depending on whether you can take it or not.

800. Never fear criticism — unless you've already resigned yourself to fate.

801. Most people bark at criticism instead of taking advantage of it.

802. People who never indulge in the criticism of a single person astonish many and chastize more than a few.

803. One of the surest marks of good character is a man's ability to accept personal criticism without malice to the one who gives it.

804. A man's character is determined not by the criticism he gives but by the criticism he forgives.

805. The most beneficial criticism in the world is self-criticism.

806. People who criticize self-made men usually haven't been able to make much of themselves.

CRITICS

807. A famous man's most merciless critic is the public.

808. You know a critic is not a quack if he does things to help the people he criticizes.

CROOKED

809. One of the surest ways to become crooked is to be bent on avoiding hard work.

CROWD

810. The fellow who believes in following the crowd ends up in the rear.

CRUST

811. Sometimes the fellow who acts as though he has a lot of crust crumbles easily.

CRY

812. Fortunately most women can forget a good cry just as quickly as they can start one.

813. How much better a woman feels after a good cry often depends on what she got out of it.

814. When a woman starts jumping down a man's throat the chances are that she's about to cry on his shoulder.

815. Every woman knows that a good cry is one that gets more out of her husband than she had planned it would.

816. Before a woman decides to cry over something she usually makes sure she has a worthwhile audience.

CYCLES

817. Everything that has a beginning has an end, and everything that has a maximum has a minimum.

DAD

818. No matter how much disagreement there is in a family they can always get together when it comes to buying a tie for dad.

DAILY NEWS

819. It amazes me how unimportant the daily news becomes if you don't look at it, listen to it, or read about it more than once a week.

DAME-DREAMING

820. That far-away look you see on some men's faces is a sign that they're dame-dreaming.

DANGER

821. The man in the greatest danger always is the one who has climbed to the top of the ladder.

822. Danger never is closer to you than when you are taking safety for granted.

DATE

823. About the only way a modern girl will break a date is by letting him take her out.

DAUGHTERS

824. All it takes to make your daughter dress up quickly is to bring home a brand new outfit for her.

825. Early to bed and early to rise is a sure sign that your daughter is being courted by a young man in your living room.

DEAD DEED

826. Dead deed — one on which you have just made the last payment.

827. It takes brute force sometimes to bring a careless motorist to a dead stop — like a locomotive.

DEATH

828. Maybe death is like a ship that carries you out to sea beyond the view of all others and towards an endless horizon.

829. Death exists in two states: one when the last dream one ever had moves beyond reach; the other when the heart stops beating for good. There usually is only a short span of time between the two.

830. Too many persons who worry about death love to kill time.

831. You know a man loves his wife if he says he hopes to join her soon afterwards if she dies first.

832. Each of us starts to put nails into the coffin of our character after we leave kindergarten!

833. Death is the one final exam we all fail.

834. Death seems to come slowest for rich individuals who have no living blood relatives.

835. In my judgment, death deserves a new definition — namely, that instant in any person's life when the last vestige of hope disappears.

DEBTS

836. People who think nothing of going into debt are usually even less concerned about getting out of it.

837. The trouble with a lot of people who give you the

impression they are going places is they may only be running into debt.

838. A person never realizes his debt to the medical profession until after he receives the doctor's bill.

839. Many people fall into debt because they are foolish enough to spend what their neighbors think they are making.

840. There are two ways of getting rid of your debts; work harder so that you may earn more money, or live within your means.

841. There are two ways to catch up with the Joneses — go into debt trying to catch up with them, or take it easy until you meet them coming back.

842. Nothing makes some people go into debt like trying to keep up with people who already are.

843. The reason some people are living far beyond their income is they aren't afraid to owe up to things.

DECEIT

844. Deceit is like a smudge mark on your face — you may not know that it shows, but everybody else can plainly see it.

845. Deceit is exhausting, especially to men who try to hide the fact that they are bald . . . or short.

846. Deceit is more vicious than outright lying — and in the end more self-destructive.

DECEMBER

847. December is the month when most family ties — are purchased.

DECISIONS

848. When it comes to making the safest and best decision, there is no better preparation than gathering together complete knowledge about the problem.

849. I have found that the best decisions I have made in life were made within ten minutes after getting up from a good night's sleep.

850. The most valuable decisions you will ever make are those you make with the courage of your convictions and without regard to the consequences.

851. The greatest advantage a man of mediocre talent can have over one of great genius is the ability to make decisions and act upon them.

852. Nothing helps you to decide that you got up on the wrong side of the bed like a futile search for your bedroom slippers.

853. Never make an important decision after 6 p.m. unless there is no way that you can hold off until you get up the following morning.

854. Nothing helps you to make the right decision like being bold about it.

855. In industry, the harder the decisions to be made, the better an executive must be to make them — right.

DEDUCTIONS

856. All year long people assume all kinds of deductions, but when April 15 comes along they're usually lost for proof.

DEEDS

857. Sometimes a man's deeds can be a worry to him . . . especially if they're heavily mortgaged.

DEFEAT

858. Defeat is never more assured for an individual than at the moment when he resigns himself to it.

DEFICIENCIES

859. Nothing is more damaging to you than denying the existence of your own deficiencies.

DEGREES

860. A lot of men who have college degrees will admit that their real education didn't begin until they began supporting a son or daughter at college.

DELIVERY BOYS

861. What we need to do is train a generation of newspaper delivery boys who will have the accuracy of attendants who park cars.

DENTIST

862. A dentist is a person who expects you to answer his questions after he fills your mouth with everything but the kitchen sink!

863. Modern dentists who believe in mass production run from room to room drilling for gold.

864. I think dentists have more faith than anybody. It's a miracle that more of them don't get their fingers bitten off.

DENTS

865. Most people become much more outraged over a dented fender than they do over having their character dented.

DEODORANT

866. There are times when the most valuable thing a man can have up his sleeve is a pleasant smelling deodorant.

DEPENDENT

867. Some women get rich by becoming dependent on as many husbands as possible.

DEPRECIATION

868. Nothing depreciates a car faster than a neighbor buying a new one.

DEPRESSION

869. You can tell that a depression is coming when businessmen start reducing the number of unemployed on their payrolls.

DESPAIR

870. Nothing proliferates more despair than giving into a little bit of it.

DESSERT

871. There are two times when a closed mouth can be of help to you — when you're about to say something against a person, and when you're offered dessert.

DESTINATION

872. In this life, nothing helps one to reach his first

destination more than knowing exactly what time he is due in the second one.

DESTINY

873.   Always treat the other person as though he holds your destiny in his hands — and he will never let you down.

DESTRUCTION OF MAN

874.   Now that man has learned to control nature, his next biggest challenge is to be able to control his half-wittedness.

DETACHED GARAGE

875.   A detached garage is one of the few remaining reasons that forces some people to take a walk.

DETAILS

876.   Details are boring things, to be sure, but the man who ignores them will ultimately discover that they will overcome him.

DETECTIVES

877.   It is a pity that more women do not become detectives — where can you find a more foolproof lie detector!

DETERIORATION

878.   The state of the world has deteriorated to the point where too many people are driving psychiatrists crazy!

DEVIL

879.   The devil is like a certain kind of friend; if you run into a lot of money, you'll find him right beside you.

DIAMONDS

880. A girl's idea of expanding her base of operations is to acquire a bigger diamond.

DICTATORS

881. America is a country infested with dictators, and they are all under six years of age.

882. The power structure of a dictator always is built upon rotten pillars.

883. As soon as you notice that everyone has started to agree with you, you had better amend your dictatorial ways.

DIET

884. The main trouble with our modern diet seems to be that it contains so little food for thought.

885. If man had to survive on eating his own words he would most surely die from overeating and malnutrition.

886. The best way to throw your weight around is by dieting.

887. A good diet is one that can deal you a heavy blow below the belt.

888. A fathead is one person who cannot be helped by a diet.

889. Life Insurance statistics prove that millions of people would rather die than diet.

890. Millions of Americans claim to be on a diet, but the trouble is that they don't observe it between meals.

891. Nothing will take the starch out of a man like a wife who is on a strict carbohydrate-free diet.

DIET ADVICE

892.   Diet advice — control thighself.

DIETING

893.   Most attempts at dieting are similar to going into debt —
they both inch up on you.

894.   A sure-fire formula for losing weight would be to gauge
your appetite by your salary . . . after taxes.

DIFFICULTIES

895.   One man who becomes spurred on to action by
difficulties can get more done than a dozen men who lose their
initiative by success.

896.   There are no really difficult jobs; there are only people
who make easy jobs difficult.

897.   The fellow who refuses to face a difficulty should not
be surprised if it sneaks up and kicks him from behind.

DIGNITY

898.   The hidden root of all dignity is complete self-confidence and security.

899.   Dignity is the art of making yourself heard without
boasting.

900.   Nothing adds dignity to a person like being able to
attract the respect of anyone holding a high office.

DILEMMA

901. One sure way to land yourself on the horns of a dilemma is to keep shooting the bull.

DIME

902. About the only time a dime is worth as much as ever is when you have to use it in the absence of a screwdriver.

DINNER

903. A good housewife is one who spends two hours getting the dinner ready, and five minutes prettying up to greet her husband at the door when he comes home.

904. The simplest way for a husband to get out of doing the dishes is to take his wife out to dinner.

905. Few sounds are more conducive to making a fellow feel right with the world than the sound of his wife in the kitchen getting ready to serve dinner.

DINNER DISHES

906. The surest way to get out of helping your wife with the dinner dishes is to buy her expensive china.

DIPLOMACY

907. Diplomacy is frequently the art of making a good impression unexpectedly.

DIRECTIONS

908. When a person stops, listens, and looks at you, he may only be getting ready to give you misleading directions.

909. In the course of my travels I have found that the world is filled with people who are willing to give you directions; the only trouble is that most of them don't know how to get there either.

DIRT

910. You never realize how expensive dirt is until you buy some by the truckload.

DISCARDS

911. If there is something around the house that you are not sure you will need or not, you can always find out tomorrow by throwing it in the trash can today.

DISCIPLINE

912. The secret of bringing up a child properly is in knowing when to give it a big hand. . .and where!

913. You can train a child to do many things by strict discipline except to run into your arms when you come into the house.

914. Somebody ought to write a book on how to raise children by disciplining their grandmothers.

DISCONTENT

915. Nothing makes a person respond more creatively than a level of discontent that approaches the unbearable.

DISCOUNT

916. Nothing prompts you to pay a bill like the arrival of a reminder with the discount added.

DISCOVERIES

917. Most great discoveries were made by a trifle stubbing its toe.

918. The history of science reveals one consistent conclusion — nobody ever set out deliberately to make THE GREATEST discoveries; they always were found unexpectedly along the way.

919. A woman's idea of making an exciting discovery is to recognize the strange man who has been visiting her neighbor regularly.

920. A disillusioned young man is one who finally discovers a young girl made to order, and finds out he has to obey her.

921. Some women manage to make the most exciting discoveries each day — about their neighbors.

922. Nothing makes something more valuable to you than throwing it away a day before you discover how badly you need it.

923. By the time most people discover that health is everything they've lost it.

DISCRIMINATION

924. Knowledge alone will dispel all forms of discrimination. Not until man realizes that the atoms in all persons are identical and are constantly being interchanged will prejudice and discrimination vanish from this planet.

DISHES

925. A woman can always find plenty of interesting things to tell her husband as long as he is willing to stay around and help with the dishes.

926. A housewife's idea of talking shop is to keep the conversation going while her husband does the dishes for her.

927. One time I really hate to hear the telephone ring for my wife is when we're halfway through the dishes.

DISHONESTY

928. Everybody is dishonest except that some are better than others in covering it up in Sunday clothes.

DISILLUSIONMENT

929. The most disillusioned girls are those who got married because they were tired of going steady.

DISPOSITION

930. Nothing improves a man's disposition like discovering a better girl in his wife than he bargained for.

931. Nothing improves a woman's disposition like a bouquet of flowers from an old flame who still thinks she's single.

932. Nothing improves a golfer's disposition like finding a better ball than he went looking for.

933. Nothing bolsters a man's disposition like having enough courage to admit he was wrong.

934. Nothing improves the disposition of a middle-aged man like good news from his dentist.

935. There are few things that will do more to improve a man's disposition than owning up to a mistake.

936. A happy marriage is one that improves a woman's looks and a man's disposition.

937. There is nothing better for a woman's disposition than a very successful husband.

DISTANCE

938. Distance is a relative matter, especially when they find out that you've fallen into money.

DISTRACTION

939. If distraction could be classed as a form of arithmetic, some women would be mathematical geniuses.

DISTRIBUTION

940. Distribution is the world's biggest problem whether its distribution of money, hair, or parking space.

941. Many a man with hair on his chest would love to transplant it on his head.

DISTRUST

942. When a woman doesn't distrust her husband it may only mean she knows his weaknesses.

943. Nothing makes a marriage rust, like distrust.

944. Distrust is to marriage what termites are to an old frame building.

DIVIDING LINE

945. The fellow who says he'll meet you halfway usually thinks he's standing on the dividing line.

DIVORCE

946. If you want to find out how silly this divorce business is ask a couple celebrating their golden wedding anniversary.

947. Judging from the divorce rate it is a pity young people don't use more horsesense before they get hitched.

948. A really poor person is one who can afford to get married, but cannot afford to get divorced.

949. When it comes to some women making fortunes, their prizewinning strategy is to force a divorce.

DO

950. The secret of making dough still is do.

DOCTOR

951. The average heart specialist can usually check the condition of his patient's heart simply by sending him a bill.

952. Doctors used to be more concerned about a patient's malaise than they were about a patient's inclination to a malpractice suit.

953. A considerate doctor is one who never mails his bills until he's sure that the patients are well enough to receive them.

954. An honest doctor is one who will admit that he also needs the patient — to help him pay his bills.

955. A successful doctor is one who is a specialist at getting his patients to pay his fees.

956. When it comes to selecting a good doctor, it pays to check out ahead of time how often he gets sick.

957. Every good doctor knows that some of his best patients are those who aren't very sick, but who are prompt at paying their bills.

958. A doctor usually has two kinds of charity patients — those who can't afford to pay him and those who can.

DOCTOR BILLS

959. When it comes to mailing doctor bills you can't accuse the average physician of a lack of practice.

960. Too many modern doctors are preoccupied in searching for tax loopholes.

961. The trouble with some doctors who believe in shock treatments is they use bills instead of pills.

962. Some doctors believe in shock treatments — mailed out the first of every month.

963. A new father never realizes how deeply indebted he is to society until he receives the obstetrician's bill.

964. The good old fashioned family doctor has vanished with the horse-and-buggy, and the man who has taken his place has developed a bank-side manner.

965. Most doctors can spot a charity patient before they even start the examination.

DOG

966. A dog is one of the few remaining reasons why some people can be persuaded to go for a walk.

967. Personality is what a man has if his dog starts running for him the moment he comes into sight.

968. The reason dogs are such popular friends is they'll do exactly as they're told.

DOG-TIRED

969. The fellow who growls all day long is bound to be dog-tired by the end of the day.

DOLLAR

970. All you have to do to stretch a dollar these days is try to hold on to it.

DOUBLE TALK

971. When people tell you either how young you look or how thin you are you can be sure that they are double talking.

DOUGH

972. The trouble with dough that you manage to get your hands on these days is that its buying power is only half-baked.

973. The only way you can get dough to stick to your fingers today is to bake your own bread.

974. Anybody can make dough in America if he needs bread badly enough to pay his bills.

975. These days before a person can rise to the uppercrust he's got to make plenty of dough.

976. A badly needed invention in America today is some kind of dough that really sticks to your fingers.

977. The wrong time to be getting down to earth is when you're in the undertaker's hands.

DREAMERS

978. The only person with some justification of dreaming that money grows on trees is a waiter, but even he knows it's more likely to be found on tabletops.

DREAMS

979. The average girl dreams of marrying a man who can afford to buy her lovely furniture, and also be strong enough to keep moving it around for her.

980. No matter how horrible a dream may be you can always count on somebody to make it come true.

981. A dream is like a spike poised on a railroad tie — until the sledge hammer of determination drives it home it is useless.

982. The dreams that have really changed the world have been those of a restless individual so overwhelmed by an idea that he would rather work at testing it than sleep.

983. More people have been shown the way to success by dreams than by studying books.

984. Overestimating your own capabilities is one of the surest way to make at least a few of your dreams come true.

DRESS

985. Most young girls don't dress to kill: they're more interested in bagging their man alive.

986. Girls who dress to kill not infrequently cook that way too.

DRINK

987 The safest way to drink yourself to death is with water.

988. There are just about as many people in the nation who wear glasses as drink from them.

DRIVE

989. All it takes to put new drive into some men is the obligation to meet alimony payments.

DRIVERS

990. A careful driver is one who has just received a traffic ticket.

991. All we need to do to make good drivers out of the women is to teach them to be as careful about curves when they're driving as when they're getting all dressed up.

992. From the way some motorists drive you would think they had graduated as parking lot attendants.

993. A careful driver is one who is following a traffic cop.

994. The fellow who drives with one hand on the wheel has one foot in the grave.

DRIVING

995. A lot of motorists risk their necks speeding to work in the morning just so they can sit at their desk and read the newspaper.

996. Nothing improves a person's driving like a police car right in back of him.

997. The surest way to lose control of your car is to fall behind on the payments.

998. Many people who are extra careful behind the wheel of their car don't do nearly as careful a job driving their bodies.

999. The trouble with many Sunday drivers is they don't drive any better during the week.

1000. Judging from the accident statistics there is a high turnover among automobiles.

DRUGS

1001. The best miracle drug yet invented is a pat on the back.

DRUNKENNESS

1002. Getting soused to cure your worries is like cleaning a gas tank with a blowtorch; the results are a lot more certain than your chance to enjoy them.

DYNAMO

1003. No matter how big a dynamo a man may be, he still needs a good wife to provide the spark.

EARLY BIRD

1004. The early bird not only catches the worm, but also the parking place.

EARLY RISERS

1005. The trouble with some early risers I know is the way they have to struggle to stay awake on the job.

EARTH

1006. The trouble with sitting on top of the world is that our planet is so unsteady.

EASE

1007. Nothing is more exhausting for a conscientious man than trying to take it easy.

EASY CHAIR

1008. An easy chair is one that is hard to get in and even harder to get out of.

EAT

1009. The secret of good health lies not so much in eating half of what you do as in saying one-tenth of what you say.

EAVESDROPPING

1010. You may hear some awful things said about yourself if you are foolish enough to go eavesdropping.

ECCENTRIC

1011. In our modern day, soon the most eccentric people in the world are going to be those exceptional few who are genuinely happy.

ECONOMY

1012.   The time to be economical is when you're prosperous; you won't have any choice in the matter when you're not.

ECUMENISM

1013.   Ecumenism has dealt a severe blow to Catholics and Protestants alike — now neither can get much pleasure out of converting the other.

1014.   The ultimate in ecumenism will only be achieved when all peoples reach a minimum standard of knowledgeability.

EDUCATION

1015.   A well-educated man is one who handles his knowledge like a time piece, and waits for you to ask the question before he gives you the answer.

1016.   A well-educated man is one who is married to a brilliant woman that he likes to listen to.

1017.   The object of a college education should be to teach a man how he could get along in life if he was unlucky enough not to have gotten one.

1018.   Man will show very little improvement until society sets up rules that will make it easier to learn to be good than it is to learn to be bad.

1019.   It always amazes me to observe how many brilliant scholars emerge from parents who could not even read or write.

1020.   Education in the United States will not reach its full stature of influence until school children will clamor to have their school terms extended.

1021. Learning how and when to hold your tongue is the best formal education of all.

1022. An educated person is one who knows how to be ignorant intelligently.

1023. A person with a great reservoir of knowledge is not well educated unless he knows when to turn the spigot on and off.

EFFICIENCY

1024. You can tell a lot about the efficiency of an executive by examining his wastebasket.

EFFORT

1025. Middle age is good for a man because it teaches him at last that a lot of things he would like to do aren't important enough to make him exert the effort.

1026. Nothing will make a man put his best foot forward like getting the other one in hot water.

1027. Middle age is the time of life when a little effort goes only a little way.

1028. The closest thing to an all-out effort on the part of some women is wearing an evening dress.

1029. It takes a lot of effort nowadays to save a few pennies — even more than it does to make a lot of dollars.

EGO

1030. Nothing helps to bolster your ego like an unexpected stroke of good luck.

1031. One of the surest ways to bolster your ego is suddenly to find a simple solution to what you always felt was a most difficult problem.

EGOTISM

1032. No drug has more power to cause hallucinations than egotism.

1033. Egotism is a form of drug addiction on the part of those who are the least able to control it.

1034. Most persons who are self-centered act as though they're off-balance.

1035. An egotist is a man who aims to please — himself.

1036. An egotist is a person who suffers from an error of superiority.

1037. A egotist is a person who can match two I's against each one of yours.

EIGHTEENTH HOLE

1038. Life is like golf — the score doesn't count at all unless you stick it out and finish at the 18th hole.

ELBOW GREASE

1039. Any man who can combine push with elbow grease today can get along without pull.

ELECT

1040. If the elect are those who will be allowed into heaven, the plight of the elected seems rather dismal.

ELECTIONS

1041. As soon as the elections and Thanksgiving Day are both over it is easy to understand why one follows the other . . . in that order.

ELOPEMENT

1042. Something engaged couples wish they could do the day before the wedding.

ELOQUENCE

1043. There is much more éloquence in one's ears than in one's tongue.

1044. Eloquence is the ability to say the right thing when you think of it.

ELUSION

1045. A bachelor is a man who can elude a pretty airline stewardess even though she's just strapped him to his seat.

EMBARRASSMENT

1046. The most embarrassing of all questions a man could be asked while under oath would be for an honest opinion of himself.

EMOTIONS

1047. The difference between bashfulness and arrogance is often nothing more than good control over one's emotions.

EMPLOYEE

1048. A well-adjusted employee is one who can begin the second week of his vacation without getting nervous about being missed back at the office.

1049. A reliable employee is one whose disposition doesn't change whether the boss is with him or not.

1050. A good employee always keeps one jump behind the boss.

EMPLOYERS

1051. People who work only for themselves eventually discover what a poor employer they are.

1052. It always pays to listen to your boss — whether you pay any attention to what your wife says or not.

ENCOURAGEMENT

1053. Nothing encourages a man to put his tongue in his cheek like finding a new cavity in a back tooth.

1054. Nothing encourages a man to do a good day's work like a pat on the back of his wallet.

1055. These are the days when nothing encourages a young man to burn the midnight oil like a tank full of gas in his father's car.

1056. Nothing encourages a man to do a good day's work like just having completed one.

ENDS

1057. The wrong way to try and make ends meet is in a sitting position.

ENDURANCE

1058. The secret of being able to take things as they come is to stagger the unpleasant ones far enough apart.

ENEMIES

1059. No enemy is more dangerous than a friend who isn't quite sure he is for or against you.

1060. There is no safer way to get rid of your enemies than by speaking and acting as though you did not know that any existed.

1061. You can never be sure that you have really won an enemy over to your side until he asks you for a loan.

1062. Love your enemies; but if you really want to make them mad, ignore them completely.

1063. At no time is praise more valuable to you than when you praise your enemies.

1064. Character is what it takes to destroy your enemies by praising them.

1065. Many persons who pray for their enemies are most unkind to their friends.

1066. Unless you give credit to your enemies, you can expect to go into debt with your friends.

1067. Nothing will increase the vigor with which your enemies will attack you like letting them know you're not paying any attention to them.

1068. There's no surer way of getting rid of your enemies than by outliving them.

1069. The only time an enemy can really do you much harm is if you can't muster enough charity to forgive him.

1070. One of the most lasting pleasures you can experience is the feeling that comes over you when you genuinely forgive an enemy — whether he knows it or not.

ENERGY

1071. It is amazing how a surplus of energy can frequently make up for a deficit in qualifications.

1072. All men would be truly created equal, only if each were parcelled out the same amount of energy for a lifetime.

1073. Nothing will sap your energy quite so fast as trying to hold on to your own reputation.

1074. It takes a lot of energy to say very little. That's why those who say nothing get so much done.

ENGAGEMENT

1075. A woman's idea of licking the problem is to get engaged.

1076. Nothing improves the use of a young girl's left hand like a new engagement ring on it.

1077. Most young girls sport an engagement ring like a young boy coming home with a straight "A" report card.

ENGLISH LANGUAGE

1078. A perfect command of the English language permits you to develop a reputation for being an excellent conversationalist without having to say anything meaningful.

ENIGMA

1079. It is an enigma of the human scene that almost to a

man people will say nothing but good about the dead, and almost nothing but bad about the living.

ENJOYMENT

1080. The real enjoyment of living, like the real enjoyment of eating a steak, comes when you put your teeth into it.

1081. Solitude is a reward you can enjoy just by being punctual.

1082. The declining years in a man's life are those when he starts to enjoy lying down on the job.

1083. Nothing helps you to enjoy your job like an independent income.

1084. Nothing makes a man enjoy a pipeful of tobacco like a wife who helps him light it up.

ENTHUSIASM

1085. The greatest achievements of man have always depended upon a marriage between intense enthusiasm and creative genius.

1086. Enthusiasm for hard work is a necessity — especially if you are the boss!

1087. I would rather have one man with enthusiasm working with me than 10 who are complacent.

1088. We need a new generation of Americans who will carry their enthusiasm for getting ahead of traffic over into their jobs.

1089. Every successful organization or manager that I know of learned to live with enthusiastic employees no matter how eccentric they may have been.

1090. Enthusiasm is an essential to success as is a switch to lighting up a darkened room.

1091. When a man is enthusiastic about hard work he is either self-employed or paying to have it done.

1092. The man who roars to success is one who is on fire with enthusiasm inside, but who appears calm on the outside.

1093. The most valuable thing I have or ever expect to have is enthusiasm, and I would rather pass this on to my children than anything else.

1094. One of the best tests of the state of your health is the enthusiasm with which you can approach a soft boiled egg at breakfast.

1095. Next to getting enthusiastic about your job, the most important requirement to get ahead is to become enthusiastic about your boss.

1096. Enthusiasm is like premium gasoline; it helps to take the knocks out of living.

1097. Enthusiasm is as essential to success as is water to reviving a dying plant.

1098. Always remember it is much easier to calm a person's enthusiasm than it is to start a fire under him in the first place.

1099. Enthusiasm is what leads some people to pay $3 for a golf ball and a $10 greens fee to chase after it.

1100. Almost anyone can develop enthusiasm — but the kind of enthusiasm that will get you somewhere is the kind that possesses you!

ENTREPRENEUR

1101. An enterprising young man is one who becomes

interested in a company because the owner would make a good father-in-law.

ENVY

1102. Never envy the other fellow; chances are he is just as envious of you.

1103. Envy is a contagious disease which you are most likely to catch from your neighbors.

EPIGRAMS

1104. There is so much wisdom condensed into some epigrams that it is little wonder people refuse to believe them. For example, it took me and my wife eighteen years to realize fully that, "Nature to be commanded, must be obeyed."

EPITAPH

1105. No man ever discovers what a wonderful fellow he is unless he insists on having his epitaph prepared while he's still alive.

EQUALITY

1106. All men are created equal but, alas, only in the eyes of God!

EQUAL RIGHTS

1107. Women who scream for equal rights are probably unable to find husbands who can support them in the manner they would like to be.

ERASER

1108. The best way to erase a mistake is to admit it.

1109. The best eraser in the world is a good night's sleep.

1110. The best eraser in the world is an eight-hour dose of hard work.

ERR

1111. To err is only human, especially when the boss is looking over your shoulder.

ERRORS

1112. Nothing has more lives than an error you refuse to correct.

1113. An error can have a happy ending, if your boss accepts the explanation.

1114. Some errors are things you did when you were younger and wish you were now able to repeat.

1115. The quickest way to lose the seat of your pants is to refuse to own up to an error.

1116. An error is like a leak in the roof of your house . . . the amount of damage it can do depends on how soon you correct it.

1117. The trouble with a lot of childish errors is they are made by adults.

1118. People who try to cover up errors end up like squirrels who hide rotten nuts.

ESCAPE

1119. About the only way a man can get away from a woman who is after him is with a car that has more horsepower.

ESSENTIALS

1120. A recession is a period during which you discover how much money you were wasting on nonessentials.

ESTATES

1121. The trait most people enjoy inheriting from their ancestors is trust — in the form of an estate.

EVANGELISTS

1122. There always have been two kinds of evangelists — some were genuinely interested in the flock, the others in their fleece.

EVENING

1123. The way most Americans like to kill an evening is to put plenty of life into it.

EVIL

1124. Most persons who are determined to destroy the roots of evil have trouble calling a spade a spade.

1125. You can prove that man has an insatiable appetite for reading about evil by picking up any metropolitan daily newspaper.

1126. Money may be the root of all evil, but it's hard to pick some of life's cutest blossoms without it.

EXAGGERATION

1127.   A fool exaggerates how much he is worth, a wise man exaggerates how happy he is!

EXAMPLE

1128.   People are stimulated by example — those under you won't work unless you do.

1129.   A man knows he's doing right by his children when he finds himself trying to live up to their good example.

1130.   The best compliment a child can pay his parents is to set a good example for them.

1131.   People are stimulated by example — especially little people under six.

EXCELLENCE

1132.   Always remember that BIGNESS does not insure excellence — the mind still is mightier than the brawn.

EXCUSE

1133.   In cooking up an excuse, you're in danger of getting burnt.

EXECUTIVE

1134.   A good executive is a man who can take a back seat among his men without losing his grip on the steering wheel.

1135.   A valuable executive is one who can tell you exactly how much money his job is saving the company.

1136.   The kind of executive timber that becomes dead wood is a man with a chip on his shoulder.

1137. Sometimes an executive who manages to keep his desk clear has a couple of assistants who are buried under the stuff he's routed to them.

1138. The real mark of an outstanding executive is how hard he works at making himself unneeded by his staff.

1139. When it comes to carrying a heavy executive load it is amazing how strong a pretty, highly capable secretary can be.

1140. A wise executive is one who is more preoccupied with the best way to get a thing done than he is with the speed with which he does it.

1141. A successful executive is one who returns home from the office refreshed by the fact that all who work for him went home exhausted.

1142. One of the first things that every top executive learns is that a very high percentage of his salary goes just to pay him to listen.

1143. A good executive is one who can keep his mind on his work — no matter how pretty his secretary is.

1144. A good executive is one who is to his organization what the mainspring is to a watch.

1145. A good executive is one who can't stand "yes" men because he knows they are either lazy — or scared stiff of him.

1146. The key quality of a top executive is the ability to convince his associates that they have far more ability than they thought they had.

1147. Nobody adds more to an executive's output than a secretary who works through his lunch hours.

1148. A happily married executive is one who insists on hiring a male secretary.

1149. A good executive is a man who believes in sharing the credit for the work somebody else does.

1150. A modern executive is a man who wears his clothes out at the seat of his pants.

1151. A good executive is one who never complains about having to do any job — unless it is an easy one.

1152. A modern executive is a man who wears out several suits to every pair of shoes.

1153. Nothing adds to an executive's leisure time like making decisions.

1154. A modern executive is a man who believes in getting the other fellow to do his best for him.

1155. One way to make a high pressure executive slow down to a walk is to ask him to be a pall bearer at another one's funeral.

1156. A good executive is one who doesn't believe in wasting his energy on easy tasks that he knows the members of his staff can do just as well.

1157. It is far more important for a good executive to be able to recognize and support ability than it is for him to have it himself.

1158. A good executive is one who can get the most feathers in his hat with the least squawk from those who work for him.

1159. The highest paid executives that I know are best at spotting outstanding talent in those they hired!

1160. Nothing insures the success of some executives like a hard-working secretary they have to keep up with.

1161. Most executives are not nearly as interested in having a big office as they are in having a pretty secretary.

1162. The one subject an executive usually gives plenty of attention to is a pretty secretary who worships him.

1163. Some of the hardest working executives I know, including me, have indefatigable secretaries.

1164. The true stature of a modern executive is determined by the heights he will climb to tackle the toughest problems.

EXERCISE

1165. The kind of exercise that wears most people down and out is running out of money.

1166. The most exhausting form of exercise is trying to run away from expenses.

1167. The best thing to get out of exercise is rest.

1168. Rolling in money is a painful exercise today, because it is spiked with hidden taxes.

1169. The average father is willing to admit that the most exhausting form of exercise is child's play.

EXHAUSTION

1170. Nothing is more exhausting than searching for easy ways to make a living.

1171. These are days when it is hard to find a Mr. Jones who isn't exhausted from trying to keep up with himself.

1172. A man has reached middle age when all it takes to exhaust him is an evening of television.

1173. Middle age is the time of life when the two steps a man used to take at a time he now takes to get exhausted.

1174. People who are in a run-down condition usually get that way by being too wound-up in themselves.

EXHILARATION

1175. Nothing is more exhilarating than saying the right thing at the wrong time.

EXPENSES

1176. A rich man is one who doesn't consider anything an expense, if it saves him some money.

1177. The most costly thing in the world to support is a cover-up — of anything.

1178. Most people have a good time traveling on an expense account until they sit down and have to fill one out.

1179. Nothing puts a man's honesty to the acid test like sitting down to fill out an expense account form.

1180. A completely honest person is one who always ends up in the red when he travels on an expense account.

1181. The two most costly things to try to keep up with are the Joneses and appearances.

1182. Today there is no surer way to meet expenses than by doing nothing but standing still.

1183. The most exhaustive form of exercise is trying to run away from expenses.

EXPERIENCE

1184. Experience is what makes a man check the basement for termites when he buys his second house.

1185. A man with a lot of experience is one who has just built a house on one.

1186. The best substitute for experience is to check with your wife beforehand.

1187. Experience is the only thing I know that becomes more valuable each time you have to use it.

1188. Experience is what makes you do a thing right when somebody is looking.

1189. Success consists in selling experience at a profit.

1190. An experienced gardener is one who knows a weed when he sees one.

1191. Experience is to life what enzymes are to chemistry — it permits you to get results with maximum speed and minimum energy.

1192. It often happens that persons who speak in short sentences put them together from long experience.

1193. Experience is like money; just when you think you've got enough something happens to make you wish you had a lot more.

1194. Experience is never more valuable to a man than when it permits him to do a tough job right the first time.

1195. Experience is a marvelous asset — especially when it permits you to do what others think is impossible at the first try.

EXPERIMENTAL FACT

1196. An experimental fact differs from any other kind of fact in that it does not depend on who repeats it.

EXPERT

1197. The easiest way to stump an expert is to ask him a question that has an obvious answer.

1198. An expert is a man who is especially careful only to make little mistakes.

1199. The best time to stump an expert is when he's a long distance from his reference books.

1200. An expert is a man who can tell you what will happen, and have a knockout explanation ready for you if it doesn't.

1201. Many experts I know owe their success to their ability to keep their mouth shut when they aren't sure of the right answers.

1202. Never take what a scientists says on faith alone. Some scientists can be as biased and pigheaded as some politicians and clergymen.

EXPRESSION

1203. Nothing controls the other person's mood like the expression on your own face.

EXTRAVAGANCE

1204. An extravagant neighbor is one who lives beyond your means.

EXTREMES

1205. Women are creatures of extremes — you can make them deliriously happy by putting something new on their head or on their feet.

EYE ON THE BALL

1206. One of the nice things about keeping your eye on the ball is that you are more likely to find it when you get in the rough.

EYES

1207. The fellow who enters into marriage with half-shut eyes ought to keep them only half-open afterwards.

1208. Tolerance consists in seeing things with your heart instead of with your eyes.

1209. When two married people see eye to eye on something, chances are they're giving each other the high sign to break up the party.

1210. Any man who claims he sees eye to eye with his wife probably means that he's exactly her height.

FACE

1211. How you wear your face is more important in determining the impression you make on others than is the way you dress.

1212. Always look a man in the face unless you distrust him. Then, look at both his faces.

1213. One of the big differences between a man and a woman is that a man is usually taken at face value.

1214. One of the first things you should think about when you face yourself in the mirror each morning is that dozens of persons will have their day brightened or dulled by the kind of face you present to them.

FACTS

1215. An experimental fact differs from any other kind of fact in that it doesn't depend on who says it.

1216. Every minute you think you may save in not getting a difficult fact straight will cost you hours, days, even possibly years of your life later.

1217. Facts become ghosts that will haunt you the minute you turn your back on them.

1218. A man can talk for years about the facts of life and suddenly discover that he runs out of material in sixty seconds when he tries to explain them to his little boy.

FAILURE

1219. Some wonder why they are failures, when their only mistake was in choosing themselves as models.

1220. Never give a man up as long as he doesn't.

1221. All through life remember that the world will gauge you more by what you fail to do than by what you do.

1222. A man doesn't become a failure until he is satisfied with being one.

1223. A man is a failure long before he starts blaming his boss — at home or at work.

1224. The reason a lot of people fail is they keep trying to better the other fellow when they should be trying to better themselves.

1225. The road to failure is often decorated by the flowers of past achievements.

1226. Most failures that I have known were experts at making excuses!

1227. A failure never becomes a hopeless mistake unless it stops you from trying again.

1228. No man is a failure as long as he refuses to take it lying down.

1229. Life will give you anything that you are satisfied with — especially failure.

1230. A failure is a man who overdraws his experience account.

1231. The surest way for a person to fall down on the job is to do nothing but sit.

1232. The worst kind of failure I can think of is a fellow who never even tried to succeed.

1233. Nothing encourages failure more than a conviction that failure is inevitable!

FAIR-WEATHER FRIEND

1234. A fair-weather friend is one who isn't any more dependable than the weather.

FAITH

1235. It is always easier to believe the unexplainable than it is to understand the explainable.

1236. The best way I know of to make a person believe something is to make it so complicated that he cannot understand it.

1237. At no time can one's faith appear more reassuring than when word has reached you that your rich uncle just died.

FALL

1238. The man who insists on getting down to earth probably remembers a very hard fall.

FALSEHOOD

1239.   There is only one legitimate use for a falsehood; to test a friend before trusting him with a secret.

FAME

1240.   There is no hotter flame than fame to test the true mettle of men.

1241.   Fame is never more fleeting than after the Internal Revenue Service examines it.

1242.   Fame, like flame, is harmless until you start inhaling it.

1243.   Too many persons who thirst after fame succeed only in becoming infamous.

1244.   Sometimes it is a short interval between giving autographs and getting fingerprinted.

1245.   The anticipation of fame always is so much sweeter than actually tasting it.

1246.   People who have the most contempt for fame are those who have long ago resigned themselves to mediocrity.

1247.   About the only thing that I know that is more unsettling than fame is — quicksand.

1248.   For years a prominent Dallasite told me he has been using my Quotoons in his lectures and writings liberally. And then, he discovered I was not a relative of John The Baptist, but alive and living within 40 miles from him.

1249.   Fame that is achieved by self-promotion usually burns brightly for a very short time.

1250.   Some children are born famous — but few adults die that way.

1251. The feeling of fame is as fleeting as the touch of a beautiful women — and just as thrilling.

1252. Fame makes great men greater and little men lesser.

1253. Anyone can become famous if he isn't afraid to publicize his vices and his dishonesty.

FAMILIARITY

1254. Nobody tries to breed familiarity with you like a political candidate who is only one week away from election day.

FAMILY

1255. A man knows he's doing right by his family when his teenage son won't let him cut the grass, his wife won't let him touch the dishes and his daughter still likes to sit on his lap.

1256. Nothing holds a modern family together like good behavior on the part of the parents.

1257. One nice thing about admitting that you are wrong is there's always the chance that the rest of the family will disbelieve you.

1258. Raising a family is more satisfying than getting rich because eventually you reach a point when you're willing to admit that you have enough.

FAMILY TREE

1259. Sometimes the shade from the family tree comes in handy for covering up an unsightly past.

1260. Before most people start boasting about their family tree, they already have done a good pruning job on it.

FANATIC

1261. A fanatic always reminds me of a windshield wiper working when it isn't raining.

FANCY

1262. When a smart woman takes a fancy to a man she makes sure that he gets more than just a passing look at her.

FARCES

1263. The biggest farce of man's history has been the argument that wars are fought to save civilization.

FARMERS

1264. A lucky farmer is one who raised a bumper crop of boys.

1265. It takes a lot of harrowing experience before a farmer can cultivate a good crop.

1266. One reason farmers are such neighbor-loving people is that their neighbors usually are more than a stone's throw away.

1267. A successful farmer is one who can turn his harrowing experiences into profit.

FAST DRIVER

1268. The difference between a slow driver and a fast driver frequently is a few quick ones.

FATE

1269. As soon as a fellow resigns himself to fate, his resignation is promptly accepted.

1270. The trouble with resigning yourself to fate never starts until you do.

1271. Fate is a great respecter of action because action is the surest way to change it.

FATHEAD

1272. A fathead is one person who cannot be helped by diet.

FATHER

1273. A father of five children is deathly sick when he doesn't show up for work.

1274. All a father has to do to knock the badness out of his son is to beat the tar out of him on a tennis court.

1275. How much a father spends for his son's toys isn't nearly as important as how much time he spends playing with him.

1276. The average father is willing to admit that the most exhausting form of exercise is child's play.

1277. Nowadays a father is more likely to take after his son — especially when he's looking for the family car.

1278. Nothing is better for a father than being beaten now and then by his teen-age son at ping-pong.

1279. One thing you can't do with a father of five boys is catch him off guard.

1280. A father of five boys will hardly agree that there is safety in numbers.

1281. A truly rich father is one who can get his children to run into his arms even when he comes home emptyhanded.

1282. A father never realizes how deeply indebted he is to society until the time comes when he has to pay for his daughter's wedding.

1283. A father knows that he is doing right by his children if they leave their seat before the T.V. set and run into his arms the minute he comes home from work.

1284. A new father never realizes how deeply indebted he is to society until he receives the obstetrician's bill.

1285. No father has really tasted the thrill of fatherhood until his six-year old daughter starts waiting on him hand and foot.

1286. The sensible father of a teen-ager looks for the car before he searches for the keys.

1287. The average father today wears out a pair of shoes while the rest of the family wears out a set of tires.

1288. These days a courageous father is one who can take advice from his son like a man.

1289. The man who frequently calls the game of love on account of darkness is the girl's father.

1290. Fathers without sons and fathers with sons are frequently sorry for each other.

FATHER-IN-LAW

1291. The best preparation a young man can have for marriage is to find a successful future father-in-law.

1292. An enterprising young man is one who becomes interested in a company because the owner would make a good father-in-law.

FATIGUE

1293. A truly tired woman is one who can't drum up enough energy to tell you she is.

1294. Nothing breeds fatigue like inactivity.

FAULTS

1295. One serious fault that surfaces in a man can cause a total eclipse that blackens out a hundred virtues.

1296. The most universal of all human faults is that of trying every way possible to avoid having to correct any of them.

1297. Take heart if you have faults — they were the source of success of some of the greatest men who lived.

1298. It is a good thing our faults are so hard to see or everybody would have an inferiority complex.

1299. About the only time a person doesn't expect you to agree with him is when he's telling you about his faults.

1300. A spoiled child is one who isn't content with only imitating his parent's faults — he insists on acquiring a few of his own.

1301. When a man starts to brag about his faults it usually pays to check his statements for accuracy.

FAVOR

1302. The same persons who raise a fuss when they don't receive an expected favor are the ones who wouldn't appreciate it if they got it.

1303. It has been my experience that the most difficult thing in the world to do satisfactorily is to confer a favor.

1304. Some persons are so grateful for favors, that they are looking for more.

1305. The politeness of some persons who ask for favors is exceeded only by their impoliteness once they've obtained them.

FEAR

1306. Fear is not always bad or dangerous — without the fear of falling on ice, for example, more persons would have broken hips.

1307. Usually the persons who live in constant fear of losing their health have seldom become seriously ill.

1308. I never have feared the law because I have always tried to live well within it, and religion never has worried me for the same reason.

1309. Some people who live in fear that they will make a mistake are bound to succeed.

FEELINGS

1310. You never know for sure how you feel about a person until you read his obituary.

1311. How much better a woman feels after a good cry depends on what she got out of it.

1312. A successful doctor is one who is a specialist at getting his patients to pay their bills without hurting their feelings.

FEET

1313. Sometimes the reason a fellow doesn't let any grass grow under his feet is they're both in hot water.

1314. Nothing will help a young man to stand on his own two feet today like being too young to get a driver's license.

1315. Nothing improves the value of the ground beneath your feet like building a house on it.

FIGHT

1316. It is not the size of a man's fist that counts, but the amount of fight that lies behind it.

FIGURE

1317. The motivation that makes some women keep in shipshape is other women who are seeworthy.

FINGERNAILS

1318. What the country needs is more men who will wear their fingernails down without a nail file.

FIRST IMPRESSIONS

1319. The effectiveness of first impressions is not unlike the reaction to a first kiss — it all depends on whether the response is "Come again" or "Drop dead, brother!".

FISCAL FITNESS

1320. In the final analysis, what a woman looks for in a man is fiscal fitness.

1321. When it comes to sizing up a prospective husband, most girl's prefer to use a yardstick calibrated in dollars than in feet.

FISH

1322. Nothing increases a man's chances of catching fish like going fishing.

1323. There are few times in a man's life when he is more genuinely happy than when the fish are biting.

1324. Sometimes a fisherman catches more than he expected . . . when he returns home to his wife.

1325. Nothing improves a fisherman's luck like fish in a biting mood.

FISHERMEN

1326. Some of the bery best fishermen I know are now. married because a woman got onto their line.

FISHING

1327. Fishing is never more exciting than on the first day of spring.

1328. Nothing will lift a weight off your mind quite as effectively as a cork bobbing on a fishing line.

1329. A happily married man is one who can go to a party with his wife with the same enthusiasm with which he goes on a fishing trip without her.

1330. At no time does the end of the day come faster than when the fish are biting.

FISHING TRIP

1331. A man knows his wife loves him if she suggests that he go off on a fishing trip by himself.

FITNESS

1332.   Of all the forms of fitness that man can aspire to none is more important or more lasting that fitness of the mind.

FLAMES

1333.   A woman worries about a man's other flames until she puts them all out.

FLATTERY

1334.   When it comes to a flattering diet some people possess insatiable appetites.

1335.   One of the ironies of human relations is that we seldom, if ever, want to flatter those we really love.

1336.   Flattery is the art of making a person dream while he's wide awake.

1337.   One of the most sincere forms of flattery is to have a nine year old girl insist on sitting beside you at a wedding party.

1338.   Sometimes the trouble with the guy who showers you with flattery is that he doesn't know you well enough to spell your name.

1339.   Flattery is as slippery as a banana peel beneath the feet of one who is proud.

FLAVOR

1340.   Money that is spent before it is earned may buy food, but most of the flavor is lost.

FLEAS

1341. Human fleas are just as common as fleas that attack other animals — the main difference is that the human variety is much bigger and has only two legs.

FLOWER

1342. Happiness is like a delicate flower — and frequently just as subject to wilting.

FOG

1343. When a fellow starts blowing his own horn, it's a sure sign that he's in a fog.

FOLLOWERS

1344. The fellow who believes in following the crowd always ends up in the rear.

FOLLY

1345. One man's folly sometimes is much more interesting than another man's fame — at least in book form.

FOOD FOR THOUGHT

1346. Despite our scientific age, one of the least popular items on the menu today seems to be food for thought.

1347. Before swallowing food-for-thought it often pays to check it for boners.

1348. If people had to live on food for thought imagine how hungry some of them would get.

FOOL

1349. The difference between a wise man and a fool is in their hides . . . a fool can be skinned more than once.

1350. A fool is a man who, because he runs into a few bits of good luck, assumes he's now a genius.

1351. One big difference between a fool and a wise man is in their way of thinking; the fool thinks publicly, the wise man privately.

1352. Sometimes a man has to act like a genius to make a fool out of himself.

1353. Wisdom consists in not exceeding the "fool limit".

1354. If you are foolish enough to think about yourself too much, you soon will come to the conclusion that you are the most miserable person in the world.

FOOT

1355. Nothing makes a man put his best foot forward like getting the other one in hot water.

FOOTBALL

1356. The only fellows who get anywhere playing both ends against the middle are opposing football coaches.

FOOTSTEPS

1357. The easiest way to get your son to follow in your footsteps is to promise him the keys to your car.

FOREIGNERS

1358. One of the first thing many foreigners notice about the American family is that the parents usually obey the children.

FORTITUDE

1359. Fortitude is what helps some persons to go through life hearing the trials of others.

FORTUNE

1360. Fortune is like a seesaw: every time it lowers one person to the ground, it raises another to the sky.

1361. Fortune is very generous at times, but when she gives you anything she never tells you for how long.

1362. One man's fortune all too often becomes the same man's misfortune.

FORTUNE TELLERS

1363. The most accurate fortune tellers in America are full-time employees of the Internal Revenue Service.

FRAGRANCE

1364. There is no flower in the world that breathes a sweeter fragrance than a freshly bathed new baby.

FREEDOM

1365. The only time a husband can feel free to shift for himself is when he's all alone in the car.

1366. Of all the freedoms a man may enjoy, none can quite match that which comes from being completely free of debt.

1367. Freedom is like a lock — it is useful only if every person has equal access to the key that can open it.

FRESH PAINT

1368. A man of faith is one who will believe a "Fresh Paint" sign without checking it with his hand.

FRIEND

1369. A friend is one who will continue to talk to you over the back fence even though he is missing his favorite television program.

1370. A friend is a person who wouldn't think of saying nasty things about you except to your face.

1371. A friend is a person who stops, looks and listens to you.

1372. A man's best friend is his mouth provided he doesn't take advantage of it.

1373. A friend is a person you can count on after everybody else has counted you out.

1374. A true friend is one who knows how poor your credit is but lends you badly needed money anyway.

1375. Man has only ten fingers — just enough on which to count the number of true friends one can find in a lifetime.

1376. The most dangerous friends are the fifty-fifty kind who aren't sure they are for or against you.

1377. Friends who are interested in you because you have money are always looking for a way to shortchange you.

1378. A true friend is one who, knowing your faults, boasts about your good points.

1379. A true friend is one who cannot be bought, but can be borrowed from.

1380. The wrong way to pick your friends is to pieces.

1381. Friends that you can buy are a dime a dozen, and each one of them will shortchange you if given a chance.

1382. Some friends I know buy the latest things, but they seldom get to use them because they have to work longer hours to pay for them.

1383. A friend in need is one who never has any trouble finding you.

FRIENDSHIP

1384. A true friend is one who can be trusted and borrowed from.

1385. A true mark of friendship is to be asked for a loan only as a last resort.

1386. Too many people start out to cultivate a friendship and end up harrowing it.

1387. Sometimes a friend in need is a good person to steer clear of.

FUEL

1388. All it takes to rocket some men to the top is the right woman to provide them with the fuel.

FUEL BILL

1389. Nothing leaves a man colder in winter than adding up the fuel bill.

1390. One reason the robin is such a popular bird is that it brings the first news of a drop in your winter's fuel bill.

FUR COAT

1391. A happily married man is one who helps his wife into her fur coat — which she bought before they got married.

FURNISHINGS

1392. Children are the most wonderful furnishings in a house, even if they don't last as long as you would like them to.

FURNITURE

1393. The easiest way to break in new furniture is to bring up a family.

1394. A man usually doesn't give the furniture a second thought until his wife asks him to move it.

1395. The easiest way to break in new furniture is to rent your house — furnished.

1396. There are two kinds of antique furniture — the kind that is too uncomfortable to sit on, and the kind that's too comfortable to get up out of.

FUTURE

1397. The future belongs to those who pay all of their taxes ... federal, excise, state, city, sales, etc., etc.

1398. People who worry the most about the future are usually those who are doing the least to prepare for it.

1399. Always remember that the future is the only thing you cannot lose until you reach it.

1400. The people who are doing the most to prepare for the future are those who are working like the devil in the present.

1401. A man doesn't have to worry about a good future if he marries one.

1402. We always are worrying about the future, and living as though we didn't have one.

1403. People who worry the most about the future usually do the least to prepare for it.

GAMBLERS

1404. Many Americans like to gamble . . . with their money, their wives, and their lives.

GARAGE

1405. If your garage is too small, you can always enlarge it by having your wife park your car.

1406. One advantage of a detached garage is that it forces some people to take a short walk.

1407. Most women drivers can get into their cars safely; the danger doesn't arise until they start backing out of the garage.

1408. America is the only country in the world where a man can build a three-car garage and fill it with cars he doesn't own.

GARBAGE CANS

1409. There are two things in America that are growing bigger together — garbage cans and taxes.

1410. Garbage cans were getting so big in America that somebody had to invent the compactor.

GARDEN

1411. A man is getting old as soon as he decides that it is a lot easier to run a lawnmower over the backyard than it is to plant a garden in it.

GARDENER

1412. A good gardener knows that all he has to do to get rid of weeds is nothing else.

1413. A conscientious gardener is one who believes in becoming buried in his work.

GAS

1414. Running out of gas no longer is the problem it used to be — now you can enjoy jogging to the nearest gas station.

1415. One way to get more people to follow the straight and narrow path would be to build gas stations alongside of it.

GENEROSITY

1416. One form of generosity that can lead to trouble consists in giving others a piece of your mind.

1417. Some of the most generous people in the world are those who insist on sharing their troubles with you.

1418. Before you give something to somebody or go out of your way to do somebody a favor remember ahead of time that the receiver may never forgive your generosity.

GENETIC ENGINEERING

1419. The greatest hazard of genetic engineering lies in the ability of bacteria and viruses to undergo evolutionary changes millions of times faster than man.

GENIUS

1420. The main difference between a genius and the average man in the same profession is that the genius doesn't go to bed until he is a lot more tired.

1421. A genius is a person who has more than a good mind . . . he must also have the vision to see something that everybody else misses.

1422. A genius very often turns out to be a man whose luck was a lot better than yours.

1423. A brilliant man is one who is shrewd enough to recognize you're a genius.

1424. A genius is a man who is in love with his work; a super-genius is one who is in love with his wife . . . and his work.

1425. Never confuse activity, talk, or money with genius.

1426. Sometimes one must stub one's toe badly before being struck by a spark of genius.

1427. True genius exhibits itself only when a superior mind is tied to an energetic body.

1428. The average man becomes a genius by following a hunch that turned out to be outstandingly successful.

1429. Many a flash of genius turns out to be a bolt of ignorance.

1430. One good guess doesn't make a man a genius anymore than a hole in one makes him a good golfer.

1431. Genius occurs only when a person's mind, heart, and hands all work in perfect harmony.

1432. History proves that no man ever became a genius just by claiming to be one.

1433. A man of genius must be more than a powder keg of energy — he must also have enough wisdom to know when to light the fuse.

1434. Every genius I have known loved to get things started well enough to be sure somebody else could put on the finishing touches.

1435. Individual commitment to an individual idea — that's what a genius is made of.

1436. The main difference between a genius and the average man in the same profession is that the genius doesn't go to bed until he is a lot more tired.

1437. A lot of young boys who do badly in school work are geniuses when it come to figuring out how to develop engine trouble when they're on a date.

1438. The world owes most of its progress to the geniuses it tried so desperately to destroy.

1439. Most children are too lazy to prove that they're the geniuses their parents claim them to be.

1440. Geniuses usually behave towards each other like chips of wood on two separate shoulders.

1441. A gentleman is a man who will stand up and take his hat off to his wife.

1442. A gentleman is a man who tells his wife he loves her — even when he doesn't have a reason to.

1443. A gentleman is a man who gives a lady his seat on a bus without first checking to see whether or not she's wearing a wedding ring.

1444. A gentleman is a man who tips his hat and his headlights.

1445. A gentleman is a man who tastes the food before he starts telling his hosts how delicious it is.

1446. A gentleman is a man who understands women, but acts as though he doesn't.

1447. A gentleman is a man who treats people he likes and people he doesn't like with the same consideration.

1448. A true gentleman is a man who treats a woman like a lady no matter how pretty she isn't.

1449. A gentleman is a man who rakes the leaves on his side of the street before you do.

1450. A gentleman is a man who makes it a cinch for a woman to remain a lady.

1451. A gentleman is a man who has trained himself to yawn in such a way that you think he is smiling at you.

1452. A gentleman is a man who wouldn't think of telling a lady anything but the unnaked truth.

1453. A true gentleman is a man who is very careful not to scratch your car in a parking lot.

1454. A gentleman is a man who will slip a nickel in an expired parking meter when he sees a cop coming . . . and do a perfect stranger a good turn.

1455. A gentleman is a man who never misses an ash tray.

1456. A woman can spot a gentleman at ten paces behind her.

1457. A gentleman is a man who can read a woman like a book — to himself.

1458. A gentleman is a man who will never criticize a person except in private.

1459. A gentleman is a man who will step aside for a lady in a crowd, and let her make a path for him.

1460. A gentleman is a man who doesn't believe in misleading women or statements.

1461. The one human characteristic that can make a person stand out above all others in a group is a mannerism of complete gentleness.

GET AHEAD

1462. You can always tell how well a fellow gets along with people by how far he gets ahead of them.

1463. Persons who are itching to get ahead don't have to worry about where to start scratching.

1464. You can always tell how well a fellow gets along with people by how far he gets ahead of them.

GET-A-WAY

1465. No self-respecting girl will chase after a man she's interested in unless he tries to get away.

GETTING ALONG

1466. The secret of getting along with others consists in first mastering the art of getting along with yourself.

GETTING THINGS DONE

1467. I hear a lot of executives declare that you must get things done through other people ... and they double the payroll to prove it.

GETTING TO THE BOTTOM

1468. Many a man who was intent at getting to the bottom of things has become a millionaire through mining.

GET-UP-AND-GO

1469. Middle age has arrived when a man's idea of get-up-and-go is to go to bed.

GHOSTS

1470. The world is filled with ghosts — one for each thing you failed to do when you should have.

GIFTS

1471. One sure way to get a person's wholehearted attention is to describe something you are going to give to him.

1472. A man exhibits true vision when he succeeds in buying his wife a Christmas gift that she does not want to exchange.

1473. Nothing adds to a guest's popularity like a punctual arrival — with an armful of gifts.

1474.   Before a woman gives her husband a gift she's got to be sure he can afford it.

1475.   Money is the only gift you can give at Christmastime — and be sure no one will want to exchange it later.

1476.   One of the best gifts a woman can give her husband is a couple of extra inches of closet space.

1477.   A rare gift is something a man gives his wife — and she doesn't want to exchange it.

GIRL

1478.   A smart girl gives a man just enough rope to lead her to the altar.

1479.   Many a girl has caught a man by being a dye-head.

1480.   A smart girl is one who knows all the hazards of parking.

1481.   Before a young girl hitches her wagon to a star, she usually determines what kind of a trail he might blaze.

1482.   No self-respecting girl will chase after a man that she's interested in — unless he tries to make a get-away.

1483.   There is nothing wrong with a man's blood pressure as long as a smile from a pretty girl will bring color to his cheeks.

1484.   Girls who dress to kill not infrequently cook that way too.

1485.   What most girls search for is a man who can afford them.

1486.   A girl will wait for the right man to come along as long as the one she's going with doesn't try to make a getaway.

1487. Nothing will do more for a young girl's complexion than a handsome man who has fallen in love with her.

1488. Today an old-fashioned girl is one who is 30 and still married to her first husband.

1489. A girl who goes to the trouble of knitting socks for a man will go to a lot more trouble to keep him tied in a knot.

1490. Most girls know what they want in marriage as long as they're still single.

1491. The subjects that give college students the most trouble live in sorority houses.

1492. No modern girl will bother to knit socks for a fellow unless she expects to take over the job of darning them too.

1493. These days the only girls who manage to keep going steady are the married ones.

1494. A smart girl is one who knows how to make opportunity wait when he whistles.

GLASSES

1495. Glasses are becoming to some people until they start drinking from them.

GOOD IDEA

1496. A good idea is one that hits the other fellow with a bolt of envy.

1497. All it takes to make a good idea generate steam is a person who can get all worked up over it.

GOVERNMENT

1498. The biggest problem facing our government is that of living within our means.

1499. Nowadays the government seems intent on helping those whom God refuses to.

GOAL

1500. The best test of how important a goal is to you is the depth of your convictions that you can succeed in reaching it.

1501. Clearly define for yourself the long-range goals you aspire to, and you will find that all the obstacles in your way will become hills instead of mountains.

GOD

1502. The most successful men I know have always admitted that they would most surely have failed without God's help.

1503. A man's true cash value is how much he is worth if he were suddenly asked by God to check in.

1504. God always helps people to get over a hill, but he seldom lends a helping hand until they make it at least halfway on their own.

1505. Some men who boast that they are self-made must look pitiful in the eyes of God.

1506. People who think they can charge their sins up to experience are going to be shocked when they discover how poor their credit is with God.

1507. People who have the highest regard for God sometimes make the mistake of acting as though they were Him.

1508. There is a lesson for all in this — God gives us wheat, but we must bake the bread. He gives us cotton, but we must convert it into clothing. He gives us trees, but we must build our homes. He provides the raw materials and expects us to make the finished products with them.

1509. God has given women tremendous powers, and some make full use of them.

1510. God loves beginnings — that is why He's so good to people who get things started.

GOLDEN RULE

1511. The trouble with many persons who preach the Golden Rule is they are blind to the fact that they aren't practicing it themselves.

GOING PLACES

1512. Nothing makes a man go places like a woman who likes to.

1513. The trouble with a lot of people who give you the impression they are going places is they may only be running into debt.

GOLD DIGGER

1514. A gold digger is a girl without a heart who takes over a man without a head.

GOLD

1515. Some persons are worth their weight in gold, but only on their own market.

GOLF

1516. One of the best ways to help a man get out of the woods is to find the golf ball he's looking for.

1517. Anybody who can keep his eye on the ball is bound to be a success, especially if he likes golf.

GOLFER

1518. All it takes to upset a serious golfer is one high ball.

1519. A really good golfer is one who always knows what your score is.

1520. A really good golfer is one who goes to church on Sunday . . . first.

1521. Nothing improves a golfer's disposition like finding a better ball than he went looking for.

GOOD

1522. There isn't a man alive who is as good as he knows he ought to be.

GOOD-BYE

1523. Some husbands kiss their wives good-bye as though they wished they were leaving them for good.

GOOD CRY

1524. A woman's idea of a good cry is one that gets the intended results.

1525. How much better a woman feels after a good cry depends on what she got out of it.

GOOD DEED

1526.   You can always tell when you've just done a good deed
. . . the person who benefited from it thinks you're the last
person in the world to whom he is indebted.

GOOD EXECUTIVE

1527.   A good executive is a man who is happy because he's
just been given additional responsibilities.

GOOD HEALTH

1528.   The surest sign that a person is in good health is a
complete absence of any reference to it in his conversation
with you.

1529.   Good health just does not take care of itself, and it is
most often lost by assuming that it will.

GOOD IDEA

1530.   A good idea is one that not only gives the other fellow
a shot in the arm; it also makes him feel the needle because he
didn't think of it first.

1531.   The best way to get the other fellow all worked up
over a good idea is to plant it in his own mind.

1532.   Some of the most successful ideas in history were
thrown on the scrap-heap by others who first rejected them.

GOOD LINE

1533.   Sometimes the man who strikes you as having a lot on
the ball is just able to pitch a good line.

GOOD LIVING

1534. The trouble with modern civilization is that too many people have the mistaken idea that a good living consists in making one.

GOOD LISTENER

1535. A good listener is one who can get you to tell him more than you ever intended to.

GOOD MAN

1536. You can't keep a good man down any more than you can stop cream from rising to the top.

GOOD MEDICINE

1537. There's no better cure for mounting hypertension in the middle years of life than for two persons to fall in love all over again on their Silver Wedding Anniversary.

GOOD NAME

1538. A good life can be lost by one bullet and a good name can be equally assassinated by a single error.

GOOD NEIGHBOR

1539. A good neighbor to have is one by the name of Jones who is trying to keep up with you!

GOODNESS

1540. One of the best ways to treat yourself is to be good to somebody else.

GOOD OLD DAYS

1541.   The good old days were when the only thing a teenager would think of stealing was a kiss!

GOOD POINTS

1542.   A person who is careful to recognize the other fellow's good points never has to worry that his own will be overlooked.

GOOD REASON

1543.   When a woman seems to bring a man his pipe and slippers for no apparent reason, there's usually a good reason.

GOOD SPEAKER

1544.   A good speaker is one who knows how little time it should take to deliver his two cents' worth.

1545.   A speaker knows he has done an outstanding job if the applause is louder and longer when he sits down than it was when he was introduced.

1546.   A good speaker usually turns out to be someone who says exactly what you want him to say.

1547.   The true test of a good speaker is if you are willing to invite him to speak for a fee.

1548. A good speaker is one who starts off with a good joke and then concentrates on ending with a better one.

1549. A good speaker is one who rises to the occasion — and then promptly sits down.

GOOD STORY

1550. Every good speaker knows that the shortest distance between two points is a good story.

GOOD VISION

1551. Good vision is the ability to see the forest and the trees.

1552. A person knows his eyes are in good shape these days if he is able to keep an eye on where his money is going.

GOOD WILL

1553. Perhaps one of the reasons good will is so appropriate at Christmastime is because that's when you need it most.

1554. Goodwill can dispel coldness and animosity as effectively as the summer sun can melt a block of ice.

GOSSIP

1555. Most gossip is either indecent or invented.

1556. There's a fortune awaiting any man who can find something to do with gossip besides repeating it.

1557. My father never had to worry about neighborhood gossip because he lived in such a manner that nobody would believe anything bad about him.

1558. Sometimes the roots of neighborhood gossip can be traced to your own children.

1559. There's a fortune awaiting any man who can find something to do with gossip besides repeating it.

1560. A woman's idea of making an exciting discovery is to stumble upon a nugget of gossip.

1561. Nothing makes gossip more savory than when it is indulged in by scandal light.

1562. Nothing will help the other fellow to get the edge over you like saying cutting things about him behind his back.

GOVERNMENT

1563. What the government gives to the people is seldom more than 10 percent of what the government collects from them!

1564. Government by the people and for the people was a laudable slogan, until the government put millions of them on its payroll.

1565. A government, like a business, is in great jeopardy as soon as too much power gravitates to one man.

GRANDCHILDREN

1566. One of the greatest pleasures a parent can experience is to gaze upon his grandchildren when they're fast asleep.

GRANDMOTHER

1567. All it takes for the average women to discover her second wind is to become a grandmother.

1568. Nothing helps a modern housewife to get an average day's work done like sending the children over to grandmother's.

1569. Somebody ought to write a book on how to raise children by disciplining their grandmothers.

GRANDPARENT

1570. Nothing adds to the popularity of a grandparent around the house like an unexpected need for a reliable babysitter.

1571. Almost every grandparent will tell you that spanking is unnecessary for your children, even though they felt it was necessary for you.

1572. Grandparents can contribute a lot to a young man's success, especially if they're very wealthy.

1573. The best substitute for wealthy parents is wealthy grandparents.

1574. Our younger generation is quite safe as long as they have grandparents to protect them.

1575. As far as grandparents are concerned, one baby in a house of adults is a majority.

1576. There is no better medicine for ailing grandparents than baby grandchildren.

GRASS

1577. Frequently the fellow who doesn't let any grass grow under his feet is too lazy to plant some.

1578. The fellow who doesn't let any grass grow under his feet is kept busy cutting it.

GRATITUDE

1579. True gratitude consists in thanking God for everything when you've got everything.

1580. When someone shows their gratitude to me for something I may have done, I get the same feeling as when I count my savings and find that I have more than I thought I had.

GRAVITY

1581. The best way to overcome the law of gravity is laughingly.

GREAT GUY

1582. The fellow who says that you're a great guy often is least qualified to say so.

GREAT MINDS

1583. Great minds do not always think alike ... rather they think in extremes, extremes of good or evil.

GREATNESS

1584. No matter how outstanding teamwork may be in accomplishing something great, history will identify it with a single name years or centuries later.

1585. The greatness of a country is measured by the number of square persons in it, not the number of square miles it contains.

1586. You can tell a great man by how little you can find out about him — from him.

GRIP

1587. A smart girl is one who can hold a man at arm's length without losing her grip on him.

GRIPE

1588. Few things in life have a higher price tag on it than a gripe.

GROUCH

1589. The best thing to do with a grouch is to isolate yourself from others until it goes away.

GUESTS

1590. Two kinds of guests always make us happy — those who come with gifts, and those who leave sooner than we expected them to.

1591. Guests we prefer to know make us happy when they come, sad when they go.

1592. One way to impress a guest is to treat him to a family-size towel.

GUIDE

1593. When you let your conscience be your guide you can be sure it will keep you on a well-beaten path.

GUILT

1594. Guilt is a disease of one's conscience which makes whispers sound like thunder.

HABITS

1595. All you have to do to make a habit lose its grip on you is let go of it.

1596. One of the healthiest habits a person can develop is to keep his mouth shut — especially at dessert time.

1597. The difference between a good habit and a bad habit, frequently, is the time it takes to learn it.

1598. A good habit is to praise your wife at least once a day . . . if you don't know why you should, she does.

HAIR

1599. The best inheritance a father can give his son is a full head of hair.

1600. Bald people should be thankful that losing hair is not as painful as pulling teeth.

1601. One advantage of being bald is you never have to worry about your hair being all out of place when you remove your hat.

1602. All too often the only thing that time does to the human head is make it whiter and smoother.

1603. Many little boys who wish they had no hair to comb will get their wish when they grow up.

1604. Many a man with hair on his chest wishes it were on his head.

1605. A rich man is one who can afford to get a haircut as often as he feels like one.

1606. Nothing gives a middle aged man the jumpses like hair that combs out in bunches.

1607. The average middle-aged man can comb his hair with the palm of his hand.

1608. Middle age is the time of life when a man hopes for a silver lining — on top of his head.

1609. There's a bright side to everything — you'll find men with hair thankful that they still have dandruff, and men without hair thankful that they don't.

1610. A truly lucky man is one who can push his way to the top without losing his hair in the process.

HAIRLINE

1611. A man can get used to anything except a receding hairline.

1612. Somebody could make a fortune by inventing a mirror for home use that will de-accentuate a receding hairline.

1613. If men would put as much effort into doing their work as they do in fighting a receding hairline, we would double our gross national product almost overnight.

HALF-COCKED

1614. No matter how much some people deliberate or procrastinate they still go off half-cocked.

HALF-WAY

1615. The fellow who says he'll meet you half-way usually thinks he's standing on the dividing line.

HAMMER HOME A POINT

1616. The best way to hammer home a point is to use your head instead of your fist.

1617. There is only a split-second interval sometimes between getting someone to eat out of your hand or getting it bitten!

1618. Frequently the best way for a man to strengthen his hand is to ask the right girl for hers.

HAND-ME-DOWNS

1619. Nobody ever complains about hand-me-downs — if they are secondhand diamonds.

HANDS

1620. One time it pays to have a firm hand is when it shakes hands with a firmer one.

1621. Too many people who are looking for a helping hand don't even try to lift one of their own fingers.

1622. One time it is a lot of fun to wash your hands is after you get them dirty from counting money.

1623. By the time a woman gives a man her hand, she usually has him eating out of it.

1624. The trouble with many hands that rock the cradle today is they're hired hands.

HAPPINESS

1625. The essence of true happiness lies in being as satisfied about what you haven't got as with what you have.

1626. Two things can make a man very happy — coming through his physical exam and his tax audit trouble free.

1627. Happiness is like candy — if you got all you wanted of it, it might sicken you.

1628. The unhappiest people in the world are those who are proud of their misery.

1629. Nothing is more conductive to enjoying a happy life than the ability to be uninfluenced by what others say about you — GOOD OR BAD.

1630. A happily married man is one who can go to a party with his wife with the same enthusiasm with which he goes on a fishing trip without her.

1631. A happily married man is one who believes that one of the soundest investments he can make is for a dozen roses for his wife.

1632. Some people are happy because they know what they're missing.

1633. A happily married woman is one who is sure she didn't get married before the right man came along.

1634. Some men discover what happiness is as soon as they get married, but then it may be too late.

1635. A truly happy person is one who can smile from year to year.

1636. Usually a person can be much happier living in the slums than on the outskirts of his means.

1637. All it takes to overcome some people in the pursuit of happiness is an urgent need for the money you loaned them.

1638. When all is said and done, a truly happy man is one who smiles ten times more often than he frowns.

1639. There are only two seasons in life — happiness and sorrow, and they invariably follow one another.

1640. You reach a state of true happiness when in your heart you could want for nothing more than what you already have in your grasp.

1641. Happiness is appreciated most when it comes in installments rather than unceasingly.

1642. There are two things that every American must do to be happy: (1) pray, and (2) pay all of his taxes.

1643. I have known great happiness in my lifetime and every bit of it came about as a result of feeling needed.

1644. A happily married man is one who would rather talk with his wife at breakfast than read the morning newspaper.

1645. There are few times in a man's life when he is more genuinely happy than when the fish are biting.

1646. The secret of happiness is to search for the beauties of the world with one's heart and overlook its ugliness with one's eyes.

1647. Most Americans in the pursuit of happiness never stop long enough to determine if they've overtaken it.

1648. Happiness is the ability to laugh without any brakes on.

1649. It takes only a split-second to change a frown into a smile, yet it can control how happy you will be in the next twenty-four hours.

1650. Most Americans never get into serious trouble pursuing happiness until they try to do it at eighty miles an hour.

1651. Happiness is like a delicate flower — and frequently just as subject to wilting.

1652. Happiness is having paid all your bills and having some left over.

HAPPY LIFE

1653. Nothing is more conducive to enjoying a happy life than the ability to be uninfluenced by what others say about you — good or bad.

HAPPINESS

1654. One of the first lessons to learn in life is that you can make some people deliriously happy simply by letting them alone.

HAPPY MAN

1655. A truly happy man is one who can get the most done in bad weather.

HARD WORK

1656. Hard work consists of an accumulation of easy jobs that you didn't do when you should have.

1657. As far as hard work is concerned, some employees like doing nothing better.

1658. All you have to do to appreciate the value of hard work is hire someone to do some for you.

1659. Nothing is hard work if you can get others to do it for you.

HARVESTS

1660. We live in an age of plentiful harvests, of which talk seems to be the most abundant.

HEAD

1661. Some people fail to use their head because they are preoccupied with sitting on their butt.

1662. All too often the only thing that time does to the human head is make it whiter and smoother.

1663. One spot that needs weeding the year around is the uncultivated territory in your head.

1664. You know that a man has a block of wood on his shoulders when you hear him whittling down others.

HEAD COLD

1665. Every time a man comes to work with a bad head cold, we know it's because his wife has too much work lined up for him if he stays home.

HEADACHE

1666. Man has no right to be proud of splitting the atom until he can find a solution to the splitting headache it is causing him.

1667. Many persons who spend the day complaining about a headache frequently may be found spending the evening getting ready for another one.

HEADLIGHTS

1668. Those who complain that they cannot see their way in life ought to try dimming their headlights.

HEALTH

1669. Millions of people who know that there is nothing

more important than good health carry on as though they are trying to disprove it.

1670. It takes the average person 50 years to learn the importance of good health, and then he spends the next 25 years trying to protect what little he has left.

1671. There is nothing more important to men and women than their health — and nothing which they treat more carelessly.

1672. As you grow older, the condition of your health is not unlike the stock market — some days it is riding high, others it hits bottom.

1673. On appraising the virtues of my friends, I find that the healthiest ones never seem to worry about their health, and the best-living of them never talk to you about what might happen to them when they die.

1674. One way to test what shape you are in is to find out how upset a life insurance salesman can make you.

1675. By the time most people discover that health is everything they've lost it.

1676. Good health does not take care of itself, and is most often lost by assuming that it will.

1677. The only time overweight is a healthy sign is when it means the butcher really likes you.

1678. One of the healthiest feelings in the world is the one that comes over you after you admit a mistake.

1679. The greatest personal loss that a successful man can suffer is the loss of his health.

1680. The secret of good health lies not so much in eating half of what you do as in saying one-tenth of what you say.

1681. The serious loss of one's health seldom occurs

gradually. More often it comes like the unexpected bolt of lightning — hitting with the sudden stabbing pain of a coronary or the casual but shocking observation of a large lump you are sure wasn't there the day before!

1682. It is when you are sick that you make the best plans to keep healthy.

1683. Nothing does more to improve a man's disposition than a wife who is very healthy — and also works.

HEALTH EQUATION

1684. Happy Mind = Healthy Body. Sad Mind = Sick Body.

HEARING

1685. Nothing improves a person's hearing like overhearing.

1686. Sometimes the best way to make yourself heard is by letting the other fellow do the talking for you.

1687. Sometimes the best way to make someone hear you is to exercise silence at the top of your eyebrows.

1688. If you live with your ear to the ground, you will hear many things which your feet would have trampled over.

1689. One advantage of wearing a hearing aid is you don't have to listen to any back talk.

1690. Nothing improves the other fellow's hearing like telling him your troubles.

1691. Man is never so hard of hearing as when his opinion is being challenged.

HEART

1692. A father seldom worries about the condition of his

heart until the time comes to teach his daughter how to ride a two-wheeler.

1693. The true condition of a person's mind depends entirely on how accurately his lips reveal what is really in his heart.

1694. Tolerance consists in seeing things with your heart instead of with your eyes.

HEART ATTACK

1695. Opportunity knocks so hard these days that it knocks some people off their feet with a heart attack.

1696. When a person reaches the stage in life when his baggage is all packed and he's ready to go, the best way is by a heart attack!

HEART SPECIALIST

1697. The average heart specialist can usually check the condition of his patient's heart simply by sending him a bill.

HEAVEN

1698. I believe I have found heaven on earth; my enjoyment of each day is so intense that my fondest wish is that I could go on like this forever.

1699. If the elect are those who will be allowed into heaven, the plight of the elected seems rather dismal.

HEIGHT

1700. History shows that taller men become corporation presidents more often than short men — and short men become world leaders more often than tall men.

1701. The height of a man's ambition is a pretty girl just a little shorter than he is.

HELP

1702. The best way to help a person overcome his weak points is to do what you can to develop his strong points.

1703. There is one pleasure that the human being cannot tire of and that is the pleasure that comes from helping someone who really needs you.

1704. When it comes to stopping a successful businessman from overwork there's nothing more decisive than a heart attack.

1705. One of the best ways to do yourself a favor is to lend somebody else a helping hand.

1706. A woman will go to almost any extreme to help a man improve his bank balance, especially if she is sure she can get her hands on some of it.

HELPING HAND

1707. America is suffering from a generation of people who are demanding a helping hand without making the least effort to raise a finger.

1708. Most little boys feel that they can get along without father's helping hand . . . until they're old enough to start college.

HEREDITY

1709. The average American parent today who has teen-age children is rapidly losing faith in the laws of heredity.

HERO

1710.   One of the biggest thrills about the TV cowboy hero is the way he makes a fortune without ever having to pay any taxes on it.

1711.   Heroes are only recognized by staying in the race until they pass the finish line.

HIDES

1712.   Many a woman wears a mink coat because she threatened to expose somebody's hide.

HIKING

1713.   Scientists have not yet found a better way of putting flavor into food than a five mile hike before dinner.

HINDSIGHT

1714.   For some people hindsight is 20/20 vision — for others it is complete and total blindness.

1715.   The trouble with hindsight is that it usually improves your vision and your envy at the same time.

1716.   The trouble with many hands that rock the cradle today is that they're hired hands.

HISTORY

1717.   History proves that man is the most stupid animal on our planet, probably because he is the only animal with intelligence to direct his stupidity.

1718.   History has now proven that the most important thing that man did to separate himself from monkeys was to stand on his own two feet.

1719. History proves that no man ever became a genius just by claiming to be one.

1720. My advice to any young man is: make history yourself — don't waste time reading about it because the only conclusion you can come to if you do is that it has taught man nothing.

1721. It is a fact of history that, almost without exception, every great contributor to world society from Jesus Christ to Einstein to Alexander Calder in modern times was accused openly early in their respective careers of being either crackpots or crazy.

1722. History proves conclusively that the omissions of good people have been far more disastrous than the aggressiveness of a few bad leaders.

1723. History has taught me a lesson — facts are usually determined by who writes them, not by who measures them.

HIT-THE-CEILING

1724. There's only one time it ever pays a man to hit the ceiling — and that is when he's chasing a mosquito with a flyswatter in hand.

1725. Nothing will make a man fall on his face faster than hitting the ceiling.

HOLLYWOOD

1726. Hollywood is a city in the U.S. where someone is more likely to ask you Who's Whose than Who's Who.

HOME

1727.   At no time is the sight of home more endearing to you than after you've travelled a couple of thousands of miles trying to get away from it.

1728.   Nothing makes a man overlook the defects in his home like an opportunity to sell it to a prospective buyer.

1729.   Everytime I hear a person say that his home life is unbearable I wonder if I'm not listening to the bear.

1730.   Staying at home becomes the most enjoyable experience of all when you turn down ten invitations to do it.

HOME BASE

1731.   Most girls believe that the safest way to prepare a home base is to start with a diamond.

HOME FIRES

1732.   Every truly great man who has set the world on fire managed to keep the home fires burning.

HOME PLATE

1733.   When it comes to the game of love, a smart girl knows enough to stay close to home plate after making a perfect catch.

HOMES

1734.   The only trouble with some of these fine new homes is their location — on the outskirts of your income.

HOMEWORK

1735. You can spot those in our younger generation who are headed for big things — they always get their weekend homework done first thing Friday nights.

1736. A girl who is concentrating on her homework is one who can't hear the horn in the driveway.

HONESTY

1737. Honesty in a person means nothing until he is tested under circumstances when he is sure he could get away with dishonesty.

1738. All men are honest — until they meet up with a big enough opportunity to be dishonest.

1739. It's an honest man who will go through a dozen snap shots of himself without feeling the urge to tear up at least one.

1740. . A completely honest person is one who will put a nickel in a broken parking meter.

1741. A truly honest man is one who doesn't know the law, but he is sure that he's living within it.

1742. A completely honest person is one who will point out a mistake that the Internal Revenue Service makes in his favor.

1743. Some persons who preach that honesty is the best policy give you the impression that they haven't paid a premium in a long time.

1744. An honest man is one who never blames his mistakes on his wife or the weather.

1745. A completely honest man is one who gives as much to his church as he tells Uncle Sam he does.

1746. Nothing puts a man's honesty to the acid test like sitting down to fill out an expense account form.

1747. Some women who honestly believe that life begins at forty do not have any intentions of outgrowing thirty.

HONOR

1748. Honor is a badge that you cannot pin on yourself.

HOPE

1749. Hope is like an antiseptic ointment without which life's innumerable scratches would lead to fatal infections.

HORSEPOWER

1750. What some women drivers lack in precision they try to make up with horsepower.

HORSESENSE

1751. A dash of horsesense would stop many from getting hitched, more from getting unhitched.

HOSPITALITY

1752. When it comes to visitors the most hospitable ones are those who like to listen.

1753. True hospitality consists in lending your guest both ears.

HOT WATER

1754. Sometimes a man of action is a fellow who just got both of his feet in hot water.

1755. The fellow who displays cold feet before marriage is sure to find himself in hot water afterwards.

1756. One man who never runs out of hot water is a bachelor.

1757. Nothing makes a man put his best foot forward quicker than to have his other one in hot water.

HOUSE

1758. All you have to do to increase the value of your property is decide you want to sell your house.

1759. Nothing raises the value of your own house to you like shopping around for a new one.

1760. One of the easiest ways to acquire a bigger house is to marry off some of the children.

1761. With building costs as high as they are, the castle a man used to build in the sky, he now has to build on a small lot.

1762. Nothing raises your opinion of your immediate neighbors like a conversation with a prospective buyer of your house.

1763. Judging from what some people are willing to pay for one floor houses, it is obvious they don't have anything upstairs.

HOUSEWIFE

1764. Nothing cuts into a modern housewife's working time like putting a comfortable chair beside the telephone.

1765. There's a good reason some housewives wake up surrounded by work — they went to sleep surrounded by it.

HOUSEWORK

1766. When a woman gets a lot of housework done nowadays, the chances are the television set is on the blink.

HOUSING

1767. What really makes it so difficult anymore to build a solid house on a lot is the wobbliness of our planet.

HUMAN BEASTIALITY

1768. One of the enigmas of Christianity is that Christians have been guilty of more hedious methods of murdering each other than many non-Christian barbarians.

HUMAN BEHAVIOR

1769. There's nothing really consistent about human behavior except its tendency to drift toward evil.

HUMAN BODY

1770. Nothing wears the human body out faster than doing nothing.

HUMAN MIND

1771. The greatest hazard of intellectual power is that it can build up mountains of errors almost as easily as it builds up books of truths.

1772. Human minds are teeming with good ideas, and charitable thoughts ... the tragedy is that most of them evaporate away without ever being acted upon.

HUMAN NATURE

1773. There is a Scarlet lurking in every woman and a Rhett always on the ready in every healthy man.

1774. To observe human nature at work in its most uninhibited form, study what people say about the presidential candidates in the United States immediately BEFORE and immediately AFTER an election.

1775. Human nature is clearly unmasked by the universal prerequisite that a milkman must be married before he can get the job.

1776. Human nature still is that quirk of *homo sapiens* that drives people in desperation to fit a square peg in a round hole, which in the field of human relations is the same thing as "rubbing people the wrong way".

HUMILITY

1777. You can tell a great man by how little you can find out about him — from him.

1778. A humble man is one who is still friendly with the photographers after he is shown the proofs.

1779. All you have to do to learn humility is to take an intensive course in self-evaluation.

1780. Humility is either a sign of greatness or a handy means of camouflaging one's imperfections.

1781. Humility is a virtue until it becomes self-satisfying; then it can become as evil as pride.

1782. The best way to be right or wrong is humbly!

HUMOR

1783. At no time is it more important to laugh at yourself than when people are saying things to make you mad.

1784.   All a man has to do to humor his boss is to offer to do the dishes for her.

HUNGER

1785.   A man who eats out of his wife's hand usually goes hungry.

HURRY

1786.   Some of the busiest people I know are only hurrying to get to a cemetery.

1787.   Hurry is purely relative, depending on which one you're trying to get away from.

1788.   I am convinced that there is really only one circumstance that warrants anyone to be in a great hurry — and that is a bad case of diarrhea.

1789.   The man who seems to be in the least hurry is the man who does things when they should be done.

HUSBAND

1790.   An ideal husband is one who treats his wife with the same consideration he treats his pretty secretary.

1791.   A contented husband is one who can't think of somebody else's wife he wishes he had married.

1792.   Some husbands have a right to talk in their sleep — it's the only chance they ever get.

1793.   A contented husband is one who has a shoulder that his wife loves to rest her head on.

1794.   An obedient husband frequently is one who is just following in his wife's footsteps.

1795. You know a woman has complete control over her husband if she has him eating out of her hand.

1796. The easiest way for a woman to lose her middle-aged husband today is to work him to death.

1797. Any woman will tell you that there isn't an electronic labor-saving device that can outmatch a devoted husband.

1798. A smart woman knows how to make her husband a big success, but it's the clever woman that also keeps him after she does.

1799. A woman never knows her true capabilities until her husband loses his.

1800. The first thing a woman should do to make a successful husband out of a man is admire him.

1801. One thing every husband should learn as early as possible in marriage is how much of his own happiness depends on a word of praise now and then for his wife.

1802. A truly contented husband is one who can't think of a better girl who would have married him.

1803. Frequently a woman's idea of a household pet is a husband who will eat out of her hand.

1804. When it comes to making a good husband a woman's work is never done.

1805. The trouble with the laws governing husband-hunting today is that they do not limit the number that one woman can bag.

1806. Most husbands train themselves to listen to every word their wives say, whether they hear it or not.

1807. An enterprising young husband is one who gives his wife an electric dishwasher so that both of them can get out of doing the dishes.

HYPOCRITES

1808. The greatest of hypocrites is he who speaks the truth in whispers.

HYPOTHESIS

1809. A valuable hypothesis is one that may not hold water at first, but can eventually pan gold.

IDEAS

1810. A good idea is one which strikes the other fellow like a bolt of lightning a year or two after you've told it to him.

1811. Two things cause the greatest pain in this world — the birth of a baby and a new idea!

1812. A good idea is one that not only gives the other fellow a shot in the arm; it also makes him feel the needle because he didn't think of it first.

1813. The best thing to do with a red hot idea is build a fire under it.

1814. Oftentimes, the acid test of a good idea is whether or not it is your own.

1815. All it takes to make a good idea generate steam is a person who can get all fired up over it.

1816. How good a red hot idea is usually depends on how much heat it loses when somebody throws cold water on it.

1817. There is nothing more explosive than an old idea hitting mankind as absolutely new at the right time of history.

1818. One truly creative mind is capable of producing a single idea that will support ten thousand "geniuses".

1819. A diamond is worthless until it is found, and a new idea is equally valueless until something is done about it.

1820. Nothing is more important to the future of an idea than the first step you take to try it out.

1821. The best thing to do with a red hot idea is to bank on it.

1822. An unwelcome idea usually is a tremendous one you did not think of first.

1823. Ideas that you give away and sell at least have a chance to germinate, grow, and flourish; but ideas that are kept in secret can only remain sterile, and dormant forever.

1824. A good idea that you give away is more than a helping hand to you . . . it becomes like a pair of wings that will help you to soar above the herd and achieve heights of personal pleasure unattainable in any other way.

1825. One good idea — like one good race horse — can father a long line of later successors.

1826. Sometimes all it takes to make a chemical reaction go is a good idea.

1827. A businessman's idea of a perfect score is to cinch a big deal on the 18th hole.

1828. Despite the billions of dollars spent EACH YEAR on research, the one place where the best ideas still show up years ahead of their time is in the comic strips.

1829. One of the surest ways to kill off a good idea is to do nothing but entertain it.

1830. Nothing breeds new ideas like getting the first good one off the ground.

IDLENESS

1831. Each minute you're idle you lose sixty seconds of happiness or progress.

1832. A man can prove anything provided he is allowed to use one "if".

IGNORANCE

1833. What you don't know is bound to help the other fellow.

1834. Where ignorance is folly, 'tis bliss to be wise.

1835. The biggest handicap of ignorance is that it prevents you from ever winning an argument.

1836. Ignorance is something people may suspect, but you can't convince them of it until you open your mouth.

1837. A truly educated man is one who knows how to be ignorant intelligently.

1838. Ignorance is a poor poultice, and very bad medicine.

1839. The irony of life is the way so many flashes of ignorance turn out to be bolts of genius, 10 or 20 years later.

1840. The trouble with some ignorant people is the doggedness with which they try to convince you they are.

1841. More people get into trouble by covering up their ignorance than by admitting it.

ILL-LUCK

1842. Ill-luck, very often, is like a stranger coming up the street; if you don't go out of your way to meet it, chances are that it will stop somebody else first.

IMAGINATION

1843. A pretty girl is one who can run away with a man's imagination . . . and his money.

1844. A smart girl knows what it takes to capture a man's imagination — and it's usually very little on her.

1845. Imagination is what keeps a man awake at night after receiving a notice to bring himself and his receipts to the Internal Revenue Service.

IMPATIENCE

1846. An impatient man is one who cannot kill time without also killing a little bit of himself.

IMPORTANCE

1847. It's just as important for a person with an open mind to keep the bugs out as it is for a person with an open mouth.

1848. A snob is a person so carried away by his own importance that he trips over people at his own level.

IMPOSSIBLE

1849. A man is ninety per cent on the way to achieving the impossible once he is confident that he can.

1850. A good executive is one who asks his help to do the impossible and then shows them how.

1851. Progress always comes from daring persons who set out with a dream to take the "im" out of impossible.

IMPRESSION

1852. The trouble with some people who claim they have an

open mind is they give you the impression they've filled it up
mostly with junk.

IMPROVEMENT

1853. A happy marriage is one in which the wife notices an
improvement in her husband's interest in her as the years go
by.

1854. The world's most needed improvement is a better
living human being.

1855. Nothing improves your chances of getting up in the
world like getting up early!

1856. Nothing improves a woman's chances of catching a
man like making up her mind which man she wants to catch.

1857. Too many people follow the path of least resistance —
like trying to improve others instead of themselves.

1858. A sure sign that a person is grown up is that he realizes
that there's room for improvement at the top.

INACTIVITY

1859. Some people who can't stand inactivity are just as lazy
sitting down.

1860. Inactivity is as damaging to one's health as distrust is
to one's marriage.

1861. The only persons who don't know what to do next are
those who don't have enough to do.

1862. Nothing breeds fatigue like inactivity.

INCOME

1863. The only trouble with some of these fine new homes is their location . .,. on the outskirts of your income.

1864.   Nobody can push a man into a high income bracket like a wife who needs the money.

1865.   Some people who are being paid more than they are worth are clever enough to keep their mouth shut about it.

1866.   People who must live on a fixed income should be especially careful to prevent their appliances from needing repairs.

1867.   When you see red it is high time that you started living within your income.

INCOME TAXES

1868.   If you want a lot of attention start cheating on your income tax.

1869.   When it comes to chiseling on their income tax, most people are found out to be poor sculptors.

1870.   At no time does telling the truth make you feel better than right after filing your income tax form.

1871.   Estimating your income tax would be a lot easier if it could be based on what income you expect to have left.

1872.   There are two things in life for which we are never fully prepared — an operation and an income tax audit — and even they have much in common.

1873.   Of all the stories carried in the newspapers, none are read more carefully than the ones about income tax evaders on trial.

INDECISION

1874.   Nothing encourages indecision like an intersection posting a four-way stop sign.

1875. The only persons who don't know what to do next are those who don't have enough to do.

1876. People who are unable to make up their minds are destined to end up as only average.

INDEPENDENCE

1877. Nothing helps you to enjoy your job like an independent income.

1878. Independence is a feeling you get once you learn not to expect something for nothing.

INDISPENSABLE

1879. Most persons who believed they were indispensable are now resting under tombstones.

INDUSTRIAL RESEARCH

1880. The future success of industrial research will depend on how effectively the idea maker can communicate directly with those who have decision making control over what to do with his ideas.

1881. Most of the money that is wasted in industrial research can be traced to continuation of effort in a field of research that already has been milked dry, but is still headed by someone so personally involved that nobody asks the question regarding its obsolescence.

INDUSTRIES

1882. What many industries really need on the job are parking meters.

1883. There are three categories of people in industry — the few who make things happen, the many who watch things happen, and the overwhelming majority who have no idea what happened.

1884. In any large organization, those who complain the most usually do the least work.

INEBRIATE

1885. An inebriate is a man who thinks the whole world revolves around him.

INEXPERIENCE

1886. Inexperience is the most valuable thing a young man has, provided it will stimulate him to try out something that an experienced person wouldn't think of doing.

1887. The trouble with most people who like to build castles in the air is they have had no experience as architects.

INFERIORITY COMPLEX

1888. The surest way to develop an inferiority complex would be to see ourselves exactly as others see us.

INFLATION

1889. There is no better yardstick for measuring the true value of the dollar — than by pegging it to the cost of first-class mail.

1890. Nobody advances inflation more than people who insist on living beyond your means.

1891. Inflation and obesity have much in common — one reduces the value of the dollar, the other reduces your longevity.

1892. The best cure for inflation is not decreasing one's taxes but increasing pride in one's work.

1893. Inflation is the difference between what others think you're worth and what you think you could command.

1894. If you want to understand inflation, buy a pound of bacon and weigh what you have left after you've cooked it to a crisp.

INGENUITY

1895. When it comes to ingenuity the human mind is at its best when it is trying to cover something up.

1896. When it comes to ingenuity, it is pretty hard to beat a woman trying to push a man — into matrimony.

1897. The ingenuity of a modern teenager is best evidenced by his ability to turn on your air conditioner, find his favorite radio station, and use an ash try he just cleaned, all within the thirty seconds or so that he spends cleaning the inside of your car at the end of the car wash line.

INHERITANCE

1898. One of the best inheritances a father can leave his son is a full head of hair.

1899. Nothing does more to reduce estate taxes like having two children in college.

1900. It is a truism that the meek shall inherit the earth — and so often also poverty.

1901. When it comes to splitting a family apart you can't beat an inheritance.

1902. The best inheritance a parent can leave a child is a will to work.

1903. The best inheritance a parent can give to his children is a few minutes of his time each day.

INNOCENCE

1904. Innocence is like a pocketbook full of money; if you lose it, chances are you'll never get it back again.

INSECURITY

1905. No one is less secure in reality than the man who believes he is indispensable in fact!

INSPIRATION

1906. Always remember that perspiration is to inspiration what sunlight is to morning glories.

INSTALLMENTS

1907. Most people are now discovering that it is taking their second wind just to meet the first installment.

1908. Most people raise their standard of living installment by installment.

1909. When it comes to climbing the social ladder most people try to do it one installment at a time.

INSURANCE SALESMEN

1910. One way of getting to feel well is to let an insurance man try to sell you a life policy.

INTELLIGENCE

1911. A smart man knows a good thing when everybody else sees it as worthless.

1912. True intelligence consists in not getting upset when supposedly intelligent people think you are ignorant.

1913. Intelligence is very much like money — if you don't let on how little you've got people will treat you as though you have a lot.

1914. Intelligence alone is no more a guarantee of success than money is a guarantee of happiness.

1915. An educated person is one who knows how to be ignorant intelligently.

INTENTIONS

1916. The reason the way of the transgressor is so hard is that it is so heavily paved with good intentions.

INTEREST

1917. There's a good reason why some men maintain a lifelong interest in pretty women — they're normal.

INTERIOR DECORATOR

1918. By the time an interior decorator is through with doing over your home, your bank account has had it, too!

1919. Fat persons usually are enthusiastic interior decorators.

INTERNAL REVENUE SERVICE

1920. Whoever said you can't take it with you must have been an Internal Revenue Agent.

1921. The acid test as to whether or not a man is telling the truth is if he continues to brag about his income when he knows he's talking to an Internal Revenue Agent.

INTERRUPTION

1922. When the wise husband interrupts his wife, it is just to tell her he agrees with her.

INTOXICATION

1923. Nothing intoxicates some people like a sip of authority.

INTRODUCTION

1924. A poor speaker is one who needs a glowing introduction.

INTUITION

1925. Intuition is what prompts you to ask a man for a loan just before he gets a chance to ask you for one.

1926. A woman's arithmetic is never better than when she's using her intuition to get your number.

1927. About the only time a woman's intuition can lead her into trouble is when she is trying to decide whether to turn right or left.

INVENTIONS

1928. Now that they have self-winding watches why doesn't someone invent a better way to make the wheels go around in a man's head?

1929. The next great invention of the age will be a wife with a push-button make-up.

1930. The next great invention on the American scene is going to be a bottle with a ready-made shake.

1931. Good inventions do not come easily to man — it took him an estimated six thousand years to invent right and left shoes, and he's still trying to find a better way to get catsup out of a bottle.

1932. A badly needed invention in America today is some kind of dough that really sticks to your fingers.

1933. It does seem incredible — almost 4,000,000 United States patents, and not a single one of them is an improvement on the human being.

1934. A much needed invention is a new kind of screen which will provide exit traffic only for flies and mosquitoes.

1935. Anyone can become wealthy in America by inventing something useful that doesn't last long — like most home appliances.

1936. Americans will pay a big price for any invention that will help them to save time they won't know what to do with.

INVESTMENTS

1937. A happily married man is one who believes that one of the soundest investments he can make is a dozen roses for his wife.

1938. A smart woman is a person who handles her husband with all the attention and tenderness he deserves as her most valuable asset.

INVITATIONS

1939. Cocktail parties are distasteful things until you get an invitation to one.

1940. Staying at home becomes the most enjoyable experience of all when you turn down ten invitations to do it.

I.Q. TESTS

1941. Some people object fiercely to taking I.Q. tests — and they're really the smart-test ones.

JACK

1942. All it takes to jack some persons up is a little more of it.

JAIL

1943. The two best places to keep out of are, jail — and the newspapers.

JAM

1944. If you insist on laying on the jam, you're bound to spread it around your waist.

JOBS

1945. Most girls like to have a job for two reasons — it gives them somebody to talk to, and somebody to talk about.

1946. To get a job well done, assign it to the man who has the most to lose, not to one who has everything to gain.

1947. You can tell how well a man is suited to his job by how busy he keeps himself.

1948. The trouble with many people today is that the only time they are lost for something to do is when they are on the job.

1949. An easy job is one that you did well.

1950. The danger of sitting down on the job is it eventually will cost you the seat of your pants.

1951.   Hard work is a series of easy jobs that you failed to do well.

1952.   Some men fall down on the job by sitting perfectly still.

1953.   There are no really difficult jobs; there are only people who make easy jobs difficult.

1954.   An easy job is one chore you complete ahead of schedule.

JOKES

1955.   I have yet to discover a practical joke that has anything practical about it.

1956.   Tact is the ability to listen to your boss tell a joke and laugh at it as though he hadn't told it to you before.

1957.   A good joke is one that you read, clip, and remember.

1958.   The trouble with some people who tell you a joke is the way they insist on repeating it . . . the next time they see you.

1959.   The best test of a good joke is how many minutes you can remember it.

1960.   A good joke is one that you can laugh at and remember it.

1961.   A good joke is one that can make you laugh . . . before breakfast.

1962.   A bore is a fellow who always follows one of your jokes with a better one.

1963.   The shortest distance between two jokes makes a perfect speech.

1964. Tolerance is the ability to listen to another person tell you one of your best jokes.

1965. Some people get a lot of fun out of their jokes — otherwise they would be wasted completely.

JONESES

1966. There are two ways to catch up with the Joneses — go into debt trying to catch up with them, or take it easy until you meet them coming back.

1967. If you want to get to know the Joneses even better, start treating their kids at your home.

1968. Pretty soon the only way you'll be able to catch up with the Joneses is with a faster rocket.

1969. One time you can keep up with the Jones family is if Mr. Jones happens to work for the Internal Revenue Service.

1970. A good neighbor to have is one by the name of Jones who is trying to keep up with you.

1971. Taxes are going so high these days that even the Jones aren't going places.

1972. If you want to find out what it is like to keep up with the Joneses, ask the bill collectors.

1973. These are days when it is hard to find a Mr. Jones who isn't exhausted from trying to keep up with himself.

1974. One of the most disappointing satisfactions in life is finally to catch up with the Joneses.

JUDGMENT

1975. Nothing inflates a man's judgment like meeting the husband of a girl he nearly married.

1976. A man never knows how good his wife's judgment is until he overhears her say what a good husband she managed to bag.

JUSTICE

1977. The greatest injustice a man can endure is a flagrant misuse of justice against him.

1978. Nothing is more cruel in the world of justice than the frequent postponement of punishment.

KEYS

1979. The key to many family squabbles is the one that fits the ignition of the family car.

1980. The easiest way to get your son to follow in your footsteps today is to offer him the keys to your car.

KINDLING WOOD

1981. Kindling wood will set a man's heart on fire, especially when he uses it to make something out of it in his workshop.

KINDNESS

1982. The true test of kindness is how willingly it is shown on the spur of the insult.

1983. There is no better extinguisher for the flames of anger and bitterness than kindness.

1984. You know you are living right if you could get rich by getting one dollar for every kind word you say behind the other fellow's back.

1985. If you think that kindness has little or no value you can prove it by trying to kill someone with it.

1986. Tolerance is the ability to be kind to dumb animals, especially when they're human beings.

KISSES

1987. The girl who puts the right food on her husband's dinner plate doesn't have to worry whether he kisses her at the door or not.

KNOCKER

1988. A chronic knocker is a fellow who may always be found on the outside of opportunity's door.

KNOW-HOW

1989. Know-how is especially valuable to a man if he doesn't know who.

KNOWLEDGE

1990. Nothing will help a person keep his voice down at all times like having enough knowledge.

1991. Knowledge is to ignorance what the sun is to a morning fog.

1992. Investment in knowledge never requires you to place a stop-loss order.

1993. Knowledge will become the ultimate moral force in the world because in the final analysis it must be the true father and mother of morality.

1994. At no time is a little knowledge more dangerous than when you are using it to start a rumor.

1995. The true mark of a well-educated man is that he never tries to answer a question before being asked to do so.

1996. A little knowledge is obviously a dangerous thing especially in the hands of college freshmen.

1997. Not until knowledge and truth are respected by the vast majority of the citizens of all nations will the inherent bestiality of man ever be neutralized and universally kept under control.

1998. Knowledge, to those who spend their lives in search of it, becomes a superhighway to its true source which, however defined, is God.

1999. There is a thin line between great knowledge and great ignorance . . . and the thin line is drawn by one's lips.

2000. If knowledge of a lifetime is not accurately recorded, it dies with the man . . . and may be lost forever.

2001. Knowledge has stood all the tests of time as the world's best vehicle for better human understanding.

2002. At no time is knowledge more powerful than when it can be used as blackmail.

2003. A little bit of knowledge is never more dangerous than when you over-reach with it.

2004. Knowledge, disseminated effectively to the public, will become the world's best eraser of prejudice, hostility, and skepticism between nations.

2005. Knowledge is the master key that can continue to unlock endless new rooms in the mansion of the human brain.

2006. Knowledge and money have many similarities — each may be accused of being the "root of all evil", each may be shown to bring corruption and human suffering, and each hold the greatest promise for benefits to humanity.

2007. Great efforts are being expended today in teaching our youth and adults new knowledge without guiding them on what they should do with it.

2008. What you don't know is bound to help the other fellow.

2009. The most powerful force in the world is correct knowledge when you need it.

2010. Knowledge alone will dispel all forms of discrimination. Not until man realizes that the atoms in all persons are identical and are constantly being interchanged will prejudice and discrimination vanish from this planet.

2011. Knowledge is very much like alcohol — a little bit of it sometimes is as bad as too much of it.

2012. A person with a great reservoir of knowledge is not educated unless he knows when to turn the spigot on and off.

2013. Knowledge is a unique form of wealth; you admire those who have more of it and feel sorry for those who have less of it.

2014. If a little knowledge is dangerous, then a great many dangerous people are on the loose.

2015. Knowledge is power, especially when it is hitched to a workhorse.

2016. The most completely lost of all days is one on which a person fails to gain a new piece of knowledge.

2017. A man who is a fountain of knowledge usually recognizes that he's just the spigot not the reservoir.

2018. A little knowledge is especially dangerous when it comes to explaining sex.

2019. Money is like knowledge — the more you have of it, the less you need to brag about it.

2020. One of the troubles with knowledge is that it only takes a couple of sips to intoxicate some persons with it.

2021. Even if a little knowledge is dangerous, a lot of people are quite harmless.

LABOR-SAVING DEVICE

2022. The greatest labor-saving device of the age still is a full-time maid.

LADDER

2023. Nothing will make a man slide down the ladder of success faster than letting go of his temper.

2024. There is always room at the top for the fellow who is willing to build his own ladder.

2025. The wrong way to try to get to the top of the ladder is by hitting the ceiling.

2026. Success defies the law of gravity; it means climbing to the top of the ladder by staying on the level.

2027. The best way to get to the top of the ladder is to lose no time building one of your own.

LADDER OF SUCCESS

2028. One of the first things a person must do to climb the ladder of success is to take his hands out of his pockets.

2029. When it comes to climbing the ladder of success there's nothing like a little jack to help you get off the ground.

2030. Some men I know were so determined to climb the ladder of success that they built their own ladders.

2031. When it comes to steadying a man on the ladder of success, it is hard to beat a woman who is madly in love with him.

2032. One of the first steps a modern man must take to climb the ladder to success is to turn off the television.

2033. The best way to climb the ladder of success is to ask a helping hand from one who is already at the top of it.

LADY

2034. A lady is a woman who wants to be looked up to even though she would prefer to be looked around at.

2035. A lady is a woman who can hold a man in her grip without ever letting him come within an arm's length of her.

2036. A young girl becomes a lady as soon as her legs are able to fill a pair of nylon stockings noticeably.

2037. A lady is a woman who can make a gentleman who is on the offensive behave defensively.

2038. As soon as a girl becomes a lady the law states that only the sun can tan her hide.

2039. A lady is a woman who doesn't have to ask a man to carry her suitcase for her.

LATENESS

2040. The latest thing in clothes generally is a woman you're waiting for.

2041. A calculating woman is one who figures out exactly how late she's going to be for a date.

LAUGHTER

2042. The best way to make the most of each day is to laugh at the fact that you'll never come out of life alive.

2043. Laugh at yourself and the rest of the world will laugh with you instead of at you.

LAURELS

2044. The easiest way to crush your laurels is to recline on them.

LAWS

2045. All you have to do to get an American mad is tell him he can't do something that's still within the law.

2046. The richest people in the world are those who earn a living, any kind of living, without breaking the law.

2047. The law of success does seem unfair . . . in the final analysis, the more you do to help the other fellow get ahead, the more you are really helping yourself.

2048. One way to achieve better laws is to make our politicians spend a trial period living under them before they're finally passed.

2049. Our laws are usually made by the least experienced lawmakers: divorce laws should be made by men who are married to witches, abortion laws by women who were butchered by quacks, and religious laws by sinners.

2050. To live up to the letter of the law it sometimes helps to spend some time praying on your knees.

LAWYERS

2051.   Lawyers are the only people in the world who can get $50.00 an hour for reading briefs!

2052.   A lawyer's best friend is a rich man who writes his own will.

LAZINESS

2053.   The fellow who doesn't let any grass grow under his feet is probably too lazy to plant some.

2054.   Laziness is a disease of human beings that is responsible for more ill health than germs.

2055.   If laziness were a disease, it would wipe out 99 percent of the human race overnight.

2056.   A lazy person is one who decides to do without catsup because none came out on the first couple of shakes.

LEAD

2057.   Lead in the seat of one's pants will never turn to gold.

LEADERS

2058.   A man knows he is a good leader if he can succeed in leading an alcoholic to water.

2059.   A good leader is one who will face the music even though he must turn his back on the crowd.

2060.   Often, a leader is a man put at the top by the same public which tries its best to knock him to the bottom.

2061.   Women are born leaders; show me the man who won't follow them.

2062.   There are two kinds of leaders in the world — some are interested in the fleece, others in the flock.

2063.   The leader of every pack of geese always has his neck sticking out the farthest.

LEADERSHIP

2064.   Leadership is that ability whereby a man can get others to work their heads off for him.

2065.   The best time to lead a man out of the woods is when you know he's barking up the wrong tree.

2066.   The surest way to get your son to follow in your footsteps is to beg him to get interested in a career other than your own.

2067.   To get people to follow the straight-and-narrow path, stop giving them advice and start leading the way.

2068.   The surest way to get your son to follow in your footsteps is by leading the way.

LEARNING

2069.   A man on his way to the top is one who is still learning something from each mistake he makes.

2070.   Stubbing your toe now and then is a low price to pay for learning how to pick up your feet.

2071.   How much you learn in life depends on how long you continue to profess your ignorance.

2072.   When it comes to learning from experience, you can't beat taking advantage of the other fellow's.

LEISURE

2073. Nothing adds to a man's leisure time like doing things when they're supposed to be done.

2074. "Leisure" is the two minutes rest a man gets while his wife is thinking up something else for him to do.

2075. Nothing adds to your leisure time more than doing things now!

2076. The surest way for a man to guarantee having an hour of leisure around the house is to suggest to his wife that she go shopping for a new hat.

2077. All you have to do to capture more leisure time is to avoid killing any of it.

2078. Nothing adds to an executive's leisure time like having a group of capable assistants around him.

LETTERS

2079. The kind of letter a college student likes to receive from home is the one that shows a check when he holds it to the light.

LEVEL-HEADEDNESS

2080. A level-headed person is one who doesn't get dizzy from doing good turns.

LIE DETECTOR

2081. Nobody yet has invented a better lie detector than a woman.

2082. When it comes to detecting a lie it is hard to beat a polygraph.

LIES

2083. The most expensive thing in the world to support is a convincing lie.

2084. It takes a lot of experience before a man can lie to his wife so she'll believe him.

2085. Nothing lends the weight of truth to a lie like saying it in a whisper.

2086. Perhaps the reason lies never stand still is they don't have a leg to stand on.

2087. Live in such a manner that if your tombstone could speak, it would not call you a liar.

LIFE

2088. Life can't be all that bad — for only ten dollars you can buy a good book that you can enjoy for a lifetime.

2089. Life is more like a ball of twine than it is like a bowl of cherries — and like twine it has many "nots" in it.

2090. The secret of long life consists in living moderately and silently.

2091. The best things in life never raise the white flag of surrender; they got to be taken by storm.

2092. Life will taunt you with a million and one cheap things, but it will punish you if you accept anything less than the best it has to offer.

2093. Life so often consists in trying to repair in our old age many of the toys which we wore out or broke when we were young.

2094. Life is that way — just about as many persons are trying to lose weight as are trying to put it on.

2095. Nobody has a harder time going through life than the fellow who tries to take it soft.

2096. The best time to stand up to any of life's situations is immediately after you get up from praying on your knees.

2097. The man who is getting the most out of life has already made ample provision for the worst.

2098. Life is a constant battle between facing problems and finding their solutions, and success for most of us is to end life pretty much at a draw.

2099. There are two things in life for which we are never fully prepared — an operation and an income tax audit — and even they have much in common.

2100. Your life will become overrun with weeds as soon as you fail to hoe the line of the law.

2101. The best way to lighten life's load is by lifting a weight off somebody else's back.

2102. The trouble with a lot of people who try to lead a model life is you know they're only posing.

2103. Whenever you feel that life's crowding you, remember that there's always room for improvement.

2104. Life is very much like golf ... no matter how many times you get in the rough, what counts in the end is your final score.

2105. Life is a great bundle of breathing spells between predicaments.

2106. Each person's life is an unending struggle between right and wrong, between poverty and wealth, between strength and weakness, between pride and humility, between health and sickness, between order and disorder, between victory and defeat, between God and Mammon, between life and death.

2107. The best way to keep on the sunny side of life is to walk away from shady deals.

2108. If you live with your ear to the ground you will hear many things which your feet would have trampled over.

2109. Life is a one-way street with a dead end.

2110. The secret of getting the most out of life is never to expect too much out of it.

LIFE INSURANCE

2111. One of the hazards of buying life insurance is the way you have to kill yourself to meet the premium payments.

2112. Life insurance statistics prove that millions of people would rather die than diet.

LIFE INSURANCE SALESMEN

2113. One of the greatest pleasures of growing old is the freedom you enjoy from life insurance salesmen.

LIGHT

2114. As soon as a man discovers the light in his life, he willingly turns over control of the switch to her.

LIGHTNING

2115. Tact is the ability to make a person see the lightning without letting him feel the bolt.

LIMELIGHT

2116. The trouble with some people who get in the limelight is they do very little reflecting.

2117. Sometimes a man who strikes you as having a lot on the ball is just able to pitch a good line.

LISTEN

2118. There are two ways a man can make sure of getting his wife to listen to him: talk about buying something for himself, or for her.

2119. It is a good rule to listen attentively to every word a person says at least for the first 60 seconds.

2120. One of the virtues of silence is that people will think the world of you for it and you don't have to listen to a word they say.

2121. The best way to get the other fellow to listen to you is by saying nice things about him behind his back.

2122. The only time it pays to listen to someone who is trying to stop you is if he happens to be a traffic cop.

2123. A successful man is one who can get a woman to listen to reason, or anything else for that matter.

2124. Most husbands train themselves to listen to every word their wives say, whether they hear it or not.

LISTENERS

2125. The surest road to a man's heart is to get him to talk to you about himself.

2126. Nothing helps a person to be a good listener like knowing he's going to be the next person to be called to the platform.

2127.   The trouble with people who are good listeners is you usually end up telling them more than you ever intended to.

2128.   The charm of a good listener lies in the patience he can exercise to keep his mouth shut.

2129.   If you have trouble finding listeners, try talking about somebody else besides yourself.

LISTENING

2130.   The greatest compliment any person can pay you is to repeat word for word exactly what you said — because that proves he was really listening to you.

2131.   Loan a man your ears and you will immediately open a pathway to his heart.

2132.   If you are willing to listen to someone else tell you about his fishing successes in life you will never have to worry about the size of the fish you catch yourself.

2133.   A man knows he has reached the pinnacle of success when he can get his wife to listen to him.

LITTLE BOYS

2134.   All some little boys need to keep busy is to be left all alone in the house with a full refrigerator.

2135.   Most little boys feel that they can get along without father's helping hand, untill they are old enough to start college.

2136.   All you need to get a little boy to use soap is a dirty pup.

2137.   It is easy to tell when a little boy is telling the truth as long as he's telling you something about one of your neighbors.

2138. You know a little boy loves his mother when he reminds her to clean behind his ears.

2139. One of the nicest things about a little boy is the way he can dislike you when you wash his face and love you a few seconds later when you fill it for him.

2140. Little boys prefer to get their hides tanned while on vacation.

2141. In our neighborhood, soon after school is over for the summer there are two things you've got to watch out for when they become very quiet — mosquitoes and little boys.

LITTLE THINGS

2142. Watch out for the little things in life; a fish bone is much more dangerous than a soup bone.

LIVE WIRE

2143. Many a fellow who appears to be a live wire has close connections with the daughter of the power house.

LIVING

2144. We seem to be living in such a fast moving age that it is impossible even to keep up with the time payments.

2145. A person who doesn't believe that the world owes him a living will always outdistance anyone who believes that it does.

LOAFING

2146. The trouble with some people who can't stand still is they prefer to loaf sitting down.

LOAN

2147. A loan is a sum of money which you cannot give your best friend without the risk of making him your worst enemy.

2148. A dollar still goes a long way — when you loan one to another person.

2149. Never loan a friend money unless you can afford to live without the interest from it.

2150. What some people save for a rainy day is a request for a loan.

2151. Tact is the ability to ask a person for a book you loaned him and succeed in getting back the other half dozen he borrowed from you.

LOGIC

2152. Logic is that line of reasoning by which some people try to explain why wicked people get rich and good people get crippled.

2153. Logic is any line of reasoning which proves you are right.

2154. Everybody claims they're being logical, especially when they're in complete disagreement with you.

2155. Nothing is harder for two or more persons to agree on than the same logic.

2156. There's only one satisfactory way to follow a woman's logic — and that is agreeably.

2157. All you have to do to appreciate logic in a person is to recognize how clearly he supports your own convictions.

2158. A logical person is anyone who can prove that you are right.

LONGEVITY

2159. Nothing improves your chances of reaching a ripe old age like making up your mind that you really want to.

2160. Nowhere is long life more important for getting ahead than in a large corporation.

2161. Longevity still is the surest way to overcome competition or failure.

2162. A lot of old people who credit their diet for their longevity aren't being fair to their parents and grandparents.

2163. When it comes to lengthening your life, it is hard to beat shortening the gait at which you try to take it.

LOOKING GLASS

2164. Nothing puts a man's honesty to the acid test like a looking glass.

LOSER

2165. A good loser is a person who can stick to a diet.

LOSS

2166. The greatest personal loss that a successful man can suffer is the loss of his health.

LOT

2167. A man owes a lot to his wife, including a decent home built on it.

2168. One of the best ways for a man to improve his lot is to get down on his hands and knees and pull out the weeds.

2169. When some people have a lot to get off their chest it may be that they have just had a house built on one.

LOVE

2170. A man who is very much in love with his wife always mails her letters.

2171. Even though love may be blind it can tie a knot in the dark.

2172. Love is never so treacherous underfoot as when it gets started on thin ice.

2173. Love is one game that is never called off on account of darkness.

2174. Love is the world's most powerful weapon against illness and disease, the world's most wonderful, wonder drug.

2175. Love is indeed a tender emotion — you can make it blossom with a smile, or completely crush it with a frown.

2176. A young man experiences the moment of truth as soon as a young girl can make him wish that time would stand still for him.

2177. You know that a woman still loves her husband if she suggests that he can use more room in her clothes closet.

2178. One way to tell how much a man loves his wife is to watch him cut a grapefruit in half and see if he dices both halves.

2179. Married people who always stay up to watch the late, late, late TV shows can't be very much in love.

2180. Next to falling in love with a beautiful woman, nothing is more satisfying than falling in love with your work.

2181. Nobody can do more for a young girl's complexion

than a handsome young man who has fallen in love with her.

2182. There are just two ways to make a woman love you: (a) show her you feel sorry for her, and (b) get her to feel sorry for you.

2183. Nothing strengthens a double-ring ceremony like two people who are madly in love with each other.

2184. The man who frequently calls the game of love on account of darkness — is the girl's father.

2185. The most stimulating person in any man's life is a wife who is madly in love with him.

2186. The trouble with many young people who put their heads together is they only think they're in love.

2187. There are some things you can't buy for love or money, but it is amazing how well money does on its own.

2188. Tolerance is the ability to love people when they don't deserve to be.

2189. You know a woman is in love with her husband if she smiles at him the way she does a traffic cop.

2190. Love will surely endure as long as it retains its stamina.

2191. Love is the eternal flame of immortality.

2192. A man is still very much in love with his wife if he jumps up the moment she walks into the room.

2193. True love is achieved only when the minds, hearts, and bodies of two persons work together in complete and unselfish harmony.

2194. Love is a game that is subject to the biggest penalties if not played fairly.

2195. Any man who really loves a woman doesn't bother

trying to understand her.

2196.   The strength of love between two persons lies not in a vow, or a chain, or a wedding band — but rather in an understanding of complete freedom from each other.

2197.   There is a tremendous difference between marrying for love or money or marrying for love and money.

2198.   A truly contented woman is one who asks for no greater calling in life than to mother the children of the man she loves.

2199.   When it comes to the game of love a smart girl knows enough to stay close to homeplate after making a perfect catch.

2200.   The most stimulating person in any man's life is a wife who is madly in love with him.

2201.   Love is so much like the sun ... it can bring new life and warmth and health to millions of persons on every part of our globe ... and all at the same time.

2202.   A woman is really in love with her husband if she will sew a button on his pajamas or patch a pant's pocket before he asks her to.

2203.   All it takes for a man to fall in love is the right girl to push him into it.

2204.   Some men are lucky in love — the girl they were interested in married another man.

2205.   A woman is really in love with her husband if she will help him to light up his pipe in the living room.

2206.   All it takes some teenage girls to grow up quickly is a young man to fall in love with.

2207.   Any married man who is in love with his boss is happily married.

2208.   Blind love can tie a tight knot.

2209.   In married life the best thing to save for rainy days is your love for each other.

2210.   Two people will remain in love as long as they still feel crazy about each other when the man's head grows smooth and the woman's face grows wrinkled.

2211.   Anytime you try to understand what makes you love a person you can be sure it's the kind of love that won't last long.

2212.   True love doesn't consist of holding hands — it consists of holding hearts.

2213.   Two people who are really in love with each other can't keep it a secret.

2214.   When it comes to steadying a man on the ladder of success, it is hard to beat a woman who is madly in love with him.

2215.   You don't have to convince a young couple in love that two heads are better than one.

2216.   You know a man really loves his wife if he will let her break in a new car.

2217.   You know a man is still very much in love with his wife if he brags about how pretty she is even at breakfast.

2218.   You know a man is still very much in love with his wife if he uses all of his free time at a convention to catch up on his sleep.

2219.   You know a woman is in love with her husband if she smiles at him the way she does at the baby.

2220.   You know a woman is in love with her husband if she isn't ashamed of him even in a bathing suit.

2221. Puppy love is what a father must have to keep walking the dog he bought his son.

2222. A man will have no trouble getting along with people if he helps them to love themselves a little bit more.

2223. You know a woman really loves her husband when she will never criticize him even in jest.

2224. It takes more skill and courage to stop love than it does to start it.

2225. No man has experienced true love until a woman has possessed him — body, soul, and bank account.

2226. Love is something a man can fall into as quick as the wink of an eye.

2227. You know a woman is still very much in love with her husband if she jumps for her make-up the minute she hears him pull the car into the driveway.

2228. I do not believe the love between two persons can possibly grow with the years unless it was infinitely deep from its first awakening.

LOVER'S LANE

2229. One road that is never paved with good intentions is lover's lane.

LOYALTY

2230. Treat your loyalties as you would a pregnancy — and remember there can never be just a little bit of either.

2231. Loyalty based only on preserving one's financial security is tantamount to personal slavery.

2232. Luck is very much like certain relatives. You never know when they'll pay a visit and when they do you never know how long they'll stay.

2233. Nothing makes life look brighter than a stroke of good luck immediately following a stroke of bad luck.

2234. Nothing helps you to trap luck like a tremendous amount of deliberate preparation.

2235. The surest way to keep pushing your luck is . . . uphill!

2236. Luck looks everyone straight in the eye, but blesses only those who are attentive enough to spot when it gives a "go-ahead" wink.

2237. Sometimes the best eraser in the world turns out to be a stroke of somebody else's bad luck.

2238. Nothing inflates a man's opinion of himself like a stroke of good luck.

2239. I am sure that luck is of the female gender: you must not only catch its eye, and woo her diligently, but you must also overcome her.

2240. Nothing improves a man's luck like betting all he's got — on himself.

2241. Luck may make men rich, but only adversity will make men great!

2242. Luck really is a charitable thing — note how frequently it visits people who work the hardest.

2243. A lucky man is one who is happy because the main thing he got out of marriage was children.

LUGGAGE

2244. One of the most pleasureable moments in air travel is the one when you arrive at the baggage claim location and spot your luggage.

LUXURY

2245. Some people who spend almost a lifetime getting used to being poor have no trouble at all getting accustomed to being rich.

2246. The difference between a luxury and a necessity depends on whether your neighbor has it and you don't.

2247. Anybody who is in a big hurry to buy luxuries usually ends up selling his necessities.

MACHINE AGE

2248. We are moving so fast towards a machine run age that some people do not realize it when they talk back to a telephone recording.

MAID

2249. When the modern housewife isn't ashamed of her housework she can thank her lucky stars that she has a conscientious maid.

2250. Nowadays it is just as hard to find a maid as it is to get one to work when you do.

2251. The average housewife today has to give her maid far more service and attention than she does her husband.

MAILMAN

2252. One man who is the first to meet his bills early is the mailman.

MAJORITY

2253. One beautiful woman among any number of men constitutes a majority.

MAN

2254. Man will show very little improvement until society sets up rules that will make it easier to learn to be good than it is to learn to be bad.

2255. One advantage of being a man is that you don't run the risk of catching a cold in evening clothes.

2256. History proves that man is the most stupid animal on our planet, probably because he is the only animal with intelligence to direct his stupidity.

2257. The disadvantage of being a man is that you can't even cry for a good reason.

2258. The man who stands on his own feet is usually popular on a dance floor.

2259. Being a man would be an unbearable task — if it weren't for women.

MAN NEXT DOOR

2260. The best way to get along with the man next door is to live at least a half a mile away from him.

MAN OF THE HOUR

2261. The man of the hour never watches the hands of the clock.

2262. Sometimes the man of the hour is one who is married ... and waiting patiently for his wife.

MAN'S STUPIDITY

2263. Man is the only creature on this planet that refuses to take any heed of warnings that clearly will endanger his well-being.

2264. One of the easiest things to prove is that man is the most stupid creature in God's universe.

MAN'S WORLD

2265. The only way a woman will honestly believe that it's a man's world is if the man who owns a lot of it happens to be hers.

MAN-IN-THE-MOON

2266. Now that we have had a TV look at ourselves from the moon, it is easy to understand why the man-in-the-moon always appears to be laughing at us.

MANAGERS

2267. Manager's Creed: Don't ask the management what it can do for you. Rather, ask yourself what you can do for management.

2268. The first rule a man must learn if he is to be a successful manager is that ACTION and REACTION on his part must NOT be equal and opposite.

2269. A good manager is one who can convince those under him that his job depends on them.

MANIPULATORS

2270. Every great leader, political or religious, manager or crook is a manipulator — each in his own way trying to attain his respective goals.

2271. Everybody is a manipulator; some in less obvious ways than others.

MANIPULATION

2272. Manipulation is like sin — it is always recognized in somebody else.

MANKIND

2273. Mankind can be divided into two groups — those who pass the salt and those who pass the check.

2274. Soon mankind will be faced with a desperate decision — it will have to choose between global peace or picking up the pieces of the globe.

MANNERS

2275. At no time is it more important to mind your manners than when you are driving a car on an expressway.

MARRIAGE

2276. When two married persons find that their aches and

pains seem to be increasing there is no better medicine in the world for them than falling madly in love with each other all over again.

2277. Marriage will fast disappear unless it is limited strictly to only one to a customer.

2278. The trouble with some men who can spot a woman just like the one who married dear old dad is they've already married somebody else.

2279. No single thing will disintegrate a marriage more effectively than a single act where one partner uses the other for a unilateral advantage.

2280. Nothing strengthens the bonds of matrimony like equal access to and control over each other's money.

2281. Marriage is a constant duel of checks and balances, with the wife holding a .45 over both of them.

2282. A happily married man is one who never remembers his wedding anniversary and never gets into trouble because he doesn't.

2283. A happily married man is one whose personality remains unchanged — whether his wife is with him or not.

2284. A happy marriage is one where a husband spends as many evenings at home with his wife as he did dating her as his fiancee.

2285. A happily married man is one who can go to a party with his wife with the same enthusiasm that he goes on a fishing trip without her.

2286. A happily married man is one who greets his wife when he comes home from work with the same enthusiasm with which he did when he left for work.

2287. Nothing makes a marriage work smoothly like plenty of fiscal lubrication.

2288. One of the best vows a young bride can take on her wedding day is to promise to keep her waistline constant over the next 30 years.

2289. A happy marriage is one in which a man kisses his wife at the door when he leaves in the morning as well as when he returns in the afternoon.

2290. Today an old fashioned girl is one who is still married to her first husband.

2291. Marriage is always a gamble, but when the chips are down, nothing beats a full house.

2292. If marriages are made in heaven somebody is certainly not taking much pride in his work.

2293. Marriage is an indissoluble contract in which one party obtains from the other party more than either ever may hope to repay.

2294. There would be fewer divorces if young people had to pass a written examination before they could get a marriage license.

2295. One of the best things that can be said in favor of marriage is that it has a great track record for changing fools into men.

2296. All men are born free and equal, but the majority of them get married.

2297. Young couples who refuse to get married until they can afford to seldom do.

2298. Nothing tests a marriage's mettle like illness on the part of one partner.

2299. When it comes to getting a marriage off to a flying start you can't beat a parent who supplies the airline tickets for the honeymoon.

2300.   Marriage today is a 50-50 proposition; a man shares half of his pay check with his wife and the other half with Uncle Sam.

2301.   Many a marriage that is started with love at first sight ends up with hate at the first fight.

2302.   The marriage ceremony is to marriage what buying a lot is to building a home.

2303.   The future of a marriage depends a lot on how a man holds his wife . . . responsibly or reverently.

2304.   Those who marry as an escape from something can be sure they'll find a mother-in-law.

2305.   A happy marriage is one in which each party understands perfectly when money matters, and when it doesn't.

2306.   Marriage statistics prove that some of the marriages that were thought to have been joined in heaven have to be separated in court.

2307.   The kind of disagreements that can tear a marriage out at its roots are almost inevitably based either on money or sex.

2308.   Some of the greatest satisfactions a parent gets out of marriage grow up and leave home.

2309.   The best preparation a young man can have for marriage is to resist it until he reaches 30.

2310.   In no institution is it more important to maintain good personnel relations than in marriage.

2311.   A happy marriage is the world's best bargain.

2312.   A happy marriage is one that improves a woman's looks and a man's disposition.

2313.   Most women don't mind letting their husband wear the pants in the family . . . as long as he does the dishes willingly.

2314. A happily married man is one who, on his first wedding anniversary, is more convinced than ever that he married the right girl.

2315. A good marriage is one in which an abundance of temptation is moderated by friendly consideration.

2316. One consequence of marriage is to half what you hold.

2317. You know that your marriage is in excellent working order if you can approach breakfast each morning humming a tune!

2318. Nothing improves the advancement of marriage more than a husband's advances.

2319. Marriage seldom makes a fool out of a man, but it has made many a man out of a fool.

2320. A happy marriage is a 50-50 situation; with the wife always standing on the dividing line.

2321. Marriage does one of two things to a girl — it either improves her complexion or ruins her figure.

2322. One of the troubles with many modern marriages is the race that has developed between husband and wife . . . the race to beat each other home from their jobs.

2323. A girl with good vision is one who can visualize what her suitor will look like ten years after she marries him.

2324. A girl never agrees to marry a man until she makes up his mind for him.

2325. A good wife is one who spends two hours getting dinner ready and five minutes trying to look prettier before her husband comes home from work.

2326. A happily married man is one who would rather talk with his wife at breakfast than read the morning newspaper.

2327. A happily married man is one who can feel his wedding ring tighten around his finger when he's alone with a pretty single woman.

2328. A happily married man is one who holds the car door open for his wife so she can get into the driver's seat.

2329. A happily married woman is one who doesn't worry because her husband doesn't wear a wedding band.

2330. A happily married woman is one who can enjoy a good cry without having a good reason for it.

2331. A happy marriage is one in which two persons find their love never grows stale on them.

2332. A man who has been married five years can always surprise his wife by passing the salt to her before she asks for it.

2333. A man knows he is master of the house if he can turn off the television without being challenged.

2334. A man who doesn't have a will of his own is probably married.

2335. A married man can always surprise his boss by coming home from the office a half hour early.

2336. An attractive girl can find a man in a matter of minutes, but it usually takes her the rest of her life to make a good husband out of him.

2337. An ideal husband is one who treats his wife with the same consideration he treats his pretty secretary.

2338. A successful man is one who has been married for 20 years and finally finds himself out of debt.

2339. A happily married man is one who believes that one of the soundest investments he can make is a dozen roses for his wife.

2340. A man knows his wife loves him if she suggests that he go off on a fishing trip by himself.

2341. A young woman who finds a man who suits her to a tee marries him, and then spends the rest of her life trying to change him.

2342. Babies may not be able to lift much, but they're strong enough to hold most marriages together.

2343. Few sounds are more conducive to making a fellow feel right with the world than the sound of his wife in the kitchen getting ready to serve dinner.

2344. Hollywood is a place where some married couples seem to believe in love the first night — only.

2345. How strong the bonds of matrimony are depends on how much interest they still can command.

2346. How successful a young woman is at marriage determines how long she has to wear the clothes she bought herself before she got married.

2347. How well a woman looks usually depends on how satisfied she is with the man she's married to.

2348. It is especially true that the meek shall inherit the earth if a man is married and his wife loves gardening.

2349. A woman will go to almost any extreme to put a man back on his feet if he's comfortable and her husband.

2350. It is not easy for a man to forget his mistakes — especially if he is married.

2351. It's hard for a woman to tell you why she married the man she did — as long as he's still alive.

2352. Marriage is a union of a man and woman, with the woman in the position of shop steward.

2353. Most women who are happy to belong to a man treat him as though they owned him.

2354. Nothing makes a marriage rust, like distrust.

2355. Nothing can bring a marriage to a head quicker than the appearance of some strong competition.

2356. One of the troubles with some men who get interested in blondes is they're married to brunettes.

2357. Opposition makes a great man greater . . . and that's why some married men are so successfull.

2358. Some bachelors would be willing to marry if they could find a girl who was too proud to let them work.

2359. Most wives are experts at beating their husbands to the withdraw.

2360. Some married men are lucky . . . not only do their wives like to cook, but they also know how!

2361. Some married women who waited for the right man to come along will tell you they didn't wait long enough.

2362. Some men who wonder what kind of a state they're in should remember they're married.

2363. Some women who get married to wealthy men discover that the bonds of matrimony are negotiable.

2364. Sometimes the young girl who spoils a fellow before she marries him, also ruins him afterwards.

2365. Some women have very little regard for men, especially if they're already married to one.

2366. Soon after a man gets married he starts losing the space originally assigned to him in the bedroom clothes closet.

2367. The average married woman's idea of framing her husband is to get him to wash the windows for her.

2368. The best things to get out of marriage are children.

2369. The fellow who enters into marriage with half-shut eyes ought to keep them only half-open afterwards.

2370. The marriage ceremony is to marriage what buying a lot is to building a home.

2371. The most disillusioned girls are those who got married because they were tired of going steady.

2372. The one thing every husband should learn as early as possible in marriage is how much of his own happiness depends on a word of praise now and then for his wife.

2373. The surest way for a young man to settle his future is to get married.

2374. The trouble with some men who are itching to go places is they're already hitched.

2375. The trouble with some men who can't even remember what happened last week is they've been married for years.

2376. There are few things more conducive to the making of a happy home than that of speaking at all times in a soft voice.

2377. When a bachelor has to eat his own words, it may only mean that his meals are now prepared by the girl he said he would never marry.

2378. When a young man gets married he should check all of his personal belongings for old love letters before his wife does.

2379. When a young man makes up his mind to apply himself diligently, he sometimes applies for a marriage license.

2380. When it comes to bringing a courtship to an abrupt end, sometimes you can't beat marriage.

2381. When it comes to making a good husband a woman's work is never done.

2382. When it comes to making your job fireproof it is hard to beat marrying the boss's daughter.

2383. When it comes to making a marriage last it is hard to beat hot homemade apple pies.

2384. When it comes to seeing through a man, most wives are not hindered by the morning newspaper.

2385. A patient man is one who is very punctual and married.

2386. A contented married woman is one who can't think of a better man she could have married.

2387. When two married people see eye to eye on something, they're reading the baby's temperature and its 104.

2388. You know a man is still very much in love with his wife if he jumps to his feet when she walks into the room.

2389. You know a woman is in love with her husband if she smiles at him the way she does a traffic cop.

2390. Whether or not the wolf will knock on your door depends on the marriageability of your young daughters.

2391. A man is happily married in direct proportion to the effort he makes to get out of going on expense-paid business trips.

MATCH

2392. A man is no match for a woman who knows how to set his heart on fire.

2393. As soon as a man discovers the light of his life, he's met his match.

2394. Some persons make a perfect match, especially after a little friction.

MATCHES

2395. It's with men as with matches — the fellow who gets lit loses his head.

MATHEMATICS

2396. Mathematics will always work against you when you try to get even with somebody.

2397. Many persons who are good at arithmetic do not know how to count even ten of their blessings.

2398. Algebra always seems like simple mathematics until the time comes when you have a daughter taking the course.

MATRIMONIAL BONDS

2399. Women who are financial wizzards usually realize that the most negotiable bonds are matrimonial.

MATURITY

2400. Nothing matures a cute girl like discovering why boys are interested in her.

2401. Maturity is in evidence when a group of persons with widely divergent views can meet for a week and disagree without being disagreeable, can express completely un-inhibited points of view without making enemies, and can part with a warmth and love for each other far greater than they had ever before known.

MEALS

2402. Some of the best meals a young married man is served were cooked by his wife's mother before he came home.

MEANS

2403. The fellow who wants to be happy and live within his means usually has to borrow money with which to do it.

MEANNESS

2404. Of all the forms of meanness that man can display, none is more heart-breaking than flagrant ingratitude.

MEDICAL CONCLUSIONS FROM PERSONAL EXPERIENCE

2405. The best medicine in the world is to love your work and your enemies.

2406. Two full glasses of warm water on getting up each morning can do more to purify your blood stream and keep you healthy than any of the expensive tonics.

2407. Regularity — the systematic disposal of the ashes from the human machine — is as important to sustaining good health as is the cleaning of spark plugs in an automobile to maintain its top performance.

2408. Many of the more serious ills of modern man arise because he applies the therapies of modern medicine before the body is given a fair chance to prove that it can clean up the problem on its own.

2409. The therapeutic benefits from Christian Science lie in its practice of making it possible for the body to have every chance to cure an illness of its own — and whenever this is possible an apparent success is claimed.

2410. Millions of persons — especially beautiful young women — who are so intent on baking their near-naked bodies in the sun to get tanned — are inviting shrivelled skin in middle-age as well as exposing themselves to grave pre-cancerous hazards. Take heed for science can prove that the sun is not the beneficial creation that its worshippers believe it to be.

2411. More baldness is created by man-made hair lotions and potions than is prevented by them.

2412. Any young adolescent with a good crop of hair stands a good chance of keeping it if: (1) starting at 18 he massages his scalp with his fingertips thoroughly before going to bed, (2) combs his hair often using nothing but tap water to control it and (3) gives his hair a thorough washing not more than once every month.

2413. My personal experience has revealed that painful arthritic-like pain develops in certain joints when I consume more than two ounces of alcohol within a twenty-four hour period. These repeated observations lead me to believe that there is a tie-in between alcohol consumption, arthritis, and bursitis, and the body's ability to dispose adequately of the build-up of alcohol or its breakdown products. The threshold level at which these by-products trigger joint inflammation and pain, must vary widely from individual to individual. In my case, however, this threshold value must be extremely low because the tie-in between alcohol consumption and the onset of joint pain is so dramatic and so reproducible.

MEDICINE

2414. Some persons never realize how indebted they are to the medical profession until after they receive a bill from their doctor.

2415. The best medicine in the world is patience, enough patience to wait until you are sure its absolutely necessary to take some.

2416. Modern medicine, if it continues to use the tools of science almost with abandon — the pill, chemicals, X-rays, lasers, etc. — without more thorough determination of their true risk-to-benefit ratios will ultimately prove to be the Achilles' heel of human health and well-being.

2417. The best medicine in the world is what your body makes when it needs it.

2418. There is no better medicine for ailing grandparents than baby grandchildren.

2419. Now that they've gotten medicines to taste so good, we've got to devise safeguards to prevent people from taking them when they don't need them.

2420. The best form of self-medication consists of doing others a good turn.

MEDITATION

2421. Perhaps the reason meditation is so popular today is that it passes as an acceptable way to get out of working.

MEDIOCRITY

2422. The danger of mediocrity is that it could erroneously lead you to believe that everybody else is inferior.

MEMORY

2423. One good memory can be used to blot out a pack of troubles.

2424. The only time an indelible memory is an advantage is when it works best at remembering your blessings.

2425. No one is to be more pitied in this life than a person with an indelible memory.

2426. If you have forgotten about a mistake you may have made, don't worry about it. You'll be surprised at how many persons will remind you of it.

2427. The true test of a man's memory is how well he remembers that he's married when he's alone with a beautiful lady.

2428. A good joke is one that you can laugh at and remember.

2429. There are a lot of people with a perfect memory if you count those who can remember everything they ever did

2430. A good memory is one that can remember the day's blessings and forget the day's troubles.

2431. An old timer is one who remembers when giving a woman some more rope meant she would string up another length of clothesline.

2432. Memory is a marvelous thing — it enables you to remember a mistake each time you repeat it.

2433. The best thing you can do about a poor memory is be thankful.

2434. There are two things a person never forgets — a dent in his car or a blow you give to his ego.

2435. Man can learn a lot from fishing — when the fish are biting no problem in the world is big enough to be remembered.

2436. A well-trained memory is one that permits you to forget the things that troubled you yesterday.

2437. A person with a good memory is one who can remember where he placed last year's list of people who sent Christmas cards.

2438.   A man with a really good memory is one who can forget that he forgave.

2439.   Nowadays a woman with a good memory is one who can tell you the names of her husbands and the order in which she divorced them.

2440.   One of the worst afflictions a person can suffer from is a good memory for all of life's little irritations.

2441.   Nothing is more refreshing or more revealing than reading letters you wrote 25 years ago — love letters especially.

2442.   Most of us have terrific memories if we gauge them by how well we remember all the things we would like to forget.

2443.   A well trained memory is one that permits you to forget everything that isn't worth remembering.

2444.   A good memory is one that can forget pain and dwell on pleasure.

2445.   Nothing makes the good old days look better than a memory that has already forgotten yesterday.

2446.   A retentive memory is a good thing for remembering facts, but it is an almost unbearable disadvantage if it cannot forget the past.

MEN

2447.   Most men lead with their chin by opening their mouth.

2448.   Some men who enjoy running things around the house are mighty proud of their powermotors.

2449.   Most men have two sides to them — the side their wives know, and the side they think she doesn't know.

2450.   The trouble with men who can read a woman like a

book is they're always in the market when another one comes along dressed up in a better jacket.

2451. Nothing will make a man brag about getting a tough job done like being forced to do it over his objections in the first place.

2452. Many men are like popcorn — you can only tell what they're made of when you put enough heat under them.

2453. When a man becomes alarmed at what his wife is wearing, the chances are that he just found out what she paid for it.

2454. All it takes for the average man to discover his second wind is to become a grandfather.

2455. Any man who can't stand his wife lecturing to him might find it a little easier to take sitting down.

2456. You've got to admire the fellow who hits the nail squarely on the head for keeping his eye on his thumb.

2457. A man who has been married a few years can always surprise his wife by passing the salt and pepper to her before she asks for them.

MENOPAUSE

2458. If you want a book on why a woman should never be President ask a man who is experiencing the emotional travail of his wife's menopause.

MENTAL ALERTNESS

2459. The surest way to keep your mind in top running order is to keep your stomach on the hungry side.

MENTAL ILLNESS

2460. The height of mental sickness has been reached when a person can no longer compliment anybody else but himself!

MERIT

2461. Real merit, like truth, always wins out — but only rarely is it recognized within the lifetime of the person who has it.

METTLE

2462. The true test of a man's mettle is his behavior when his adversary thinks he has him completely at bay.

MIDDLE AGE

2463. A man knows he has past middle age when his wife starts paying the premiums on his insurance policies long before they are even due.

2464. Middle age is the time of life when the hardest thing to raise in your garden is your knees.

2465. Middle age has set in when a man finds that he has to move the side parting of his hair closer and closer to the middle.

2466. Middle age is the time of life when most men and women read everything they see in print — about sex improvement.

2467. Middle age is good for a man because it teaches him that a lot of things he would like to do aren't important enough to make him exert the effort.

2468. A man reaches middle age as soon as he has to throw his shoulders back to maintain his balance.

2469. Middle age is the time of life when most men are in the market for a new pair of swimming trunks.

2470. A harrowing experience for a middle-aged man can be nothing more than a request from his wife to hoe the weeds in the flower bed.

2471. Middle age has set in when a man is more interested in what his wife's clothes cost than in how they fit her.

2472. By the time most young men reach middle age they are more interested in saving their hair than they are in saving the world.

2473. A man knows he has passed middle age when he finds the easiest way to fight graying hair is to get a haircut every week.

2474. Middle age has definitely arrived when your wife suggests that you comb your hair differently so that it will look as though you have more left than you really do.

2475. Middle age is when a man feels he gets less for his money each time he goes to the barber.

2476. Middle age is the time of life when the fellow who always acted like a human dynamo starts showing signs of ignition trouble.

2477. Middle age is the time of life when a man starts blaming the cleaners because his suits are shrinking.

2478. For most people, middle age is the time of life when a man gets fat from having to eat all of the brash conclusions he made in his youth.

2479. Middle age is the time of life when you can write a book about the things you talk yourself out of doing.

2480. Middle age is the time of life when a man can get exhausted simply by wrestling with his conscience.

2481. Middle age is the time of life when you wonder how you could be stupid enough to have organized a picnic for a group of ten-year-olds.

2482. Middle age is the time of life when a man fights a losing battle between the number of gray hairs that appear and the number he loses.

2483. Middle age is the time of life when a man's hair starts thinning out a bunch at a time.

2484. Middle age is the time of life when a man starts spreading in the middle and shedding on the top.

2485. Middle age is the time of life when a man needs a belt only as an ornament for his trousers.

2486. A woman reaches middle age when she is willing to wear shoes that fit her comfortably.

2487. Middle age is the time of life when a man starts to play both ends against the middle.

2488. A man reaches middle age when his waistline clearly marks the halfway mark.

2489. A man has reached middle age when all it takes to get him exhausted is a little bit of child's play.

2490. A man reaches middle age when he has to bend his knees to pick something up.

2491. A man knows he has past middle age when he notices that his wife starts paying the premiums on his insurance policies before they are even due.

2492. Nothing stumps a middle-aged man like trying to get into last summer's bathing suit.

2493. A man reaches middle age when he can't wear the same swimming suit two summers in a row.

2494. A middle aged man's idea of a roaring good time is to enjoy it all from a sitting position.

2495. A sure sign of middle age is the size of the obstacle that gets in your way when you tie your shoes.

2496. Middle age is the time of life when a man convinces himself that green lawn would look better than a vegetable garden in his backyard.

2497. Middle age is the time of life when you're lucky if you can reach the phone before it rings three times.

2498. Middle age is the time of life when the only time a man will run for anything is for political office.

2499. Middle age is the time of life when the price you pay for a little fun goes up each time.

2450. Middle age has already arrived when the thought of doing weight lifting exercises is enough to exhaust you.

2501. Middle age is the time of life when a man starts declining almost everything.

2502. Middle age is the time in life when a person gets set in his ways so much that he just sets, sets, and sets.

2503. Middle age is the time of life when a man becomes determined to diet each time he buys a new suit.

2504. Middle age is the time of life when most men find it much harder to throw their weight around . . . or away.

2505. Middle age is the time of life when the fellow who was once a human dynamo shows signs of ignition trouble.

2506. One way a man can tell whether or not he's reached middle age is to baby-sit for his first grandchild.

2507. Middle age is the time of life when a man fights a

losing battle between the number of gray hairs that appear and the number he loses.

2508.   Middle age is the time of life when a man who used to go like 60 now has to push himself just to go like 30.

2509.   Middle age is the time of life when a man knows how much work he should do, but manages to get by on half of it.

2510.   Middle age is the time of life when a man doesn't believe in making a run for anything.

2511.   Middle age is the time of life when a harrowing experience for a man is to listen to his wife brag about the big garden she wants.

2512.   Middle age has arrived when a man's idea of get-up-and-go is to go to bed.

2513.   Middle age is the time in a man's life when the five o'clock shadow doesn't show up until nine — because his beard has turned so much whiter.

2514.   Middle age has set in when a man knows how to double his income but convinces himself it's not worth the effort.

2515.   Middle age is the time of life when a man who eats his cake has to buy larger clothes.

2516.   Middle age has set in when a man starts making up excuses to do nothing.

2517.   Middle age is the time of life when you can count on seeing your dentist at least once every six months.

2518.   Middle age is the time of life when the things that once struck you as a lot of fun now seem like a lot of work.

2519.   Middle age is the time of life when most men feel terrible after they have the time of their life.

2520. Middle age is when you hope nobody will invite you out next Saturday night.

2521. Middle age is the time of life when a man is faced with a constant struggle between going to pot or to seed.

2522. Middle age is the time of life when a man gives up taking two steps at a time, and takes two pills at a time instead.

2523. Middle age has arrived when a man's urge to hit the hay comes around 9:00 o'clock every evening.

2524. Middle age is the time of life when a man hopes for a silver lining — on top of his head.

2525. The average middle-aged man would enjoy washing his face more if it were easier for him to know where to draw the line.

2526. Middle age is the time of life when a person tries to control his weight by increasing his use of laxatives.

2527. Middle age is the time of life when a man is willing to give up the chase — and let the youngsters get away.

2528. Middle age is the time of life when a little effort goes only a little way.

MIDDLE-OF-THE-ROADER

2529. Nowadays, most people are getting to be middle-of-the-roaders about religion — they think they're standing on the dividing line between heaven and hell.

MILLIONAIRES

2530. All a man has to do to become a millionaire in America is invent a low calorie diet that tastes good to eat.

2531. People who are envious of millionaires are usually too lazy to try to become one.

2532. Money does not necessarily ruin a man — many great millionaire philanthropists learned true charity only after acquiring their millions.

MIND

2533. The surest way to keep your mind in top running order is to keep your stomach on the hungry side.

2534. Of all the forms of fitness that man can aspire to none is more important or more lasting than fitness of the mind.

2535. Nothing helps to stretch one's mind like a good idea that you can get all excited about.

2536. The easiest way to find out what's on your wife's mind is to sit yourself down in a comfortable chair.

MINISTER

2537. A minister is a man who has to pray for a living.

MINK COATS

2538. Many a woman wears a mink coat because she threatened to expose somebody's hide.

MINORITY RULE

2539. A perfect example of minority rule is a pretty girl surrounded by men.

MIRRORS

2540. Each person sees us as differently as we see ourselves in different mirrors.

MISCHIEF

2541. Every young mother knows that when it rains it pours — mischief.

2542. The trouble with a quiet child is that the mischief is usually already done.

2543. What most children save for a rainy day is mischief.

2544. Children aren't always haphazard in their ways — sometimes they plan their mischief.

MISERS

2545. People who are misers with their money often are philanthropists with their troubles.

MISERY

2546. Most people always are amazed to find the extent of their compassion when it comes to enduring the misery of others.

2547. The unhappiest people in the world are those who are proud of their misery.

2548. People who love misery do the least to end it.

2549. A miserable person is one who insists on sharing his misery with you.

MISFORTUNE

2550. No misfortune can befall a man that will prove more disastrous than his loss of self-confidence.

MISTAKES

2551. To err is human, but alas to admit it seldom is.

2552. An error doesn't become a mistake until you refuse to correct it.

2553. When it comes to profiting from your mistakes, you can count on the Internal Revenue Service.

2554. There are few things that will do more to improve a man's disposition or digestion than owning up to a mistake.

2555. The most urgent mistakes to correct are those you make deliberately.

2556. Don't be afraid to admit a mistake; you'll never be critized for doing so.

2557. I always feel at home with a person who admits he makes mistakes because I like my own kind of company.

2558. How much a mistake really costs you can best be determined by estimating how much you could have saved by not making it in the first place.

2559. One of the healthiest feelings in the world is the one that comes over you after you admit a mistake.

2560. The man who isn't afraid to make mistakes will always achieve much more of lasting value in a life time than the man who always plays it safe.

2561. I want nothing to do with a man who makes the same mistake only twice — it means he's superconservative!

2562. Anyone who succeeds by not making some mistakes does so through luck or an inheritance.

2563. Mistakes of the tongue have destroyed more people, ruined more marriages, and cost more businessmen their jobs and their futures than any other kind of mistakes.

2564. Mistakes, after all, do serve a purpose — our friends find such pleasure in pointing them out to us.

2565. There are few thrills in this life that can come up to the one you get when you correct a mistake you're sure you could have gotten away with.

2566. Statistics prove decisively that the gravest mistake thousands of Americans make each year is to drive while intoxicated.

2567. The man who isn't afraid to make mistakes will always achieve more of lasting value in a lifetime than the man who always plays it safe.

2568. Most people can do a fair job of profiting by the mistakes of others ... but it is only the exceptional ones who can profit by their own mistakes.

2569. To make mistakes is human and so is trying to get out of correcting them.

2570. The greater a person's wealth and the more power he acquires, the greater is his risk of making a calamitous error.

2571. A completely useless mistake is one that doesn't give a friend a chance to tell you about it.

2572. A good executive is a man who is afraid to make a mistake but makes a few anyway.

2573. Mistakes are good for you ... if you make them seldom enough.

2574. A man on his way to the top is one who is still learning something from each mistake he makes.

2575. A failure never becomes a hopeless mistake unless it stops you from trying again.

2576. Just because some people never make the same mistake twice doesn't mean that they make fewer ones.

2577. Nothing has more lives than an error you refuse to correct.

2578.   The heaviest chip on a man's shoulders is a mistake he refuses to correct.

2579.   A good executive is a man who's not afraid to correct a mistake made by his secretary . . . no matter how pretty she is.

MODERATION

2580.   Moderation in life is as important as spikes in a railroad track; without it you are bound to end up a wreck.

2581.   Moderation is never more virtuous than when you're about to let off steam.

2582.   The secret of long life consists in living moderately and silently.

2583.   About the only time over-indulgence will not harm you is when it is overindulgence in moderation.

MODERN CHILD

2584.   Nothing annoys the average modern child today like a disobedient parent.

MODERN EXECUTIVE

2585.   A modern executive is a man who believes in getting the other fellow to do his best for him.

2586.   A modern executive is a man who wears out several suits to every pair of shoes.

MODERN FAMILY

2587.   Nothing holds a modern family together like good behavior on the part of the parents.

MODERN GIRL

2588. By the time a modern girl starts knitting socks for a fellow she knows that she's got him all sewed up.

2589. No modern girl will bother to knit socks for a fellow unless she expects to take over the job of darning them too.

MODERN PHYSICIAN

2590. A modern physician is a man who works 18 hours a day telling others to slow down or they'll get high blood pressure.

MODESTY

2591. Modesty increases as a virtue the less you have to be modest about.

MODIFIED GOLDEN RULE

2592. Modified Golden Rule — treat others first the way you hope they will treat you later.

MONDAYS

2593. There's nothing wrong with my Mondays that ten hours of solid sleep Sunday night cannot cure.

MONEY

2594. Nowadays when you save money for a rainy day you would be wise to pray for just a passing shower.

2595. Funny how a dollar still seems like a dollar when you loan it to somebody!

2596. Money still talks, but lately it has developed a bad case of laryngitis.

2597. These are days when most people aren't interested in doubling their money — they would be satisfied if they could hold onto what they've got.

2598. When it comes to putting zip into a man's step and making him throw his shoulders back one of the best drugs of all is money.

2599. People who like to borrow money usually dislike paying it back.

2600. Money isn't everything, really, until you are old, retired, and want to retain your independence.

2601. Whenever a man is accused of having more money than brains — you can be sure he inherited it.

2602. One time that money is useless is when you try to create an idea with it.

2603. A badly needed invention in America today is some kind of dough which sticks to your fingers.

2604. When it comes to making money you can't beat putting somebody else's money to work for you.

2605. People who can count all their money these days don't have to be very good at arithmetic.

2606. A borrower is a man who tries to make ends meet by stretching your dough.

2607. Nothing is more exhausting than searching for easy ways to make a living.

2608. A man can get used to anything except an empty wallet.

2609. When it comes to dulling the pain of poverty, the best novacain of all is money.

2610. What most people save for a rainy day is a request for a loan.

2611. Nothing improves a person's disposition like money in the pocket — or pocketbook.

2612. Money still talks, but it seems to be getting more aloof all the time.

2613. Of all the things you may give away, money is the least permanent in the pleasure it produces and the most likely to backfire on the giver.

2614. The poorest man in the world is one who has all the money he wants, but nothing else.

2615. A girl with a shapely figure can get by with half as much clothes' money.

2616. Nobody can push a man into a high income bracket like a wife who needs the money.

2617. These days a person doesn't try to make ends meet; he just tries to keep track of how far beyond his means he's going.

2618. How low the value of the dollar falls depends on how far some people will stoop to make one.

2619. Money and brains may provide a man with the fuels of life, but he still needs a good wife to provide the spark.

2620. People who really know what to do with money are best at holding onto it.

2621. Thrift is the ability to want to hold onto money until the urge to buy something you can do without passes away.

2622. When it comes to making a man cough up his money you can't beat the Internal Revenue Service.

2623. Money that is earned by blood, sweat and tears is seldom spent like water.

2624. Money is like knowledge — the more you have of it, the less you need to brag about it.

2625. Money does not necessarily ruin a man — many millionaire philanthropists learned true charity only after acquiring their millions.

2626. Nowadays when you say good-bye to your money you can't accuse it of loitering.

2627. Money may be the root of all evil, but it is hard to pick up some of life's cutest blossoms without it.

2628. Most people in the world under-estimate the true value of money because they never get hold of enough of it to over-estimate its value.

2629. It is the man with money who is watched closely both by robbers and Internal Revenue agents.

2630. Money still talks, of course, but only what is left after taxes.

2631. The same people who preach that money is evil and contemptable enjoy sumptuous dinners.

2632. Nine times out of ten when members of a family refuse to talk to each other . . . you can blame it on money.

2633. Money still makes the best kind of gift for any occasion, and you can be sure it will fit . . . any pocketbook.

2634. Money isn't everything, but it does provide you with a magnificent cloud cover.

2635. The most expensive way to make money is to spend

your whole lifetime doing nothing else.

2636. There are two great dangers underlying monetary success ... the danger of your mind going to seed and your waistline going to pot.

2637. Money always comes to you either directly or indirectly because you render somebody else a service.

2638. Money doesn't burn holes in pockets any more — it doesn't stay around long enough to even warm the lining.

2639. One of the greatest pleasures that you can get from hard-earned money is to spend it with abandon if and when you choose to.

2640. Usually it is better to let your wife handle the money because in the end it will amount to the same thing.

2641. Money is one thing we hoard in this world that we won't have any use for in the next.

2642. All you have to do to stretch a dollar these days is to try and hold onto it.

2643. Nothing is more chilling to a man of importance than hot money.

2644. A man's finances rather than his geographical location determines the number of distant relatives that he has.

2645. A dime is as valuable today as it ever was only if you use it to put in your two cents' worth.

2646. The only trouble with some of these fine new homes is the location — on the outskirts of your income.

2647. All it takes to overcome some people in the pursuit of happiness is an urgent need for the money you loaned them.

2648. A small town is a place where you can always count on someone to tell you what you did with your money.

2649. It takes lots of money to make ends meet nowadays — as a matter of fact, it takes twice as much.

2650. A dime is valuable today, especially if you want to put in your two cents' worth.

2651. All a man needs to keep a woman happy is enough money to keep her from running out of it.

2652. A pretty girl is one who can run away with a man's imagination . . . and his money.

2653. A happy marriage is one in which each party understands perfectly when money matters, and when it doesn't.

2654. A rich man is one who counts his dollar bills twice before he lets go of one of them.

2655. A rich man is one who refuses to give up the search for his golf ball, even after he finds a better one than he lost.

2656. About the only thing worse than returning from a vacation broke is running into your friends who didn't even know where you were spending all your money.

2657. About the only reason some people worry about money is they find it convenient for making down payments.

2658. After all is said and done, the thing that we go through the most in life is money.

2659. A borrower is a man who tries to make ends meet by stretching your dough.

2660. A bargain is something that is priced so low that you can't resist buying it even though you don't need it.

2661. A recession is a period when you discover how much money you were wasting on non-essentials.

2662. Any time you race a traffic cop you're giving him a race for your money.

2663. A rich man is one who can afford to get a haircut as often as he feels like one.

2664. A completely honest person is one who will count his change to prevent you from short-changing yourself.

2665. A dollar still goes a long way — when you loan one to another person.

2666. A rich man is one who checks the meters in a row of empty parking spots before he parks his car at the one that still has some unexpired time.

2667. The surest way to lose track of your money is to go to the races with it.

2668. A rich bachelor is a man who has enough time and money for both golfing and fishing.

2669. A practical man is one who looks for a wife that will make him a wealthy son-in-law.

2670. Hard work is what you need today to hold on to money once you've made some.

2671. How much a man is paid usually depends on how many people he can get to do a job as well as if he did it himself.

2672. One of the surest ways to enjoy money is to earn it before you spend it.

2673. If people would only learn to live according to what they can afford, they would be much happier and thinner.

2674. In America when something becomes popularly priced it simply means that millions who can't afford it are buying it.

2675. Most people who can't live within their means will have an even harder time living up to the hilt of their credit.

2676. Nothing helps you to become a self-made man like

having a wife who has more than enough to support the both of you.

2677. Nothing gives a man a shot in the arm like a loaded pocketbook.

2678. Nowadays about the best a fellow can do with the money he saves for a rainy day is pay his taxes with it.

2679. One kind of heat that is especially pleasant comes from money burning a hole in your pocket.

2680. People who are misers with their money often are philanthropists with their troubles.

2681. Shopping bags are getting bigger all the time; and so are the pocketbooks you need to bring along enough money to fill them.

2682. Some people who try to keep up with the Joneses succeed only in getting out of breath, and broke.

2683. The amount of money required by the average person to make ends meet is always about five times more than he's making.

2684. Marry for money and you will always live in fear of losing the change.

2685. Money still talks, but the pause between pay days does seem to be getting longer and longer.

2686. Money still talks, of course, but it has to stop and catch its breath more often these days.

2687. Money talks as much as ever, except that it has to shout a lot louder to be heard.

2688. Money certainly is a relative matter; the more you get the more relatives you discover you have, too.

2689. A practical young man is one who looks for a fiancee who would make him a wealthy son-in-law.

2690. Some people aren't interested in doubling their money; they would be satisfied if they could hold on to what they've got.

2691. Money talks, but not the fellow who has plenty of it.

2692. Money still talks, but in faint infrequent whispers.

2693. Most persons never realize how much time they wasted making money until God asks them to cash their life in.

2694. Most women are satisfied to get along on their husband's salary, but they usually expect him to find some additional means for his own support.

2695. Most wives are experts when it comes to beating their husbands to the withdraw.

2696. The man who doesn't know where his money is going these days just can't see fast-moving objects.

2697. When you see red it is high time that you started living within your income.

2698. The best way to appreciate how much $100 still is, is to try to borrow it from somebody.

2699. Nothing gives a woman a greater feeling of security than a tight grip on a man's pocketbook.

2700. Nothing makes a man run out of money like trying to catch up with the Joneses.

2701. Nothing makes a paycheck look better to a man than being the father of five children.

2702. Nothing makes money lose interest like talking about how much of it you've got.

2703. Nothing will put out the fire in a woman's voice like showering her with cold cash.

2704. Nothing will whittle away a man's income like the belief that money grows on trees.

2705. Nowadays money is so hard to get a hold of that you can get out of breath just trying to keep up with the installments.

2706. One thing you can't say about a man who marries for money is that he's a no-account.

2707. One way to test your vision today is try and keep an eye on your money.

2708. One of the easiest ways to become poor is to try and live up to a reputation for being rich.

2709. People who believe that money grows on trees usually get caught out on a limb.

2710. People who can count all their money these days don't have to be very good at arithmetic.

2711. People who claim they can't see any change in the dollar mean they never get any back.

2712. Rolling in money is a painful exercise today, because it is spiked with hidden taxes.

2713. Some men have more money than brains and they usually have no trouble proving it.

2714. Some of the hardest people to catch up with are those who are running into debt.

2715. Some people are not nearly as interested in how much talent they've inherited as they are in its cash value.

2716. Some people manage to make a fortune throwing money away . . . but first they take careful aim.

2717. The ambition of every modern American businessman inevitably is to increase his income until his taxes are higher than his take-home pay.

2718. The average young girl puts all of her money into clothes that she cannot get all of herself into.

2719. The best substitute for wealthy parents is wealthy grandparents.

2720. The best way to ask for a raise at the top of your voice is to let your work do the talking for you.

2721. The first sign of a recession is when people who own Cadillacs start buying gasoline a dollar's worth at a time.

2722. The man who can't see anything funny about a woman's hat is the one who has to pay for it.

2723. The most serious mistake a young girl can make is to try and capture a man's checkbook instead of his heart.

2724. The only man who can make more money than his wife can spend is a widower.

2725. The only really poor people in the world are those who pretend they're rich.

2726. The people who have very little to complain about are probably nearly broke.

2727. The reason economy is hard to practice today is that first you must have the money to practice it with.

2728. The richest people in the world are those who are making ends meet without breaking a law.

2729. The secret of making dough still is do.

2730. The trouble with most of these fine new homes they're building is they are located on the outskirts of your income.

2731. The trouble with some people who fall into debt is they do it with your money.

2732. The trouble with most women who come home from a shopping spree is their pocketbook is as spent as they are.

2733. There are two times when money is dangerous — when you're crazy about it, and when you are completely out of it.

2734. These days before a person can rise to the uppercrust he's got to make plenty of dough.

2735. There are some things you can't buy for love or money, but it is amazing how well money does on its own.

2736. There's nothing like a recession to make it easier for everybody to understand money when it starts to talk.

2737. Today a man with 20/20 vision is one who can see where his money is going.

2738. We appreciate praise and money most from people who are thrifty with them.

2739. There is only one time that the value of money does not fluctuate with inflation — and that is when you offer a penny for someone's thoughts.

2740. You'll never hear anyone complain about getting their hands dirty as long as they're counting money.

2741. If you don't think much of money, then try paying your bills with a smile.

2742. Nothing will make you realize the importance of money like retirement.

2743. When a man has money to burn he can always find a woman to provide the match.

2744. When money starts talking, a good conscience perks up its ears.

2745. When it comes to spotting a fool with money, you can't beat a good looking waitress.

2746. When it comes to effective personal public relations, you can't beat plenty of money in the bank.

2747. When money starts talking out loud it is a sure sign that it is about to lose its power of speech.

2748. When a man builds his "castle in the air" today, he discovers that the price of it, at least, is sky high.

2749. When it comes to beating a policeman to the draw, it pays to put money in the parking meter.

2750. When a new car runs into money it is usually by accident.

2751. When a man becomes alarmed at what his wife is wearing, it may be she forgot to remove the price tag from it.

2752. You can make a child do a lot of things by spending money lavishly on him, except run into your arms when you come into your house.

2753. You know you are living right if you could get rich by getting one dollar for every kind word you say behind the other fellow's back.

2754. You soon lose interest in people with a lot of money who keep telling you how hard up they are.

2755. Money that is spent before it is earned usually buys nothing but more misery.

2756. There are two times when money is dangerous — when you're crazy about it, and when you're completely out of it.

MOOD

2757. Nothing controls the other person's mood like the

expression on your own face.

MOON

2758. Our astronauts have proved the truth of an old saw; they proved that the pastures on the other side of the moon are not greener either!

2759. Now that we have had a TV look at ourselves from the moon, it is easy to understand why the man in the moon is always laughing at us!

MOONLIGHT

2760. Some girls try to move heaven and earth to catch a man, but the really smart ones just use a little bit of moonlight.

2761. Most young girls believe in setting the bait out under the sunlight and springing the trap by moonlight.

MORTGAGES

2762. A man who has a lot to be thankful for is one who just paid the last installment on his mortgage.

2763. Sometimes a man's deeds can be a worry to him ... especially if they are heavily mortgaged.

2764. Nothing lightens the average working man's load like a final payment on a mortgage.

2765. Some persons are kepy busy by painting off their mortgages.

2766. You can't blame some people for worshipping the ground they stand on — especially once it is mortgage-free.

2767. A man doesn't know the real meaning of being blood thirsty until he finds himself in a closed room that is infested with mosquitoes.

2768. A patient man is one who never hits the ceiling — unless he's after a mosquito on the loose.

2769. One of the most distressing sights is a mosquito gliding in your direction with its landing gear down.

2770. Next to hooking a rainbow trout, few pleasures are more comforting than swatting a mosquito before it left the spot where you thought it was.

2771. In our neighborhood, soon after school is over for the summer there are two things you've got to watch out for when they become very quiet — mosquitoes and little boys.

MOTHER-IN-LAW

2772. My publisher told me that I was the only author they knew who dedicated a best seller to his mother-in-law!

2773. A dangerous mother-in-law is one who is not satisfied with being a coach, but insists on taking over as referee.

2774. The best kind of mother-in-law to have is one who takes her son-in-law's side.

2775. The first thing you must do to get along with your mother-in-law is to kiss her each time you meet her . . . and really mean it!

2776. There is only one thing worse than a mother-in-law who lives in your house — and that is a mother-in-law in whose house you must live.

2777. When it comes to holding a home or a family together it's hard to beat a good mother.

2778. The reason a mother gets so much done in a day is that her children give her so much to do.

2779. There's much more to being a mother than having babies — like the housework that never ends.

2780. The trouble with some mothers who raise their children by the book is they use the comic books.

2781. When a modern mother gets a lot done in a day, she's got to give the children most of the credit for it for making the work in the first place.

2782. A family that is always in agreement can thank a wonderful mother for it.

2783. When a mother reaches the end of her rope, it is usually too late for the children to start behaving.

2784. A modern mother is one who never worries about her daughter getting into trouble as long as marriage is the way to get her out of it.

MOTIVATION

2785. Motivation is sometimes demonstrated in its most vigorous form by a man who is living far beyond his income.

2786. If men were as motivated at doing their work as they are in fighting a receding hairline, we could double our gross national product almost overnight.

2787. Most of the people with whom you will come into contact in life will have one common thirst, one common inner drive, namely your acknowledgement that they are right about something, about anything.

2788. People always are motivated by at least two things; the one they tell you about, and the one they don't tell you about.

2789. Motivation is a tremendous virtue provided it is not used to practice dishonesty.

2790. If you want to discover what makes some people tick, try winding them up.

2791. Whatever it is that motivates a man you can be sure that in one way or another it is soothing his ego.

2792. Money may not be the elixir of life ... but it is a wonderful match with which to build a fire under someone when applied as a bonus.

MOTIVES

2793. Most people have two motives for doing things — alternative and ulterior.

MOTORISTS

2794. There would be fewer accidents if the law required motorists to own their cars before they could drive them.

2795. Just because some modern cars don't have a clutch you can't stop some motorists from acting as though they were asleep at it.

2796. A careful motorist is one who knows he's not wasting time when he's waiting for a green light.

2797. All you have to do to get a big hand from a sullen motorist is to give up your parking space to him.

2798. Nothing would stop some motorists from driving around in circles like a handy spot to park their cars.

2799. Most reckless motorists drive as though they didn't own their cars, and they usually don't.

2800. Nothing makes a motorist obey a traffic light like a cop standing beside it.

2801. The average motorist isn't dangerous as long as he's a pedestrian.

2802. It takes brute force sometimes to bring a careless motorist to a dead stop — like a locomotive.

2803. Most motorists come to a full stop at a stop sign when a pretty blonde happens to be standing beside it.

2804. You can explain the way many motorists drive by the fact that they don't own their cars.

MOUNTAIN CLIMBING

2805. Mountain climbing never is more exhausting than when it is up the side of a molehill.

MOUTH

2806. When a man leads with his chin, you can be sure his mouth is wide open.

2807. At no time is it more important to keep your mouth shut than when you feel like exploding.

2808. It's just as important for a person with an open mind to keep the bugs out as it is for a person with an open mouth.

2809. Some people who are being paid more than they're worth know enough to keep their mouth shut about it.

2810. Your mouth is the window to your mind so it pays to know when to open or close it.

MOVIES

2811. The trouble with two people who put their heads ·together sometimes is they're sitting directly in front of you at a movie.

2812. Television is not only replacing movies and housework — it is also doing quite a job on furniture.

MOVIE CONTRACT

2813. One of the most valuable things a man can have up his sleeve is a movie contract.

MUD

2814. The moment you start slinging mud about somebody else, you begin to lose ground.

MUDDLING THROUGH

2815. The only time it makes sense to muddle through something is when it is the only way to get to the other side of the puddle.

MUSIC

2816. A smart girl would rather have a man dancing to her tune than stepping on her feet on the dance floor.

NAKED TRUTH

2817. Nothing is harder to see than the naked truth.

NAP

2818. All you have to do to get the world to beat a path to your door is decide to take a bath.

2819. The pleasure of an afternoon nap is hard to beat — if you can ever take one without somebody ringing the doorbell.

2820. Sometimes the difference between a good speaker and a poor speaker is a nice nap.

2821. Any man who can take a nap or a hot water shower whenever he feels like it is still a bachelor.

2822. All you have to do to get the world to beat a path to your door is decide that you want to take a nap.

NATIONAL DEBT

2823. The truly courageous people in America are the members of the younger generation who don't seem to be all upset over the size of the national debt they will have to carry.

NATURAL

2824. Most persons can act more natural when they're well dressed than they could if they were naked.

NATURE

2825. Nature is willing to give you nearly everything you could wish for, providing you take it from her in exactly the way she wants you to.

2826. If nature really knows best, how can you explain why nylon has replaced the silk worm?

2827. Most of the world's ills result from the fact that society is intent on disobeying nature.

2828. Nature uses subtle camouflage — so subtle that she can hide great scientific discoveries before your eyes for decades without you ever suspecting that they are staring you in the face.

NAVIGATION

2829. When it comes to docking a man's ship, you can't beat a woman navigator.

NECESSITIES

2830. An old timer is one who can remember when the bare necessities of life consisted of occasional trips to the woodshed.

2831. Necessity is to procrastination what the spur is to a lazy horse.

NECKLINE

2832. Nothing lowers a man's resistance like a plunging neckline.

2833. When some women get all dressed up to please a man, they obviously know where to draw the neckline.

NEED

2834. Nothing makes something more valuable to you than throwing it away a day before you discover how badly you need it.

NEEDLING

2835. Before a man climbs the ladder of success he usually finds the right woman to needle him up it.

NEIGHBOR

2836. Nobody taxes a man's income more than his neighbor.

2837. A good neighbor to have is one by the name of Jones who is trying to keep up with you.

2838. You're never quite sure how you feel about a neighbor until you run into him broiling steaks on the backyard grill.

2839. A good neighbor is one who has to take a half-hour to get to your house, and never stays more than a couple of minutes.

2840. A popular neighbor is one whose children are old enough to be away at college.

2841. A neighbor is a person who likes to borrow your equipment and loan you his troubles.

2842. A contented neighbor is one who boasts to you about the good behavior of your children.

2843. You're never quite sure how you feel about a neighbor until a "For Sale" sign suddenly appears in front of his house.

2844. A neighbor is a person who can get to your house in less than a minute and take two hours to go back home.

2845. A popular neighbor is one whose children are old enough to be away at college.

2846. A good neighbor to have is one who can get to your house in less than a minute, and seldom stays any longer than that.

2847. How much it takes to love your neighbor increases the closer your neighbor lives to you.

2848. It's the unexpected things in life that provide the biggest thrills — like a neighbor stopping you on the street to tell you what a wonderful little boy your son is.

2849. Nobody spoils faster than the fine young boy who just moved in next door.

271

2850. Nobody can ruin a good night's sleep like a neighbor who insists on making his parties a howling success.

2851. Nothing lasts as long as a car that is two years older than your neighbor's.

2852. Nothing improves your wife's attention to you like an unexpected visit from your neighbor's pretty wife.

2853. Nothing raises your opinion of your immediate neighbor like your daughter falling deeply in love with his son.

2854. Nothing helps to stabilize the family budget like an economy drive by your closest neighbor.

2855. Nothing raises your opinion of your immediate neighbor like a full tool shed you can help yourself to.

2856. Prosperity is very hard to stand, especially when it is the next door neighbor who is enjoying it.

2857. Self-denial is a virtue we value especially in a neighbor we're trying to keep up with.

2858. The quickest way to patch up a quarrel with your neighbor is to give his dog a chance to bite you.

2859. Tolerance is the ability to admire a neighbor who is much more extravagant than you are.

2860. When it comes to stabilizing the family budget nothing helps like your neighbor getting a cut in salary.

2861. You can tell how you feel about a neighbor by what you do with weeds that are within your easy reach, but are on his side of the fence.

2862. A contented neighbor is one who boasts to you about the good behavior of your children.

2863. A neighbor that is attracted to you is one who is trying to overhear what's going on in your house.

2864. No matter how much you may deride your neighbors you must admit that if it wasn't for them watching your house as closely as they do you would lose most of your security from robbers.

2865. Nothing helps you to get to know your neighbors better than a fully equipped tool shed.

2866. Getting to know your neighbors is easy if you're willing to collect funds for every charitable purpose that comes along.

2867. You are never quite sure how you feel about a neighbor until you read his obituary in the paper.

2868. The best time to establish the limits of your property is right after the neighbors on each side of you have mowed their lawns.

2869. You can tell how you feel about a neighbor by what you do with weeds that are within your easy reach, but on his side of the fence.

2870. Nothing helps you to live within your budget like living next door to an internal revenue agent.

2871. The best way to get along with the man next door is to live at least a half a mile away from him.

2872. No matter how far fetched a little boy's story is, it always sounds like the truth when it is about one of the neighbors.

2873. Nothing raises your opinion of your immediate neighbors like a conversation with a prospective buyer of your house.

2874. A sure sign that two neighbors get along well is a path worn between their back fences.

2875. There's no place like a viewing to get to see all of your neighbors.

2876. The other fellow's backyard always looks greener until after your children are through playing in it.

2877. A contented neighborhood is one where all the neighbors think they're doing just a little bit better than each other.

2879. One reason farmers are such neighbor-loving people is that their neighbors usually are more than a stone's throw away.

2879. One of the easiest ways to meet your neighbors is to own the best tool shed in the block.

2880. A good neighbor to have is one by the name of Jones who is trying to keep up with you!

2881. All you have to do to make your neighbor pay attention to what you are saying is to get into an argument with your wife.

2882. Nothing raises your opinion of your next door neighbor like being given an extra key to his house and his tool shed.

2883. Give the neighbor's kid an inch of your backyard and you'll never have to cut the grass again.

2884. A popular neighbor is one whose handsome sons are old enough to keep your pretty daughter close to home.

NEUTRALITY

2885. You will find a very shallow reservoir of courage in any one who is most comfortable taking a neutral position.

NEW BRIDE

2886.   A new bride sometimes is a girl who is beginning to wonder if she did catch the perfect husband.

NEW DRESS

2887.   Nothing makes a new dress age faster than cramming it into a closet filled with old ones.

NEW FATHER

2888.   A new father never fully realizes his debt to society until he receives the obstetrician's bill.

NEW GENERATION

2889.   We need a new generation of Americans who will carry their enthusiasm for getting ahead of traffic — over into their jobs.

NEW LEAF

2890.   Sometimes when a man turns over a new leaf, he gets a new lease on an old one.

2891.   When a husband turns over a new leaf he seldom has a rake in his hand.

NEW PRODUCTS

2892.   The most important ingredient for development of a new product is the man who first got the idea for it.

NEWS

2893.   It amazes me how unimportant the daily news becomes if you don't look at it, listen to it, or read about it for even a week.

2894. If you want to be sure to get some news spread around casually misplace an opened letter marked "Personal and Confidential."

NEWSPAPER

2895. Nothing helps you decide that you got up on the wrong side of the bed like reading the morning newspaper.

2896. A lot of motorists risk their necks speeding to work in the morning just so they can sit at their desk and read the morning newspaper.

2897. A happily married man is one who would rather talk with his wife at breakfast than read the morning newspaper.

2898. A dangerous newspaperman is one who is never quote sure of himself.

2899. Newspapers depend for their existence on printing millions of words about people and events that are of interest only to people who are desperately unhappy with their lot in life.

2900. The two best places to keep out of are jail and the newspapers.

NEW SUIT

2901. Breaking in a new suit is no trouble at all if you have five children.

NEW WORLDS

2902. There lies within each human being the potential of more unexplored territory, more new worlds of excitement and progress than even the New World that Columbus discovered.

NEW YEAR'S DAY

2903.   New Year's Day is the time of the year when you resolve to do your Christmas shopping earlier next year.

NEW YEAR'S RESOLUTION

2904.   The two hardest things in the world to keep are a New Year's resolution and a diet.

2905.   The hardest thing on a New Year's Resolution is a New Year's Eve party.

NICE GUY

2906.   I've known many nice guys in my life, and they were all about mid-way between the top and the bottom.

NIGHT CLUB

2907.   One place where people are forced to take a dim view of things is in a night club.

NIGHT OWL

2908.   You can always spot a night owl by the large circles around his eyes.

NOBEL PRIZE

2909.   Any day now, a designer of women's clothes will receive a Nobel Prize for revealing naked art!

NOBILITY

2910. The nobility of a man is directly related to the conscientiousness with which he pulls out weeds and plants flowers, with which he dispels ridicule and promotes praise.

NOSE

2911. The best way to keep one's nose clean is to keep one's mouth shut.

NOTHING

2912. Nothing wears the human body out faster than doing nothing.

NOTORIETY

2913. How really famous a person is depends on with whom such a person is being compared.

NOVOCAIN

2914. Nobody helps the dentrifrice business more than dentists who drill cavities without novocain.

NUMBER

2915. When a woman starts putting two and two together, she's got your number.

NURSE

2916. Nothing dispels the beauty normally evident in a pretty nurse like a hypodermic needle in her hand.

2917.   All a nurse has to do to get a patient's mind off of her is put a hypodermic needle in her hand.

NURSERY

2918.   The door to the nursery in our home is equipped with a fine mesh screen through which the troubles of a busy day cannot pass.

OBESITY

2919.   Inflation and obesity have much in common — one reduces the value of the dollar, the other reduces the length of your retirement.

OBITUARY

2920.   The only newspaper column that can boast of the least errors, unfortunately, is the obituary column.

2921.   If you want to find out how many friends you really have, publish your obituary prematurely.

2922.   You never know for sure how you feel about a person until you read his obituary.

2923.   The wrong place to have your reputation bolstered is in an obituary write-up.

OBJECTIVES

2924.   Now that man has demonstrated that he can travel faster than sound, wouldn't it be wonderful if more people knew where they want to go and why?

2925.   Nothing helps you to reach your objectives faster than being faced with disastrous alternatives if you stand still.

OBJECTORS

2926. The trouble with some people who object to doing a full day's work is they're such conscientious objectors.

OBSTACLE

2927. Sometimes the biggest obstacle in a man's life is a woman who likes to make up his mind for him.

OBSTETRICIAN

2928. One man who really knows the value of getting as many men working for him as possible — is an obstetrician.

2929. An obstetrician has more security than any other specialist of the medical profession — largely because he can count on the backing of so many men.

OCCASION

2930. A good speaker is one who can rise to the occasion, and sit through the ovation.

2931. The trouble with some people who rise to the occasion is they don't know when to sit down.

OLD AGE

2932. A man is getting old when he encourages his wife to go out so he can have the house to himself.

2933. A sure sign than you have passed the peak of your maturity is when you can find time to look back at the past ... and enjoy it!

2934. Old age is the time of life when most men believe in childhood and in God for the second time.

2935. Old age is the time of life when fun not only costs more but you get far less for your money.

2936. I pity any person of 90 who reaches it with nothing more to show than how pleased he is to have reached it.

2937. Old age is the time of life when wisdom and stubbornness, are often mistaken for each other.

2938. Old age is the time of life when a man may lose his hair, his teeth, even his memory — but might still, at least, hold on to his money.

2939. You are getting old when you are bored by the thought of being left all alone in your house ... with your wife!

2940. Virtues and rheumatic pains are both increased by old age.

2941. You're getting old when you don't give a damn about anything!

2942. Old age should be to youth like the protective envelope of soft air that protects our planet.

2943. A man is getting old when he starts to ring for the elevator to the second floor.

OLD MAID

2944. Nothing makes a lady a confirmed old maid like a determination to wait until the perfect man comes along.

OLD TIMER

2945. An old timer is one who remembers when he hit a golf ball it went as far as he expected it to.

2946. An old timer is one who could have promised his fiancee the moon without any fear of having to make the promise good.

2947. An old timer is a man who remembers when a child had more brothers and sisters than he had fathers.

2948. Tomorrow's old timer will have trouble recalling these times as the "good old days."

2949. An old timer is one who can remember when getting his house debugged meant calling the insect exterminator.

2950. An old timer is a person who can remember when you could carry money around in your pocket long enough to wear a hole in it.

2951. An old timer is one who can remember that it didn't pay to get hot under the collar — because it would wilt it.

2952. An old timer is one who can remember when the only time a fellow ran out of gas was on purpose.

2953. An old timer is one who never had to look for his daughter when one of his shirts was missing.

2954. An old timer is a person who never thought he would ever see women expose as much of themselves as they do . . . for free.

2955. An old timer is one who can remember when money stayed around long enough for germs to grow on it.

2956. An old timer is one who remembers when you wouldn't upset anybody just by telling the truth.

2957. An old timer is a man who can remember when he could hold onto a ten-dollar bill long enough to fold it.

2958. An old timer is one who remembers when children didn't ask what a cow was — they were told to get up at dawn and go milk one.

2959. An old timer is one who could read a novel without having to hide it from the children each time he put it down.

2960. An old timer is one who remembers when giving a woman some more rope meant she would string up another length of clothesline.

2961. An old timer is a man who can't understand why people who make women's clothes are so intent on driving themselves out of business.

2962. An old timer is one who can remember when the wealthiest man in town owned a two-car garage.

2963. An old timer is one who can remember when the height of indiscretion was to type a love letter.

2964. An old timer is a person who believes that the best thing about the good old days was the taxes.

2965. An optimist is a person who believes he has heard his last definition of an old timer.

OMISSIONS

2966. History proves conclusively that the omissions of good people have been far more disastrous than the aggressiveness of a few bad leaders.

ONIONS

2967. Many persons are like onions — they don't smart until you try to cut them up.

ONLY CHILD

2968. The best way to rear an only child is to live next to a neighbor who has a half a dozen children.

OPEN BOOK

2969. When a woman can read a man like an open book — she means cover up to cover up.

2970. The true character of some people doesn't become an open book until you throw it at them.

OPENINGS

2971. Two good openings for a young man are the legs in a pair of overalls.

OPEN MIND

2972. It is just as important for a person with an open mind to keep the bugs out as it is for a person with an open mouth.

2973. An open mind can be as dangerous as an open manhole unless you keep your eyes wide open.

2974. An open mind, like an open window, should be equipped with a screen to keep the bugs out.

OPEN MOUTH

2975. Always remember that when you open your mouth you could be leading with your chin.

OPERATION

2976. A surgeon's most convincing proof that the operation was successful is the receipt of immediate payment for professional services rendered.

OPINION

2977. You never know how absurd your own opinion is until you hear somebody else quoting it.

2978. Man is never so hard of hearing as when his opinion is being challenged.

2979. When a man offers you his opinion, remember that he thinks the world of it.

2980. Nothing inflates a man's opinion of himself like a stroke of good luck.

2981. You can never force somebody to adopt your opinion but you're 90 percent of the way as soon as you ask him his opinion of it.

2982. We are living in an age of premature babies and opinions.

2983. Nothing will insure proving the absurdity of an opinion like holding onto one irrevocably.

2984. You will never hear anyone accuse you of having a biased opinion as long as his agrees with yours.

2985. Few things can weigh more heavily in favor of a man's opinion than having a reputation for being wealthy.

OPPORTUNIST

2986. An opportunist is a man who listens carefully to what you say you'd like to do, and does it himself.

2987. An opportunist is a fellow who takes the cold water thrown on his ideas and makes ice cubes with it.

2988. An opportunist is a person who knows how to take a hard knock and hammer something good home with it.

2989. A lot of persons look the other way when they see opportunity because it's usually ready to hand them some working clothes.

2990. An opportunist is a man who can keep ahead of the Joneses by loaning them money.

2991. An opportunist is usually envied by those who heard the same knock but refused to open the door.

2992. The same persons who criticize opportunists can seldom spot opportunities.

2993. The only time opportunity will pat you on the back is after you've taken advantage of it.

OPPORTUNITY

2994. A smart girl knows enough to make opportunity wait while he whistles.

2995. A golden opportunity frequently approaches you camouflaged as a difficult problem.

2996. Opportunity is luck's entrepreneur.

2997. A chronic knocker is a fellow who may always be found on the outside of opportunity's door.

2998. A brilliant person is one who never misses an opportunity to give you a compliment.

2999. The trouble with opportunity today is that it has got to prove itself after taxes.

3000. A popular girl is one who knows how to keep temptation and opportunity fighting each other to a draw.

3001. Opportunity is like a hit or miss proposition; whereas, temptation likes to linger around indefinitely.

3002. Always remember than when opportunity rings your doorbell, it does not expect you to sit down to dinner with it.

3003. It's easy to take advantage of opportunity — all you

have to do is beat it to the knock.

3004. Nothing dresses up an opportunity like seeing it being entertained by the other fellow.

3005. Nothing increases a man's chances of finding opportunity like setting out with a determination to find it.

3006. Nothing will shatter an opportunity like dropping it.

3007. One of the best tests of religion is to receive an opportunity to do a good turn without turning it down.

3008. Opportunity is closest at hand when everybody is against taking advantage of it.

3009. Tact is the ability to get a person to take advantage of an opportunity for you.

3010. One of the surest ways to miss out on some of life's greatest opportunities is to do nothing with a good idea but entertain it.

3011. The kind of people I can't stand are those who never miss an opportunity to sit.

3012. The world is filled with people who are out to meet an opportunity; the successful ones, however, are those who set out to make an opportunity.

3013. There is no valid excuse for missing an opportunity to make somebody else happy.

3014. When it comes to seeing the other fellow walking off with opportunity everybody has 20/20 vision.

3015. Not all opportunities are worthwhile today — some of them aren't worth it after taxes.

3016. A bachelor is a man who believes that opportunities are meant to be embraced, but not engaged.

3017. Gone are the days of the horse-and-buggy, but there's still plenty of opportunities for workhorses.

3018. The saddest of all opportunities to miss is the chance to help someone in need.

3020. Nothing will increase your chances of meeting opportunity like doing things when they are supposed to be done.

3021. It is not possible to judge the size of an opportunity by the loudness of its knock.

3022. Nothing helps opportunity to ring the bell like placing the button within easy reach of it.

OPPOSITION

3023. Opposition makes a great man greater ... and that's why some married men are so successful.

3024. Opposition is something you're sure to find if you go looking for it.

OPTIMIST

3025. An optimist is a man who will wink at a pretty girl and think that his wife won't see him.

3026. An optimist is a man who expects change from a taxi driver.

3027. An optimist is a man who holds the car door open in front of the house while he waits for his wife.

3028. An optimist is a person who believes that the government has exhausted its ability to devise new taxes.

3029. An optimist is a man who can hand his car over to a parking-lot attendant without looking back.

3030.   I would rather be an optimist and be right 50 percent of the time than a pessimist and be right all of the time.

3031.   An optimist is a man who just borrowed some money from a fellow he is going to make into a pessimist.

3032.   An optimist is a man, who, on reaching age 60, reflects on how much luckier he is than the millions before him who failed to reach it.

3033.   An optimist is a man who goes into a supermarket with a $20 bill in his wallet expecting that he'll have enough money to get past the cashier.

3034.   One of the advantages of being an optimist is it permits you to make the most out of good luck as well as bad luck.

3035.   Most optimists I have known have enjoyed a lot of hidden security.

3036.   An optimist is a man boasting about his income; a pessimist is the same man talking to an internal revenue agent who overheard him.

3037.   An optimist is a man who expects to read good news when he sits down with a newspaper.

3038.   An optimist is a man who doesn't get upset even when the bus he just missed is the last one.

3039.   An optimist is a man who thinks he's just made his final payment on the installment plan.

3040.   An optimist is a man who tries to argue a traffic cop out of giving him a ticket; a pessimist is the same fellow a little later.

3041.   An optimist is a man who hurries because he thinks his date is waiting for him.

3042.   An optimist is a borrower who brings along a blank check.

3043. An optimist is a person who believes there's more mileage to be gained in giving compliments than criticism.

3044. An optimist is a person who expects his bonus to be big enough to pay his Christmas bills.

3045. An optimist is a man who thinks he can fool his wife.

3046. An optimist is a man who thinks he can park in front of an "expired" meter and get back to his car before a cop does.

3047. An optimist is a man who thinks that he can get his wife to wear shoes that will fit her.

ORDERS

3048. When a man speaks in no uncertain terms, he's probably just carrying out his wife's orders.

3049. A meek man is one who can take orders, and is married.

ORIGINATORS

3050. No one lives more dangerously in modern society than he who dares to be an originator instead of an imitator.

OTHER FELLOW

3051. The reason a lot of people fail is they keep trying to better the other fellow when they should be trying to better themselves.

3052. Not until you learn to treat the other fellow as though your destiny were in his hands will you ever be able to develop your full potential.

OVERHEARING

3053. Sometimes the best way to make yourself heard is to be overheard!

3054. Nothing improves one's hearing like paper-thin motel walls.

OVERPAID

3055. Some people are overpaid because they are being paid for what they're supposed to know.

OVERPOPULATION

3056. The most serious overpopulation problems, alas, are on the taxpayers' payroll.

OVERWEIGHT

3057. About the only time overweight will make you feel better is when you see it on someone you nearly married.

3058. One of the best reducing incentives the average executive can get is a notice that he is due for his annual physical in three weeks.

3059. A woman is decidedly overweight when there is even the slightest chance that her friends might suspect she is having a baby.

3060. Middle age is the time of life when a man starts blaming the cleaners because his suits are shrinking.

3061. A woman is not overweight if she can feel comfortable in a modern bathing suit.

OWN WAY

3062. The wrong way to make your way in the world is to insist on having it.

PACKAGE

3063. When it comes to retieing a Christmas package, you can't beat a woman who wasn't supposed to have looked inside of it in the first place.

PAIN

3064. Bald people should be thankful that losing hair is not as painful as pulling teeth.

3065. Two things cause the greatest pain in this world — the birth of a baby and a new idea.

PAIN IN THE NECK

3066. To get rid of a pain in the neck, try borrowing some money from him.

PALLBEARER

3067. Being a pallbearer is a little like getting a flat tire — it makes you drive through life more carefully for a day or so.

PAPERWORK

3068. Paperwork has become a panacea in big organizations because it is the easiest way to camouflage a scarcity of original thinking.

PARENTS

3069. However far a man may go, he should remember always that he couldn't have gotten started without his parents.

3070. A happy parent is one who believes in waking up a new baby just to see it smile.

3071. One of the greatest pleasures a parent can experience is to gaze upon the children when they're fast asleep.

3072. Nothing annoys the average child today like a disobedient parent.

3073. Nothing holds a modern family together like good behavior on the part of the parents.

3074. Parents can never be sure how good a job they have done in raising their children until after they all reach at least 30.

3075. The greatest weakness of most parents is their inability to see any faults in their children.

3076. If parents would worry more about when their children turn in, they'd have to worry less about how they'll turn out.

3077. Some of the smartest people in the world of science owe their success largely to picking the parents they did.

3078. One of the troubles with parents who bring up children these days is they don't hit bottom often enough.

3079. Parents who have to take after their children should never have given them car key privileges in the first place.

3080. The reason it is becoming harder for children to take after their parents is they've got to decide which one they want to follow.

3081. The secret of raising a child properly is in knowing when to give it a big hand — and where.

3082. Training a child to follow the straight and narrow path is easy for parents . . . all they have to do is lead the way.

3083. Parents who wonder what the children should be reading sometimes forget that the children are reading them like a book.

3084. Too many parents think they can raise children by their voices.

3085. A parent who can't afford a tape-recorder can always count on the children for accurate play-backs.

3086. Few people are more poorly trained to raise a child than brand new parents.

3087. The two-car garage is what paved the way for three-car families and two all-day-working parents!

PARENTHOOD

3088. A thorough preparation seems essential for success in every walk of life — except parenthood.

PARKING

3089. A gentleman is a man who will slip a nickel in an expired parking meter when he sees a cop coming . . . and do a perfect stranger a good turn.

3090. A smart girl is one who knows all the hazards of parking.

3091. Although you can't admire a parking lot attendant's driving, you've got to admire his precision.

3092. Our young men have their problems these days — just as soon as they convince a girl the engine is giving them trouble they can't find a place to park.

3093. The early bird not only catches the worm but also the parking space.

PARKING LOTS

3094. The first thing you should do when you find your car in a parking lot these days — is count how many additional dents and scratches it has.

PARKING METER

3095. What many industries really need on the job are parking meters for their employees.

3096. A rich man is one who can estimate how much change to put into a parking meter to the nearest penny.

3097. Punctuality is a virtue, especially when your date is with a parking meter.

3098. Conscience is that still small voice that tells you a traffic cop has beaten you back to an expired parking meter.

3099. Time is a fleeting commodity as anybody can discover by reserving some of it on a parking meter.

3100. A completely honest person is one who will put a nickel in a broken parking meter.

PARKING SPACE

3101. The easiest way to find a parking space is immediately behind a fellow who just beat you to it.

PARTIES

3102. Parties that cause the most trouble are those that end up a howling success.

3103. What kind of a time a man has at a party usually depends on how close his wife sticks to him.

3104. When two married people see eye to eye on something chances are they're giving each other the high sign to break up the party.

PAST

3105. The nicest thing about the past is that you can forget the whole darn mess all at one time.

3106. Sometimes the shade from the family tree comes in handy for covering up an unsightly past.

3107. When a politician starts running for office, his past starts running for cover.

3108. The dreadful part of one's past is the way others can't forget it.

PATIENCE

3109. Patience: Tomorrow waiting for today to pass away.

3110. A patient person is one who is willing to let somebody teach him something he already knows.

3111. A patient man is one who likes catsup.

3112. Nowadays a patient man is often the boss waiting for his employees to show up for work.

3113. A patient man is one who can put up with himself.

3114. Every good doctor knows that some of his best patients are those who aren't sick, but who are prompt at paying their bills.

3115. Patience is a virtue you recognize in yourself when the other fellow is your boss.

3116. Patience is what it takes to talk to a service man who is fixing your air conditioner when you know he makes twice as much an hour as you do.

3117. Patience is a virtue you take credit for when the other fellow holds a bigger stick.

3118. When two equally prominent persons are placed on a balance, the one with the greater patience will tip the scales in his favor.

3119. Patience is never more important than when you are at the edge of losing it.

3120. Always remember that the mouse that gets caught is the one that gives in to temptation.

3121. You may never discover how patient you can be until the fellow who is arguing with you happens to look twice your size.

3122. Patience is that rare ability to remain silent until you find out for sure whether the traffic cop is going to write up a ticket or not.

3123. Patience is never more golden than when you have no pressing need for it.

3124. A patient man is one who is waiting for the mailman to arrive with his tax refund.

3125. The best medicine in the world is having enough patience to wait until it is absolutely necessary to take some.

3126. Patience is a camel's back waiting for the last straw.

3127. Patience is the greatest of all virtues if it permits you to put up with things over which you have no control.

3128. A patient man is one who can sit and look in rapture at a rainbow — until it evaporates from view.

3129. A patient man is one who is waiting for the last word from his wife.

3130. A patient man is one who can listen to his wife until she's exhausted.

3131. A patient man is one who is very punctual and married.

PATRIOTISM

3132. Patriotism is very much like true love — if you've really got it you don't need to shout about it from the rooftops.

PAY

3133. Premium pay will seldom do anything for an employee who enjoys complaining.

PAYCHECK

3134. Nothing makes a paycheck look better to a man than being the father of five children.

PAY DAY

3135. The size of one's problems usually depends on whether payday just arrived or still is a long way off.

3136. Sometimes the fellow who tries to stir up a little mud is only trying to find some pay dirt.

PAYMENTS

3137. Nothing will get a person down these days like the down payments.

PAYROLL

3138. The trouble with most people on the payroll today is that they shine mostly in the seat of their pants.

3139. The trouble with people who object to a full day's work is they're usually already on the payroll.

PEACE

3140. There will be no true peace in the world until man's extrasensory faculties are developed to the point that we will be able to read each other's minds accurately.

3141. True peace could come instantly to the world if we all treated each other as though today was the last day in our lives — which it could very well be!

3142. There's no surer way to bring peace into your life than by starting this minute to love your neighbors and your enemies ... even if they happen to be one and the same persons.

3143. True inner peace comes from the security which arises from being free to do exactly what you enjoy doing most.

PEACEFUL FAMILY

3144. A peaceful family is one that never has any left overs after a scrap.

PEACEMAKER

3145. Judging from the record of mankind to date, the least successful figures of world history are its peacemakers.

PEANUTS

3146. At no time do stale peanuts taste better than at a cocktail party.

PEDESTRIAN

3147. Frequently a pedestrian is a person who wishes he had left the car at home.

3148. A pedestrian is a man who enjoys walking the dog.

3149. The average motorist isn't dangerous as long as he's a pedestrian.

3150. What most pedestrians need these days is more horse-fear of automobiles.

3151. At no time is it more important for you to get the brakes in life than when you're a pedestrian crossing a busy street.

3152. The surest way for a pedestrian to live longer nowadays is to buy himself a car.

3153. The trouble with the general run of pedestrians is they aren't agile enough.

3154. A disgruntled pedestrian is one who still has another mile to go before he can reach his car in the parking lot.

3155. Pedestrians must be forever on guard against that run down feeling.

3156. A healthy pedestrian is one who is agile enough to have outmaneuvered motorists.

PEDIGREE

3157. A bore is a failure who is proud of his pedigree.

3158. If you want to stop somebody from boasting about his pedigree, ask him to trace it for you.

PEOPLE

3159. People are forever putting themselves in the other fellow's place but not in his shoes.

3160. The trouble with a lot of people who think they are on the right track is they don't know whether they're coming or going.

3161. The best way to handle people is to heart-handle them.

3162. People wouldn't hurry as much as they do if they realized that there's still tomorrow and it hasn't even been touched yet.

3163. All you have to do to get some people to shut up quickly is to throw the book at them.

3164. Our young people aren't half as bad as they might be — most of them aren't even trying.

3165. Some people waste a lot of time talking about themselves even though they'd prefer to have you do it.

3166. The trouble with many people who are hollering to get an early start in life is they're still infants.

3167. All it takes to like some people better is a chance to see less of them.

3168. The trouble with some people who rise to the occasion is that they don't know when to sit down.

3169. Most people raise their standard of living installment by installment.

3170. When you take an overall view, you must conclude that people are as changeable as the weather, and just as difficult to control.

3171. The target of too many people who aim to please is themselves.

3172. People are like plants — some go to seed with age, and others to pot.

3173. There are two kinds of people I feel lastingly sorry for — those who can't take criticism, and those who have an indelible memory.

PERFECT DAY

3174. The best way to end a perfect day is with a determiniation that you're going to repeat it tomorrow.

PERFECT MAN

3175. God help the woman who won't marry until she finds the perfect man; God help the fellow if she finds him.

PERFORMANCE

3176. When a woman is happy with her husband's performance it may only mean he is doing what she asked him to.

PERFUME

3177. Christmas is the time of year when a man who buys perfume realizes he is paying through the nose for it.

PERSISTENCE

3178. When two persons are matched in direct competition, I will always bet that the winner will be the one with the most persistence over the one with the highest I.Q.

3179. Life is a bit like unwinding a piece of badly knotted string with success coming to the few who persist to the bitter end.

3180. Persistence loses its standing as a virtue by the time you hit your head against a stone wall for the third time.

3181. Persistence is never more golden when you know exactly how it will pay off.

PERSONALITY

3182. It is easy to spot a brilliant person with a lot of personality — he reminds you so much of you!

3183. A happily married man is one whose personality remains unchanged whether his wife is with him or not.

3184. Personality is what a man has if women will look up to him and what a girl has if men will look around at her.

3185. Personality is what a person has when he makes you feel the same way about him as you do about yourself.

3186. A girl with plenty of personality is one who can make men glow after her.

PERSPIRATION

3187. Perspiration is to inspiration what water is to a dying plant.

3188. Perspiration is to success what a lighted match is to a candle.

PESSIMIST

3189. Sometimes a pessimist is a man who is optimistic only about protecting himself.

3190. A pessimist is a person who complains of exhaustion as he starts to climb a molehill.

3191. A pessimist is a man who was positive nobody would give him any ties for Christmas.

3192. A pessimist is a person who on reaching the age of 50 complains that he will never make it to 75; an optimist is a person who reaches 50 and proudly boasts that he is only halfway to reaching 100.

3193. A pessimist is a man who expects the worst to happen, and when it does he makes the worst of it.

PET

3194. Frequently a woman's idea of a household pet is a husband who will eat out of her hand.

PHOTOS

3195. Anybody who likes his passport photo took it himself.

3196. An humble man is one who is still friendly with the photographer after he sees the proofs.

PHOTO ALBUMS

3197. Family photo albums would have greater popularity if less snap and more care were used in taking pictures.

3198. The best physicians I know refuse to give their own children medicine — except as a last resort.

PHYSICAL EXAM

3199. Two things can make a man happy — coming through his annual physical and his tax audit trouble-free.

PHYSICAL FITNESS

3200. One of the surest ways to discover what shape you are in is to spend two hours on your knees — weeding the garden.

PHYSICIANS

3201. One reason physicians can be happy about their work is the feeling of security their patients give them.

PHYSICS

3202. The best way to appreciate gravity is as a law of physics.

PHYSICIANS

3203. A physician is a person who works 16 hours a day telling others to slow down or they'll get high blood pressure.

3204. The trouble with many physicians who have earned their M.D.'s is they act as though this made them G.O.D.'s.

3205. Most physicians may not realize it but they should credit most of their success to the body's ability to get better despite the medicines they prescribe.

PIANIST

3206. The fellow who plays his hands right is a successful pianist.

PIGGY BANK

3207. One of the best things a parent can teach a child is never to take out of his piggy bank all of the pennies put into it.

PILL

3208. The hardest kind of pill to take is one who insists on telling you how great he is.

PILLS & NEEDLES

3209. Today, many persons have to live, from day to day, on pills and needles.

PIOUSNESS

3210. A lot of people who act piously may only be braying.

PLATFORM

3211. Most politicians believe in building their homes of stone and their platforms of sand.

PLAY

3212. With adults, as with children, play with them for a few minutes and you can get them to do anything for you.

3213. How much a father spends for his son's toys isn't nearly as important as how much time he spends playing with him.

PLAYMATE

3214. One playmate that a little boy never falls out with is his pup.

PLEASANTNESS

3215. One of the most difficult things to do is to be as pleasant in your own home as you are in the homes of others.

PLEASURE

3216. The degree of pleasure one gets in life usually is in direct proportion to the difficulties you must overcome in getting it.

3217. The pleasures of the world are like our thirst for water ... we think we can drink a pitcher full, but start choking on the first glass.

3218. There is one pleasure that the human being cannot tire of and that is the pleasure that comes from helping someone who really needs you.

3219. One of the greatest pleasures of growing old is the freedom you enjoy from life insurance salesmen.

3220. One of the greatest pleasures a parent can experience is to gaze upon the children when they're fast asleep.

3221. One way to enjoy the pleasures of solitary moments is always to be punctual.

3222. No sound is more pleasing to the human ear than the sound of your boss telling you you're getting a raise.

3223. One of the most lasting pleasures you can experience is the feeling that comes over you when you genuinely forgive an enemy — whether he knows it or not.

3224. Few pleasures in this life exceed those that come from living the way you can afford to.

3225. Pleasures are most satisfying when you are least prepared to receive them.

PLOT

3226. The first thing a young girl does when she meets an eligible young man is to devise a plan to catch him.

PLOTTING

3227. A woman is not old as long as she does not give up plotting her way through life.

POCKETBOOK

3228. The way to a man's pocketbook is through his wife.

3229. A lady is a woman who never has to carry anything heavier than her pocketbook.

POINT

3230. If you must stick to the point, don't be blunt about it.

POISE

3231. One woman's poise is frequently another woman's poison.

3232. Nothing adds poise to an attractive woman like a successful husband standing beside her.

POKER FACE

3233. At no time is a poker face more advantageous than when you are seeing a pack of relatives off who have overstayed their visit.

POLICE

3234. Nothing improves a person's driving like a police car right in back of him.

POLICEMAN

3235. The only time it pays to listen to someone who is trying to stop you is if he happens to be a traffic policeman.

3236. You know that your conscience still is alive as long as it helps you to spot a cop in time to discourage you from jumping a red light.

3237. Nothing increases your respect for an automobile like a policeman behind its steering wheel.

3238. When a policeman sees red it's usually because a careless motorist didn't.

POLITENESS

3239. Politeness of the heart is far more important than politeness of the lips.

3240. One thing you're sure to gain by politeness is weight.

3241. Politeness is what you show a salesman who keeps his foot in the door long enough to let some flies in.

3242. The polite thing to do with a guest towel is to pretend that you used it.

POLITICAL JOKES

3243. The trouble with some political jokes is they are hard to beat at election time.

POLITICIAN

3244. What the world needs is a new breed of politicians whose enthusiasm for the welfare of the common man during his election campaign doesn't disappear as soon as he's elected.

3246. Most politicians are experts at changing campaign promises into taxes.

3247. One thing to the undying discredit of our politicians is their outstanding success at making a mountain out of a molehill of taxes.

3248. When some politicians stand on their records they could be covering something up.

3249. One of the virtues of a small-town politician is that he knows that he has to stick pretty close to the truth.

3250. The phrase "to tax one's thinking" is becoming increasingly dangerous because one of these days the politicians will come up with a way to do it.

3251. Nothing is harder on a politician's hearing than having to listen to what the grass roots are saying.

3252. The trouble with many politicians who run for office is the way they come to a dead stop once they're elected.

3253. Sheepish voters beget wolfish politicians.

3254. An agile politician is one who can always dodge an issue.

3255. An honest politician is one who is running for office for the first time.

3256. The most agile politicians are not those who know how to duck the issue, but those who can straddle it.

3257. The surest way to stop a politician in his tracks is to elect him.

POLLUTION

3258. Nowadays it is dangerous to open the window to let the fresh air in.

POPULARITY

3259. The true test of popularity is the number of people you don't know who know you.

3260. Nothing adds to a guest's popularity like a punctual arrival and a punctual exit.

3261. If you want to make your own light shine brighter, you can't beat turning up the wick on the other fellow's lamp.

3262. Nothing will add to your popularity like owning up to being wrong now and then, even when you don't have to.

3263. The most popular man in any neighborhood is the one who has the best equipped tool shed.

POOR MAN

3264. A poor man is one who spends enough to prevent his neighbors from guessing his true salary.

POOR WINNER

3265.   Many a woman never realizes what a poor winner she is until she's bagged her man.

POSING

3266.   The trouble with a lot of people who try to lead a model life is you know they're only posing.

POSITIVENESS

3267.   There are times when silence is the best way to be positive at the top of your voice.

POSSESSIONS

3268.   Most women are happy to belong to a man in return for all of his belongings.

POSTAGE

3269.   The value of the dollar has shrunk in direct proportion to the increase in the cost to mail a first-class letter.

POSTMAN

3270.   As long as there are postmen, there will be dogs to attack them.

POSTURE

3271.   There is nothing wrong with holding your shoulders back and your head high as long as you can do it without turning up your nose.

3272. Sometimes, all a woman has to do to develop her best potentialities is become a widow.

POVERTY

3273. The only really poor people in the world are those who pretend they're rich.

3274. Poverty becomes unbearable only when one has never experienced it before.

3275. Poverty is such a relative matter — some people get more pleasure out of a hot dog than others get out of a filet mignon.

3276. Poverty has its compensations — ask anybody who distributes welfare checks.

3277. Poverty has its compensations ... at least you don't have to worry about an income tax audit.

3278. The greatest men of all times, like the most majestic churches, have always had their first roots in the vicinity of poverty.

3279. The only persons I ever hear proclaiming the advantages of poverty are those who have been unsuccessful in working their way out of it.

3280. The best cure for poverty is hard work.

3281. Poverty still remains the most fertile soil from which man's greatest leaders are grown.

3282. One of the greatest handicaps of children born of affluent parents is their lack of exposure to valuable education that only poverty can teach.

3283. Poverty has its compensations — at least you won't forget your wallet in another pair of trousers.

3284. The greatest virtue of having experienced poverty is that it never will be so hard to take if you become poor again.

POWER

3285. The hunger for power is a much stronger motivating force than either sex or money.

3286. In the business world, the most powerful executive is the one who has the most people with their shoulders to his wheel.

3287. Power that rules without being questioned invariably will rule with injustice.

3288. A power structure that is devastating can be built either upon truths or upon lies.

3289. Power is the root of world evil — those who have it fight to get more, and those who haven't got any will fight to help them succeed.

3290. An insatiable lust for power is as much a cancer of the mind as is biological cancer of the body.

3291. A man's trust in God diminishes in direct proportion to the growth of his power over people.

3292. Power is never more effectively administered than when it is exercised in a steady, cool manner.

3293. Most persons are opposed to power . . . until they get a chance to get a hold of some.

3294. Power will either burn a man out or put the spotlight on him.

POWER OF THE PEN

3295. Many modern corporations are finally realizing that the pen is mightier than the Board.

PRACTICAL MAN

3296. A practical man is one who gets married because he's tired of going steady.

PRAISE

3297. We appreciate praise and money from people who are thrifty with them.

3298. A good habit is to praise your wife at least once a day. If you don't know why, she does.

3299. Praise others in public — and watch how your own reputation grows behind your back.

3300. Praise can be especially valuable to you when you shower it on your enemies.

3301. Praise is something which will make you sick if you feed on it.

3302. Praise your wife in public and watch how much better the meals will get.

3303. Praise without motive is the sincerest form of flattery.

PRAYER

3304. Nowadays when you save money for a rainy day, you would be wise to pray just for a passing shower.

3305. Many persons who pray for their enemies are most unkind to their friends.

3306. Nobody prays harder for the rain than a taxi driver who also is the father of six children.

3307. The best time to stand up to any of life's situations is immediately after you get up from praying on your knees.

3308. Those who pray for a million dollars would get better results if they prayed for a strong back and a good pair of hands.

3309. Prayer always seems to work better after a person exhausts all attempts to get the results they wanted by using profanity.

3310. One of the sad facts of our age is that the closest many people ever get to praying today is when they bend a knee to tie a shoelace.

3311. The trouble with many of the things you pray for is that most of them have a price tag on them.

3312. Nothing puts feeling into a prayer like a mighty good reason for saying it.

3313. The trouble with a lot of people who resort to prayer is they use it only as a last resort.

3314. One of the sad facts of our age is that the closest many people ever get to praying today is when they get down on their knees to weed their garden.

3315. Saying prayers to God is a poor substitute for serving him by doing things for your fellowman.

PRECISION

3316. Although you can't admire a parking lot attendant's driving, you've got to admire his precision.

PREDICTIONS

3317. The most hazardous of all predictions is to predict that something is impossible.

PREJUDICE

3318. Prejudice is any line of reasoning that proves you are right.

PREMIUM PAY

3319. Premium pay seldom will take the ping out of the man who is forever knocking others.

PRESCRIPTION FOR GOOD HEALTH

3320. Keep your wallets full and your bellies flat.

PRESIDENT

3321. One advantage or disadvantage of being President of the United States of America is that you can always find out exactly what people think of you by reading the newspapers.

PRESTIGE

3322. Prestige, like pleasure, is a relative matter — the mayor of a small town in his own right enjoys the same height of prestige as does a national celebrity.

PRETENSE

3323. Beauty may be only skin deep — but pretense is written all over your face.

PRETTY GIRL

3324. A pretty girl is one who can run away with a man's imagination . . . and his money.

PRICES

3325. The trouble with prices nowadays is they rise with the sun each morning.

PRIDE

3326. You can always tell a proud man — but the chances are he will take offense.

3327. The best cure for pride is a mirror that distorts how you think you look.

3328. The only kind of pride that has never harmed a person is pride in one's work.

3329. There is no better reducing exercise for one's ego than swallowing your pride.

3330. The greatest danger inherent in pride is the effectiveness with which our own brilliance can blind our vision.

PRINCIPLES

3331. The best principles to live by are those that don't fluctuate with the value of the dollar.

3332. To offset the increase in the cost of living, a good many persons have decreased the price of their principles.

PRIVACY

3333. Nothing is more sacred than the privacy of one's mind.

3334. There is no greater privilege that a young person can have than the opportunity to make his own way from scratch — without handouts of any kind but encouragement from his parents.

PROBLEMS

3335. One of the surest ways to bolster your ego is suddenly to find a simple solution to what you always felt was a most difficult problem.

3336. The first step to solving a problem is to bring it into a clear enough focus to recognize clearly what the problem is.

3337. The size of your problems often depends on whether payday just came or is still a long way off.

3338. One man who never hesitates to tackle a problem is worth a dozen who prefer to talk about a solution to it.

3339. I refuse to believe that problems will solve themselves — I have never yet solved a problem unless I attacked it head-on.

3340. The troubles of the world will continue to increase as long as we train people how to spot problems instead of how to solve them.

3341. One of the biggest advantages of being very busy is that you're never faced with the problem of not knowing what to do next.

3342. The trouble with most family problems is they're usually a relative matter.

3343. There are no insolvable problems confronting man . . . there are only impossible people!

3344. The fellow who believes that problems will take care of themselves better not get cancer.

3345. At the heart of every problem you will find the easiest answer to its solution.

3346. Problems, unlike shadows, can be made to disappear if you stay right on top of them.

3347. Most people find that solving problems are no trouble at all — as long as they are the other fellow's.

PROCRASTINATION

3348. Necessity is to procrastination what a spur can be to a lazy horse.

PROFANITY

3349. Profanity is a man's way of letting off scream.

PROFIT

3350. Success consists of selling experience at a profit.

3351. With the present tax structure the way it is, it would be difficult to find what profit a man had even if he gained the whole world.

PROGENY

3352. One good idea, like one good race horse, can farther a long line of champions.

PROGRESS

3353. Progress is only possible by continuing change.

3354. Despite all the progress of science, the best way to get ahead still is to use the one you've got.

PROMISES

3355. A precocious young man today is one who starts out by offering his sweetheart Mrs.

3356. The only kind of opportunity that rings the bell these days is one that holds out a promise of a capital gain.

PROMOTION

3357. There's no surer way to get a better job than by doing better in the one you've got.

3358. Sometimes the surest way to get a promotion is to out-guess your boss' boss.

PROMPTNESS

3359. Nothing increases the value of a few well-chosen words like saying them promptly.

3360. The most unpredictable thing a woman can do still is to be on time.

3361. A young man's future is in danger of being settled when his date starts being ready for him on time.

PROOF

3362. The best way to prove that you are right is to convince the other fellow that you cannot possibly be wrong.

3363. One of the advantages of trying to prove that you are wrong is that most people will be ready to believe you.

PROPOSAL

3364. Before a woman asks a man's advice on getting married, she makes sure that he's well prepared to give her the right answer.

PROSPERITY

3365. Prosperity is hard to stand, especially when it's the other fellow's that is holding you up.

3366. Prosperity may not be what it is cracked up to be, but most persons would like a chance to crack it up.

3367. People who can't stand prosperity are usually the ones who try to find it sitting down.

PROTOCOL

3368. The more a person insists on protocol or ritual, usually the less his intelligence and wisdom.

PRUDENCE

3369. Prudence is a virtue you suddenly acquire after someone talks you into paying fifty dollars for something only worth five.

PSYCHIATRISTS

3370. An honest psychiatrist is one who will admit how much some of his patients help him.

3371. It really pays to listen, especially if you're a psychiatrist.

3372. The trouble with some psychiatrists who believe in shock treatment is they use bills instead of pills.

PSYCHOLOGY

3373. Bad psychology is to draw conclusions based on statistics . . . collected by somebody else.

PUBLICITY

3374. The acid test of receiving nationwide publicity is whether or not you get burned as a result of it.

3375. The most severe test of nationwide publicity is to be able to survive it.

3376. People who love publicity usually leave the smallest shadows in the face of the sun.

3377. One of the surest ways to keep out of trouble is to keep out of the newspapers.

PUBLIC OFFICE

3378. Any public office brings with it all of the hazards of a lack of privacy.

PUBLIC SPEAKING

3379. What America needs more badly than ever in its history is more private thinking and less public speaking on the part of its leaders.

3380. A good speaker is one who rises to the occasion and promptly sits down.

PULL

3381. A smart man is one who uses his pull to lift himself up.

3382. The trouble with people with a lot of pull is they usually enjoy pushing their weight around.

PUNCTUALITY

3383.   The trouble with some people who are punctual is they never miss a chance to buy something on time.

3384.   A girl will wait for the right man to come along as long as the one she's going with doesn't try to make a get-away.

3385.   One time it never pays to take a woman at her word is when she says she'll be ready in a minute.

3386.   A patient man is one who is very punctual and married.

3387.   A punctual man is a fellow who doesn't own a watch.

3388.   The young girl who made her date cool his heels for her will insist on the same man sitting down to dinner on the button after she marries him.

3389.   Frequently a woman appreciates a man who is punctual so that she can make him wait for her.

3390.   Punctuality is never more valuable to you than when it applies to regularity.

3391.   No matter what the function may be you always can count on those who must come the farthest to get there first.

PUNISHMENT

3392.   A strict parent usually believes in stern punishment.

PURPOSE

3393.   A woman does everything with a purpose in mind, and the prettier she is the more expensive the purpose.

3394.   Nowadays a woman's clothes are designed with the same purpose as always, only it takes a lot less material.

3395. When a woman does something with a well-defined purpose in mind, you can expect some man to pay for it.

PURSUIT

3396. A successful woman is one who doesn't have to work as hard after catching a man as she did trying to catch him in the first place.

3397. A woman will play hard to get as long as you're pursuing her. If you stop, she'll play harder.

PUSH

3398. Many persons without much push hang on for dear life to their pull.

3399. Always remember that the first thing you must do to get through a revolving door is push!

QUALIFICATIONS

3400. It is amazing how a surplus of energy can frequently make up for a deficit in qualifications.

QUALITIES

3401. A brave man is one who isn't afraid to step right up and point out one of your best qualities.

QUEER

3402. Everybody is queer, each in his own way.

QUESTIONS

3403. The most valuable ability a man can develop is that of asking the right questions at the right time.

3404. Some of the most celebrated milestones in history occurred when somebody dared to ask what everybody else thought was a stupid question.

3405. Ask questions that you know a person can answer very well and two things will happen: your knowledge will increase rapidly, and so will the number of your life-long friends.

QUICKSAND

3406. Affluence is proving to be a modern quicksand into which honesty, integrity, and virtue are disappearing.

QUOTATIONS

3407. One of the reasons the remarks of some children sound so grown up is they're usually just quoting adults.

3408. A dangerous newspaperman is one who is never quote sure of himself.

QUO VADIS?

3409. Now that man has demonstrated that he can travel faster than sound, wouldn't it be wonderful if more people knew where they want to go and why?

RADIO

3410. One of the big advantages radio has over television is that you can listen to some comedians without having to look at them.

3411. Farmers may look on rain as manna from the heavens while a young mother straddled with three youngsters will say that when it rains — it pours — mischief.

RAINY DAY

3412. What most people save for a rainy day isn't usually enough to pay the bills.

3413. The whole trouble with saving up for a rainy day is you've got to work through the best weather to do it.

3414. What most little boys save for a rainy day is mischief.

3415. Those rainy days for which a man saves come before he gets a chance to.

RAISE

3416. Think the world of your job and you can almost be sure you'll get a raise.

3417. The best way to ask for a raise is to let your work do the talking for you.

3418. No sound is more pleasing to the human ear than the sound of your boss telling you you're getting a raise.

RATTLES

3419. Nothing will rattle a person like hearing one in his brand new automobile.

RATING

3420. As a general rule you will invite more trouble by

underrating yourself than by overrating yourself.

READING

3421. The best time to enjoy reading a woman like a book is long before you have to start wearing bifocals.

3422. When it comes to reading a woman's mind it is amazing how easy it becomes with the help of soft music and candlelight.

REALITY

3423. Reality is getting into a brand new shirt that you got as a gift and suddenly feeling a pin that you missed.

3424. Reality is when you find out that the boss did overhear what you said about him.

3425. Reality consists in discovering that indeed you did leave your keys in the car after having locked yourself out of it.

REASON

3426. The surest way a man can get a woman to listen to reason is to hand her a blank check.

3427. The surest mark of a successful man is a wife that boasts that he's easy to reason with.

RECESSION

3428. There's nothing like a business recession to make an old suit look like new.

3429. The first sign of a recession is when people who own cadillacs start buying gasoline — a dollar's worth at a time.

RECLINING POSITION

3430. The real hazard of a reclining position is that when you're in it there's no way that you can put your shoulder to the wheel.

RECOGNITION

3431. To receive full recognition for major accomplishments in one's lifetime it sure helps to live to be 90.

RED HOT IDEA

3432. You can tell when an idea is red hot: it burns the other fellow up because he didn't think of it first.

REDUCING

3433. One of the best reducing incentives the average executive can get is a notice that he is due for his annual physical in three weeks.

REFLECTION

3434. The object of a woman's reflection is her clothes, and the object of a man's observation is how the clothes fit.

REFORM

3435. Reform emerges from the discontented masses just as rich farmlands arise out of eroded expanses of lava.

REFRIGERATOR

3436. A refrigerator is a place where you store left-overs, before throwing them out later.

RELATIVE

3437. Hurry is purely relative, depending on which one you're trying to get away from.

RELATIVES

3438. If you have trouble getting replies from your relatives, try leaving out the signature on the next check you send one of them.

3439. Relatives who live several hundreds of miles away are usually no problem . . . unless you suddenly become famous or your wife inherits a bundle of money.

3440. Most people will put more faith and trust in a distant friend than in a close relative.

3441. Distance is only a relative matter when one of them suddenly becomes in desperate need of a loan from you.

RELATIVITY

3442. Looking at planet Earth from 100,000 miles in space, it is impossible to detect any differences between a single one of the billions of inhabitants on it.

RELAXATION

3443. A man has not mastered the art of relaxation unless he can loaf for a day and then enjoy a good night's sleep.

3444. Today the only people who seem to have enough time to sit down and relax are those who are serving it.

RELIABILITY

3445. A reliable employee is one whose disposition doesn't change whether the boss is with him or not.

3446. The trouble with so many persons who attend church on Sundays is they sit on their hearts the rest of the week.

3447. The true test of a man's religion is what he says about a neighbor he doesn't like.

3448. There are times when it is more important to obey the laws of nature than it is to obey some of the laws of religion.

3449. There always has been two kinds of evangelists — some were genuinely interested in the flock, the others in their fleece.

3450. Religious convictions can be very dangerous; never trust any that are based solely on logic or conviction.

REMARKS

3451. When a person makes himself the target of his remarks, you cannot accuse him of having a poor aim.

REPAIRMAN

3452. A repairman's best friend is the man of the house who insists he can fix things himself.

REPARTEE

3453. Repartee is knowing what to say after you've missed your chance to.

REPEAT

3454. The trouble with some of the bad mistakes people make is they usually think they are good enough to repeat.

3455. Not only is history repeating itself — it is beginning to get the hiccups.

REPORTS

3456. People who are extremely busy never write long-winded reports.

REPUTATION

3457. A reputation that is broken is far more difficult to put together than a mirror that is shattered into a thousand pieces.

3458. Our reputation is not shaped by our hands or our minds, but rather by the sum total of the words and actions of others for or against us.

3459. You know that your reputation is well founded if you find yourself on vacation in a remote part of the country and people there treat you like a celebrity.

3460. A man is responsible only for half his reputation; his friends are for the other half.

3461. A man can tell how good his reputation is by how hard it is for him to live up to it.

3462. Praise others in public — and watch how your own reputation grows behind your back.

3463. One way to find out if a man is living up to his reputation is to start praising him to the sky behind his back.

3464. Reputation is one of the few things that looks worse when you try to decorate it.

3465. A single girl's reputation frequently depends on the number of men she can keep at the end of her rope.

3466. A lot of reputations are ruined by people who enjoy running others down.

3467. One of the best ways to preserve a good reputation is to be silent about it.

3468. The fellow who is easiest to trip is one who is riding along on his reputation.

3469. Sometimes the fellow who has a reputation for being sharp turns out to be his own butcher.

3470. If you are in doubt about the track record of your relatives or your ancestors, you can always learn the unbelievable facts by running for a political office.

3471. It doesn't take much to ruin a man's reputation ... usually one newspaper headline is more than enough.

3472. When it comes to putting the finishing touches on a person's reputation, some women know exactly where to apply the brush-off.

3473. The size of a man's reputation depends on whether he's trying to hold it up or whether he lets his friends do it for him.

3474. Nothing will shatter your reputation faster than trying to hammer down somebody else's.

3475. It is much harder to live up to a reputation than it is to die for a principle.

3476. If you accept a man's reputation at face value ... just be sure that he's not two-faced.

RESEARCH

3477. Creative research requires the faith of a Columbus — a conviction that something is worth pursuing even if it turns out to be different from what you expect.

3478. The most sterile research program is one devoid of controversey because everybody on the team is afraid to challenge the boss' viewpoint.

3479. A good research director must cut burdensome red tape and paperwork to the bone so that he is able to ignore everyday problems most of the time and be free to be thinking about things that will influence the profits of his company in 5, 10, 20 years.

3480. In research, nothing encourages failure more than a conviction on the part of leadership that failure will occur — no matter how it is camouflaged.

3481. It is a wise Board of Directors who will invest in research in good times, recognizing they will have no choice but to do so in bad times.

3482. Research often is like looking for a lost golf ball; frequently when you find yourself in the rough you will find something better than what you started out to look for.

3483. An individual who undertakes a journey into the land of research should know that he will never reach a dead end.

3484. One of the most important cogs in any research organization is a man who will listen to ideas with enthusiasm.

3485. In research the only unsuccessful experiments are dishonest ones.

3486. In Research & Development one of the least note-worthy boasts of a director would be that he succeeded in operating his department last year within 1% of the approved budget.

3487. One of the most important contributors to research productivity in any organization is a member of top management who makes a point of listening to a scientist discuss his ideas . . . with both ears!

3488. Research costs a company a lot of money, especially

when the amount appropriated is only a tenth of what it should be.

3489. Nothing will dispel the gloom of a floundering research program like the bolt of light released by a bright new idea.

3490. The key to creative research is to go to the lab in search of an idea rather than to the library in search of a rest.

3491. Women should make especially good research investigators because of their intuition for suspecting hidden things.

3492. Research is expensive, but nobody has invented a cheaper way to stay in business.

3493. Not until a research man settles a week-long discussion by spending ten minutes at his work-bench does he come to appreciate fully the value of the experimental method.

3494. People who really enjoy research are content to get more fun than money out of their work.

3495. A research director who is earning more than his salary is one who has the courage and the good judgement to kill a losing research program when it has cost $100,000 instead of $1,000,000.

3496. The most valuable kind of industrial researcher to have on the payroll today is the kind who hates to re-invent anything.

RESIGNATION

3497. As soon as a fellow resigns himself to fate his resignation is promptly accepted.

RESISTANCE

3498. People who believe in following the path of least resistance usually end up trying only to improve others.

3499. If at first you succeed in resisting temptation — don't worry, it will come again.

3500. Temptations are easiest to resist with your eyes closed.

RESOLUTIONS

3501. The best resolutions in the world frequently are the ones we never kept.

RESPECT

3502. Two virtues that can earn you the highest possible respect of your peers are silence and brevity.

3503. Without exception as I look back, the people I've known who have enjoyed the most respect were those who had the most to say in the fewest possible words.

3504. The surest way to increase respect that people will have for you is to admit openly a mistake they know you could have covered up.

RESPONSIBILITY

3505. Responsibility is like old age in that it is not possible to escape from either of them.

3506. Most people are never more irresponsible at taking chances than when they make chance remarks.

3507. A good executive is a man who is happy because he's just been given added responsibilities.

3508. Some women refuse to shoulder their responsibilities because they are more attractive in a strapless gown.

3509. The man who shoulders his responsibilities has no room left for a chip.

REST

3510. The best thing to get out of exercise is rest.

RETIREMENT

3511. There is only one sure way to enjoy retirement — to go from an 8-hour day to a 16-hour day.

3512. Always plan your future in such a way that when the time comes to put you out to pasture you will be able to choose your own grazing grounds.

REVENGE

3513. Getting revenge is something you do to the other fellow to make yourself feel worse.

3514. In retrospect, one always will discover that no victory is more fruitless than a victory motivated by revenge.

REVENUE

3515. With the state the world is in, any government could raise unlimited revenue simply by taxing sins.

REWARDS

3516. The most sterile reward in life is a posthumous award.

3517. The greatest rewards in life come from doing a difficult job because it is there, not because you were asked to do it.

RICH MAN

3518. A rich man is one who has succeeded in discovering that money isn't everything.

3519. A truly rich man is one who has paid all of his taxes.

3520. A truly rich man is one who is well-liked by those who think he has nothing as he is by those who know how much he does have.

3521. A rich man is one who spends his dollars as carefully as he does his minutes.

3522. A rich man is one who can estimate how much money to put in a parking meter to the nearest nickel.

3523. A truly rich man is one who could lose most of his wealth without losing any of his friends.

RICH WOMEN

3524. Some of the richest women in America today owe their wealth to their success with at least three or four husbands.

RIDICULE

3525. Ridicule is like a fire hose that can smother fires that have great potential for providing warmth.

RIGHT MAN

3526. A girl will wait for the right man to come along as long as the one she's going with doesn't try to make a getaway.

3527. When a woman makes a hit with the right man, she's never miss-ed again.

RIGHT THING

3528. All you have to do to say the right thing at the right time is to speak softly and seldom.

RINGS

3529. A smart young girl is one who knows how to talk rings around her fingers.

RIOTS

3530. As long as the poor maintain a greater faith in God than in the dollar, they will not riot.

RISKS

3531. If you can get a bank to loan you money, you know you're a good risk.

3532. People who believe that the world owes them a living make the poorest financial risks.

ROAD MAP

3533. Nothing is more conducive to a pleasant motor trip than learning how to fold a road map quickly before you start.

ROBINS

3534. One reason the robin is such a popular bird is that it brings the first news of a drop in your winter's fuel bill.

ROCKING-THE-BOAT

3535. It is amazing how many people can be successful by following a policy of not "rocking the boat," and equally amazing to see how quickly they disappear when somebody else does!

3536. Many times the fellow who rocks the boat is the likeliest one to drown if it capsizes.

3537. Some people delight in rocking the boat you are in — as long as they are safely seated on the shore.

ROPES

3538. Any man who really knows the ropes will never let them tie him up in a knot.

ROSES

3539. A happily married man is one who believes that one of the soundest investments he can make is a dozen roses for his wife.

RUMOR

3540. Even a physicist will agree that the only thing known to travel faster than a sound is a rumor.

SAFE DRIVING

3541. Next to a policeman in the car in front of you, nothing makes for careful driving more than a woman driver immediately behind you.

3542. The best safety device in a car is a sober driver.

3543. A near-miss can be one of the best lessons in careful driving that a person can get.

SAFETY

3544. Playing things safe may get you to first base — but it will seldom bring you a home run.

3545. The man of the house is sure to be in great danger as long as he is keeping his wife in the dark about something.

3546. The safest way to cross a street is by an overpass.

SAINT

3547. A saint is a great humanitarian who is dead!

3548. Saints always are unpopular while they live because they are the most uncomfortable people for most of us to live with.

SALARIES

3549. Most women are satisfied to get along on their husband's salary ... but they expect him to find some additional means for his own support.

SALARY INCREASE

3550. Nowadays, the people who get the most out of your salary increase work for the Internal Revenue Service.

SALES

3551. All a woman has to do to take the wind out of a man's sales is spend his commissions before he makes them.

SALESMAN

3552. One of the most valuable things a salesman can learn is never to rest on his orders.

SALESMANSHIP

3553. A phony salesman's arguments resemble a sieve; they won't hold water, but sometimes they pan gold.

3554. A successful person is one who knows that the first product he must sell to the other person is himself.

3555. The only salesmen who can afford to sit around and wait for their customers are in the tombstone business.

SALT

3556. A man who has been married for five years can always surprise his wife by passing the salt to her before she asks.

SAND TRAP

3557. The most dangerous kind of sand trap for a young man is a blonde looking for a man on the beach.

SANITY

3558. True sanity is seldom reached before the age of 80.

SANTA CLAUS

3559. Some people who don't believe in Santa Claus are waiting around for him to come.

3560. One man who really believes in Santa Claus is the manufacturer of electric trains.

SATISFACTION

3561. Nothing is more satisfying in life than when timing and delivery occur in perfect sequence.

3562. Some of the happiest men in history were content to spend their lives studying the boundless mysteries hidden in a spoonful of dirt or a twinkle of stardust.

3563. Life will give you anything that you are satisfied with — especially failure.

3564. Few satisfactions in life exceed the thrill of being fussed over by people you never saw before in your life.

3565. One of the shallowest satisfactions in life is forcing others to admit that you were right.

3566. Next to falling in love with a beautiful woman the most satisfying experiences in life comes from falling in love with your work.

3567. Sometimes all it takes for a man to become dissatisfied with his walk in life is a heavy snowfall.

3568. People who never leave bad enough alone can never be satisfied.

SATURDAY

3569. Saturday is the day of the week that determines how sick a little boy was on Friday.

SCARCITY

3570. I always am amazed at how valuable a quarter or a paper hand towel can become when each of them are the last ones available to you in a rest room.

SCHOOL

3571. A little boy's arithmetic is at its best when he's counting the minutes before school's out.

3572. Maybe some drivers speed past the school because they remember how slowly they went through it.

SCHOOL BOY

3573. These days a school boy is a real failure if he has to repeat history.

SCHOOL ZONE

3574. The trouble with many who approach a school zone slowly is they're still too young to drive.

SCIENCE

3575. I have experienced more pleasures from new knowledge than I have from the harmony of symphony orchestras, religious sermons, or sex.

3576. In science, unlike in politics, misrepresentations can never be covered up because no scientist ever can insist on executive privilege.

3577. Understanding the physiology of a child is science, but delight at a child's beauty and innocence is morality.

SCIENTIFIC AGE

3578. Despite our scientific age, one of the least popular items on the menu today seems to be food for thought.

SCIENTIFIC FACT

3579. A scientific fact based upon experiment differs from any other kind of fact in that it does not depend on WHO reports it.

SCIENTISTS

3580. Most of the successful scientists I have known succeeded in mastering the art of getting along better with molecules than with people.

3581. The most creative scientists generally are more competent at watching for accidents than they are at avoiding them.

3582. A good scientist never argues with the facts unless he's gone to the trouble of checking them himself.

3583. A successful scientist is one who plants his ideas freely and then carefully waters those that take root.

3584. A smart scientist is one who gets an expert to do his glass-blowing for him . . . in the first place.

3585. The only time politics will not interfere with the quality of a scientist's work is when he happens to be a political scientist.

3586. A scientist who accepts anything less than the truth is an intellectual derelict.

3587. The best way for a scientist to prove himself right is to advance all the arguments he can in an effort to prove himself wrong.

3588. A true scientist will experience a more intense and a more lasting thrill at wrestling a beautiful new fact from nature than he would from conquering the love of a beautiful woman.

3589. When it comes to stopping a scientist from speculating, you can't beat a request to put it in writing.

3590. A contented scientist is one who can't think of anything else he would rather be doing.

3591. There are two kinds of scientists — those who are interested in the results of controlled experiments, and those who are interested in controlling the results of the test experiments.

3592. I have become very skeptical of any scientist who will not tolerate dandruff or loose hair on someone else's coat . . . or on his own!

3593. A truly enterprising scientist is more competent at watching for accidents than he is at avoiding them.

3594. A scientist is never more smartly dressed than when he's wearing his thinking cap.

3595. A brilliant scientist is one who is a fountain of knowledge and knows when to turn the fountain on and off.

3596. Every successful scientist knows how important it is to hang on and try one more experiment when he comes to the end of his rope.

3597. A scientist often is a person who makes discoveries, but resents a fellow scientist who makes money out of them.

3598. The most valuable kind of scientist to have on the payroll is one who abhors re-inventing anything.

SCORE

3599. A businessman's idea of a perfect score is to cinch a big deal on the 18th hole.

SCREWDRIVER

3600. A dime is still worth as much as it ever was only when you want to use it in place of a screwdriver.

SCULPTORS

3601. When it comes to chiseling on their income tax, most people are found out to be poor sculptors.

SECRET

3602. The secret of making life worthwhile is to believe that it is.

3603. Two people who are really in love with each other can't keep it a secret.

3604. A woman's idea of a bargain is to get the facts on a big secret in exchange for a little one.

3605. How important a secret is often depends on the number of people who think they're the only ones who know about it.

3606. Secrets, after all, do serve a purpose. Those you tell them to get so much pleasure out of telling them to somebody else.

3607. One secret it usually pays a man to keep from his wife is that he's gradually going deaf.

3608. The best kept secret in the world is the secret of one's success. Yet, if you ask anybody what this is, they'll tell you.

3609. When it comes to handling secrets, some women are mighty fast on the drawl.

3610. Oddly enough, the reason many persons tell you secrets is they want to convince you that they can be trusted.

SECRETARY

3611. A good executive is a man who isn't afraid to correct a mistake made by his secretary — no matter how pretty she is.

3612. One way a man can cheer his wife up is to come home and announce that his pretty secretary got married.

3613. When a boss starts getting interested in what his

secretary wears you know he is losing interest in what his wife wears.

3614. Nothing will sink a secretary into disgrace with her boss faster than a small leak ... of confidential information.

3615. One of the quickest ways for a man to lose his secretary is to treat her as indifferently as he sometimes does his wife.

3616. A good secretary is one who can keep up with her boss when he's dictating and ahead of him when he's not.

3617. A good secretary is one who can prevent her boss from falling down on the job.

3618. It is a clever secretary who can read her boss's mind and act as though she's stone-blind.

SECRET OF SUCCESS

3619. Almost anybody can become a success if he will bend every action, utter every word he can to raise the other fellow's esteem of himself.

3620. The first and foremost secret of success is to open a pathway that no one travelled on before.

SECURITY

3621. The sad fact of the 20th Century is that, based on TV ads, the only place in the world that can be considered secure is the appropriately deodorized armpit!

3622. The best security a parent can give his children is an insatiable thirst for hard work.

3623. The surest road to security is over the dead body of each problem you meet.

3624. Security is most dangerous when you are confident you have all you need.

3625. Anyone who works for another person should realize that his best insurance for the future is to do everything he can to insure the security of his boss's job.

3626. Persons who entertain far beyond their budget, who build homes on the basis of the salary they expect to be making in the future, who try to straddle several rungs of the social ladder at a time, are simply building a bon-fire under themselves for their ultimate financial ruin.

3627. When it comes to making your job fireproof it is hard to beat marrying the boss's daughter.

3628. The best security in a job is in having learned it inside and out.

3629. Time was when security consisted in having a .45 in your holster — now it consists of having enough money in the bank to be able to withdraw.

3630. Security is a two-edged sword; it can be either the safest or the most dangerous thing to strive for.

3631. The feeling of financial security is the first step towards true charity.

3632. Always remember that the security you get from salting money away is safer than income from your future labors.

3633. When a person can make a killing in the stock market and keep it a secret chances are he has always been wealthy.

3634. A woman's idea of security is to know that she has a man's bank account tightly within her signature.

SELF-ADMIRATION

3635. The greatest pitfall of most men is that they are apt to go overboard when it comes to believing in themselves.

SELF-APPRAISAL

3636. Seeing ourselves as others see us is usually a terrible let-down.

3637. The eye is the "window of the soul" to be sure, but it does a better job of seeing your neighbor's than you own.

SELF-CENTERED

3638. The trouble with some people who aim to please is they are too self-centered.

SELF-CONTROL

3639. At no time is self-control more difficult than in times of success.

3640. A lady is a woman who can read a man's mind like a book but has enough self-control not to throw it at him.

3641. It takes much more self-control to exercise one's freedom of thought than one's freedom of speech.

SELF-CRITICISM

3642. The most effective criticism in the world is self-criticism.

SELF-DENIAL

3643. Self-denial is a virtue we value, especially in a person who owes us some money.

3644. Self-denial is a virtue we value, especially in a neighbor we're trying to keep up with.

SELF-EMPLOYED

3645. When a man is enthusiastic about hard work he is either self-employed or paying to have it done.

SELF-ESTEEM

3646. Few people will criticize you for talking about yourself if you can make it amusing enough to entertain them.

SELF-IMPORTANCE

3647. Self-importance inevitably breeds self-destruction.

3648. The trouble with people who are carried away with their own importance is they seldom go very far.

3649. A man who is pulling his own weight never has any left over to throw around.

SELF-MADE MAN

3650. Many a self-made man had a wife who was a good sculptoress.

3651. People who criticize self-made men usually haven't been able to make much of themselves.

SELF-PRAISE

3652. God built man for humility . . . he didn't even give him a tail so he could pat his own back.

3653. Self-praise has at least one important advantage — it precludes the devastating dangers of self-contempt.

3654. No self-respecting girl will chase after a man she's interested in unless he tries to get away.

SELF-STARTER

3655. With human beings as with cars, the most valuable equipment to have is a self-starter.

SELFISHNESS

3656. The target of too many people who aim to please is themselves.

3657. When a selfish person dies he leaves this planet a better place to live in.

SENILITY

3658. A sure sign that senility is creeping up on a man is all an ocean-view vacation does is make him want to dine out.

SENSE

3659. Most persons who have sense enough use it too sparingly.

3660. How much sense there is in what a person says almost always depends on how brief it is.

SENTENCE

3661. When it comes to stopping a man's circulation you can't beat a jail sentence.

3662. September is the month when most little boys develop class hatred.

3663. September is the month teachers discover what a rough time mothers had while the school children were on vacation.

3664. September is the month when a lot of people discover what a good time the moths had while they were on vacation.

SERENDIPITY

3665. Serendipity consists of making the right discovery, while looking for the wrong thing.

SERVICE

3666. When it comes to meals, tennis, or success — always remember that it is how you serve others that counts.

3667. You can go much farther in life by service than you can by shouting or by silence.

3668. Service always is more eloquent than silence.

SERMON

3669. The real test of a good sermon is how many of its points point at you.

SEX

3670. The secret of a happy sex life is to make babies with it first and have fun with it afterwards.

3671. A man never realizes how shallow the depth of his knowledge is until he starts explaining sex to his oldest son.

3672. When it comes to controlling sex, the best tourniquet of all is marriage.

SEX-APPEAL

3673. In our super-scientific, moon-walking nuclear age of the 20th Century, nothing smacks more of dark-age witchcraft than a TV ad which promises you more sex-appeal if you brush your teeth with a new brand of toothpaste, or smoke a longer cigarette.

SHADE

3674. At no time is shade more important to you than when you're a shade better than the other fellow.

SHADY DEALS

3675. The best way to keep on the sunny side of life is to walk away from shady deals.

SHAME

3676. You know a woman is in love with her husband if she isn't ashamed of him even in a bathing suit.

SHIRT

3677. The surest way to hold on to your shirt is to roll up your sleeves.

3678. An old timer is one who never had to look for his daughter when one of his shirts was missing.

SHOCK

3679. About the only way anybody can be shocked today is by being hit by a bolt of lightning.

3680. Most people who insist on getting what they believe they deserve are shocked when they do.

3681. Anytime the truth shocks you, the chances are it is well grounded.

SHOCK TREATMENTS

3682. The trouble with some psychiatrists who believe in shock treatments is they use bills instead of pills.

3683. Some doctors believe in shock treatments — mailed out the first of every month.

SHOES

3684. When the shoes hurt, the average woman acts as though they fit.

3685. It is common practice for a young man to step into his father's shoes especially if they happen to fit him.

3686. All it takes to lift some women up into the world is a pair of high-heeled shoes.

3687. A woman reaches middle age when she is willing to wear shoes that fit her comfortably.

3688. You cannot tell how hard a woman can kick by the size of her shoes.

3689. Before you can fill the other man's shoes you had better do a thorough job of picking his brains.

3690. An optimist is a man who thinks that he can get his wife to wear shoes that will fit her.

3691. When a man boasts he can size women up he may only be a shoe clerk.

SHOP STEWARD

3692. Marriage is a union of a man and woman, with the woman in the position of shop steward.

SHORTCOMINGS

3693. When it comes to spotting the other fellow's shortcomings — everybody has 20/20 vision.

SHORT PERSONS

3694. Short persons would do well to remember that brains are measured from the chin up.

SHOULDER

3695. A contented husband is one who has a shoulder that his wife loves to rest her head on.

3696. Every time I run across a man with a chip on his shoulder I look for wood higher up.

3697. The surest way to knock a chip off a man's shoulder is with a compliment.

3698. Sometimes the biggest stumbling block in a man's career is the chip of wood on his shoulder.

3699. The heaviest chip on a man's shoulder is a mistake he refuses to correct.

3700. When it comes to stirring up trouble, some people like to use the chip on their shoulder.

3701. The man who likes to shoulder his responsibilities never has room for a chip on it.

3702. People who have a chip on their shoulder are easy to knock off balance.

3703. No amount of trouble is too heavy to shoulder — as long as it is on the other fellow's.

3704. No matter how broad a man's shoulders are they'll give under the weight of a swelled head.

SHOUTING

3705. Nothing will make the bottom fall out of your argument like raising your voice.

SIBLINGS

3706. Peace and prosperity are two siblings that seldom get along together.

SICK MAN

3707. Nothing will drive a sick man to his job like knowing how much work his wife has lined up for him if he stays home.

SICKNESS

3708. It is in sickness that one can clearly distinguish the saint from the scoundrel!

SIDES

3709. Frequently a story with two sides to it is so thin that you can see clear through it.

SIGHTSEEING

3710. When a man is looking his sharpest, he may be just sightseeing on a beach.

SIGNS OF THE TIMES

3711. Nowadays when a plumber fixes his doctor's plumbing he can expect to charge at least as much as when the doctor tries to fix his.

3712. The modern cleaning lady holds bankers' hours (10-3), gets served a hot lunch, and receives personalized chauffeur service to and from her place of residence!

SIGNATURE

3713. You can go through life with a signature that nobody can read as long as the banks will honor it.

SILENCE

3714. Silence is not always golden. Sometimes it means simply that the other fellow didn't listen to a word you said.

3715. There are times when silence is the best way to shout at the top of your voice.

3716. There is no more powerful force in the world than silence — at the right moment.

3717. Silence is never more golden than when you have nothing to say.

3718. Silence is an ignorant man's most valuable possession only so long as he can keep it.

3719. Silence is never more golden than when you keep it long enough to get all of the facts.

3720. Women who suffer in silence really do.

3721. Silence more often is yellow, not golden.

3722. Service always is more eloquent than silence.

3723. Silence is never more golden than when it is motivated by true love.

3724. I knew a person I thought was a genius — until I discovered he was tongue-tied.

3725. Silence is never more golden than when you know with absolute certainty that you are in the right.

3726. Women who suffer in silence are not bluffing.

3727. Silence is about the only known thing which cannot double-cross you.

3728. One of the virtues of silence is that it is a sure way to get others to think you are a great listener.

SILVER LININGS

3729. Silver linings would be more popular if bank tellers would cash them.

3730. The trouble with silver linings is that they're no substitute for cold cash.

SINS

3731. Sins are like termites — their ravages occur from within and when the signs show up on the outside it may already be too late.

3732. Nothing encourages sin like a clergyman committing one.

3733. If there is such a thing as a mortal sin I believe it is taking advantage of someone who believes in you.

SINCERITY

3734. Nothing helps to put sincerity into prayer more than an empty stomach.

SINS

3735. One of the hazards of sin is that the most serious ones always turn out to be the most enjoyable to commit.

3736. People who think they can charge their sins up to experience are going to be shocked when they discover how poor their credit is with God.

3737. With the state the world is in, any government could raise unlimited revenue simply by taxing sins.

3738. People who are best at forgiving sins usually are poorest at avoiding them.

SIZE

3739. How big a person's reputation is depends on how small the geographical sphere of his audience is.

SKIRTS

3740. One of the easiest things a man can spot is whether a woman lets her skirt creep above her knees deliberately or accidentally.

SLACKS

3741. The trouble with some women in play slacks is there just isn't enough play left in them.

3742. A woman with a pretty figure is one who can retain it even during the slack season.

3743. Nothing will show a woman up or let her down like a pair of slacks.

SLEEP

3744. The hardest thing for a mother of a new baby to catch is sleep.

3745. The fellow who does a good day's work seldom has to worry about getting a good night's sleep.

3746. You know a man is still very much in love with his wife if he uses all of his free time at a convention to catch up on his sleep.

3747. Sleep is the best cure for worry, providing you can do it instead.

3748. How well you sleep at night is usually determined by how much of yourself you gave to others during the day.

3749. Few things can bring on a sleepless night more effectively than a notice from the Internal Revenue Service that your return is to be audited.

3750. One of the greatest pleasures a parent can experience is a full night's sleep by the children.

3751. Nothing upsets a woman in the middle of the night like a husband who doesn't talk coherently in his sleep.

SLEEVES

3752. Men who aren't afraid to roll up their sleeves sometimes end up doing the dishes.

SLIPPERS

3753. One of the hardest things for a man to understand is

how his bedroom slippers manage to move so far away from him during the night.

SMALL BOYS

3754. When a small boy toys with temptation it is usually a destructive one.

3755. The best device for keeping a small boy out of hot water is a bathtub.

SMALL TOWN

3756. A small town is a place where babies never arrive unexpectedly.

3757. A small town is a place where balance counts, and most people in addition to the bank manager know what it is.

3758. A small town is a place where a man with a black eye is more interested in a good explanation than he is in a quick cure for it.

3759. A small town is a place where all you have to do to locate a cop is break the speed limit.

3760. A small town is a place where you can hire the Police Chief to cut your lawn during his off-hours.

3761. A small town is a place where the people enjoy reading in the newspapers what they knew already.

3762. One of the virtues of a small town politician is that he knows he has to stick pretty close to the truth.

SMART GIRL

3763. A smart girl is one who can make a young man's passing fancy stop short.

3764.   A smart girl is one who can hold a man at arm's length without losing her grip on him.

3765.   A smart girl knows when to look her best and when to stop looking.

3766.   A smart girl is one who knows a good bargain when she sees him.

SMART MAN

3767.   A smart man is one who uses his pull to lift himself up, not to throw his weight around.

SMART WOMEN

3768.   It's a smart wife who knows how to get her husband to start the dinner dishes — and then call her best friend on the phone.

3769.   A smart wife is one who handles her husband with all the attention and tenderness he deserves as her most valuable investment.

3770.   A smart woman knows how to make her husband a big success, but it's the clever woman that also keeps him after she does.

3771.   A smart woman is one who never worries about where her husband is at the moment, unless she's not absolutely certain.

3772.   A smart woman knows that the best ground rules for dealing with her husband is to insist on an open checkbook policy.

3773.   A smart woman is one who can keep her husband pursuing her after she lets him catch her.

3774. When you face opportunity with a smile, the chances are it will never dodge you.

3775. The best thing to do with a smile is to start it.

3776. The shortest distance between two points is between the ends of a smile.

3777. The best time to get a smile started is precisely when you are about to frown.

3778. The most powerful single thing you can do to have influence over others is to smile at them.

3779. When you face opportunity with a smile, the chances are it will never dodge you.

3780. You know a woman is in love with her husband if she smiles at him the way she does a traffic cop.

3781. How easy or how difficult the solution of any problem becomes depends more than anything else on whether or not you face up to it with a smile.

3782. The most powerful single thing you can do to have influence over others is to smile at them.

3783. The most important smile of the day is the first one you give yourself in the mirror when you get up.

3784. If you don't think much of money, then try paying your bills with a smile!

3785. A truly happy person is one who can keep smiling from ear to ear.

SMOKING CURE

3786. There is no better cure for cigarette smoking than

attending a younger brother's funeral who just died from lung cancer.

SNOBS

3787. Snobs are people who are just one inch from being snubbed.

3788. Snobs are persons who are so wrapped up with those above them that they can't see a thing in people on their own level.

SNOWFALL

3789. One time you won't hear some men brag about living in a corner house is right after a heavy snowfall.

SOCIAL LADDER

3790. Some people try to climb the social ladder installment by installment.

SOCIAL SECURITY

3791. The best social security that I know of is to work like the devil when you're young.

SOCKS

3792. Any girl who goes to the trouble of knitting socks for a man will go to a lot more trouble to keep him tied in a knot.

3793. By the time a modern girl starts knitting socks for a fellow, she knows she's got him all sewed up.

3794. No modern girl will bother to knit socks for a man unless she expects to take over the job of darning them.

SOFT SHOULDER

3795.   Nothing makes a soft shoulder more dangerous than leaning against one while driving a car.

SOFT SOAP

3796.   When a man resorts to the use of soft soap, the chances are that he is up to something dirty.

3797.   All a person has to do to get me in a lather is try to use soft soap on me.

SOFT-SPOKEN

3798.   Beware the soft-spoken salesman — he usually strikes the hardest bargain.

3799.   As a rule, the things that really count in this life are softly spoken.

SOLEMNITY

3800.   The more solemn a person's demeanor, the more cautious I am of his hidden intentions.

SOMETHING FOR NOTHING

3801.   There is no surer way to undermine the freedom of people than by promising them something for nothing.

SON

3802.   The easiest way to get your son to follow in your footsteps today is to offer him the keys to your car.

3803.   All a father had to do to knock the badness out of his son is to beat the tar out of him on a tennis court.

SORORITY HOUSES

3804. The subjects that give a lot of college students the most trouble live in sorority houses.

SORROW

3805. There is no better way to combat a period of intense sorrow than by doubling your normal work-load.

SOUL

3806. Few things are better for your soul than a walk through a cemetery where all of your old friends are buried.

SOUND

3807. No sound is more pleasing to the human ear than the sound of someone admitting that you're right.

SPACE

3808. The one space in the world that is becoming cluttered faster than anything else is the space between people's ears.

SPADE

3809. A righteous-living person is one who always calls a spade a spade, even when he trips over one.

SPANKING

3810. One of the troubles with parents who bring up children these days is they don't hit bottom often enough.

3811. Every child should receive an introduction to a literary background — preferably by the proper application of a book, now and then, hard enough and low enough.

SPARE-TIME

3812. The easiest way to find more time to do all the things you want to do is to turn off the television.

SPARK

3813. No matter how big a dynamo a man may be, he still needs a good wife to provide the spark.

3814. Money and brains may provide a man with the fuels of life, but he still needs a good wife to provide the spark.

SPEAKERS

3815. A good speaker is one who can say a few well-chosen words in less than fifteen minutes.

3816. The most impressive act of an after-dinner speaker is the one in which he graciously sits.

3817. A popular speaker is one who knows all the advantages of stopping sooner than his audience expects him to.

3818. The best thing a speaker can do to please his audience is to sit down at least five minutes before they expect him to.

3819. The conclusions of a speaker's speech are remembered best when they come about ten minutes after the beginning.

3820. A good speaker is one who can stop everyone in his audience from coughing or sleeping.

3821. Nothing upsets an audience more than a speaker who starts saying "And finally..."

3822. Nothing helps you to make an impromptu speech a big success like coming fully prepared for it.

3823. One advantage of being the speaker is you can turn off the conversation any time you choose to.

3824. A good speaker not only knows what to say, but also how little.

3825. A speaker should always remember that to his audience he is a live sound movie of what is going on in his brain.

3826. A good speaker is one who knows how little time his two cents' worth should take.

3827. A good speaker is one who is not afraid to take a stand and then sit down promptly.

3828. A convincing speaker is one who can make his audience roundly cheer what he says even though they don't understand it.

3829. A good speaker is one who knows how to convince you that you know what you're talking about.

3830. A good speaker is one who rises to the occasion because he's being paid handsomely for doing it.

3831. Every good speaker knows that the shortest distance between two points is a good story.

3832. A poor speaker is one who needs a glowing introduction.

3833. A good toastmaster is one who can make you whip up an appetite for a speaker even though you've just finished a meal.

3834. A good toastmaster is one who can get the speaker to

sit down before the audience starts to feel that the toast is being badly burnt.

3835. People who appreciate a good speaker the most are program chairmen.

3836. Some speakers drive their listeners home before their point.

3837. A good speaker is one who gets more applause when he is finished than when he is introduced.

3838. The recipe for successful after-dinner speaking includes using plenty of shortening.

3839. The trouble with some speakers who get carried away with themselves is they never think of looking at the clock on the wall.

3840. The best after-dinner speakers are those who are not too full — of themselves.

3841. The trouble with some people who rise to the occasion is they don't know when to sit down.

3842. A poor speaker is one who has little or nothing to say, but insists on saying it all anyway.

3843. Conclusions are an important part of speech, especially when they come as close as possible to the beginning.

3844. Sometimes the best after-dinner speaker is one who is still hungry!

3845. The trouble with a lot of speakers is they can usually remember the beginning, but it is finding the end that takes all their time.

3846. A good speaker is one who starts off with a good joke and then concentrates on a fast wind-up.

3847. A good speaker is one who can go from one thought to the next one in the fewest possible words.

3848. A good speaker is one who is made speechless by a big ovation.

SPECIALISTS

3849. The world is filled with specialists, if you count those who specialize in fixing the blame.

SPECTACLES

3850. The same persons who complain that they can't see their way on life very often make spectacles of themselves.

SPEECH

3851. You can make a good speech by taking a tip from the wheel — the shorter the spoke, the less the tire.

3852. A good speaker is one who knows how to make a one hour speech in fifteen minutes.

3853. Anybody can get invited to make speeches if he's willing to do them without receiving a fee.

3854. One advantage of thinking twice before you speak is that you will speak seldom.

3855. The shortest distance between two jokes makes a perfect speech.

3856. The most effective impromptu speeches I have ever made were condensations of long-winded orations used years previously.

3857. You've got to admire people who think before they speak.

3858. A good speech is one you can give in less than a half hour, and a good book is one based on the same speech.

3859. The shortest distance between making two points is a perfect speech.

SPEED

3860. When it comes to picking up speed from a stop position, you can't beat a bus you've just missed.

3861. The quickest way to get a hundred and one things done still is one thing at a time.

3862. When it comes to speed, you can't beat the average stenographer at the water cooler.

3863. The trouble with many young men who are going places today is they insist on breaking the speed limit.

3864. Speed is so characteristic of our day and age that people are now even jumping to wrong conclusions.

3865. Now that man has demonstrated that he can travel faster than sound, wouldn't it be wonderful if more people knew where they want to go and why?

SPEED COP

3866. Nothing is more relaxing to a motorist than the sight of a speed cop chasing a car going the other way.

SPILT MILK

3867. If you must cry over spilt milk, try and condense it.

SPIN-THE-BOTTLE

3868. Most men will agree that the fellow who invented the game called spin-the-bottle was a genius.

SPOKES

3869. Nothing will make the wheels in a man's head start turning like a few spokes from the boss.

SPRING

3870. Spring is the season of the year when most men get a passing fancy for gardening.

3871. A pessimist is happy to see the first robin because he knows his fuel bill will drop — an optimist because he knows he's paid his taxes for another year.

SQUARE PERSONS

3872. The greatness of a country is measured by the number of square persons in it, not the number of square miles it contains.

SQUARES

3873. Most people who try to talk circles around you give you the impression that they're square.

STAGNATION

3874. The flowing river never suffers from stagnation — neither does the active mind.

STAIRS

3875. Old age has set in as soon as you start getting out of breath when you go down stairs.

STANDARD OF LIVING

3876. Nobody advances our standard of living like people who live beyond their means.

3877. Nothing will make a man improve his standard of living like writing a book about how he thinks others should live.

3878. Most people raise their standard of living installment by installment.

3879. Nobody advances our standard of living like people who live beyond their means.

STANDARDS

3880. The secret of success is to keep raising your own standards.

3881. A man knows he's a success when he can measure up to standards other people set for him.

STANDING

3882. Frequently how long a man will remain standing depends on how hard he falls for a girl.

STAND UP

3883. A smart girl knows that it is more important for a man to be able to stand up on his own two feet at the office than it is on the dance floor.

STATE TROOPERS

3884. Courage is what it takes to pass a State Trooper even

when you can keep within the speed limit.

3885. The motor cycle cop hiding behind billboards has now been replaced by a state trooper aiming a radar viewer at you.

STEAM

3886. There is no better way to vent a full head of steam than a look at yourself in a mirror.

STENOGRAPHER

3887. A smart stenographer is one who is good at typing, especially at typing her boss.

STOCK MARKET

3888. Many people have learned that playing the stock market is anything but fun!

3889. Many people who have played the stock market have good reason to dispute the security of securities.

STONE AGE

3890. We are still in the stone age when it comes to using the wonders of our tongue and our ears in our own best interests and for the good of our fellowmen.

STOP SIGN

3891. Most motorists come to a full stop at a stop sign when a pretty blonde happens to be waiting beside it.

STORK

3892. The stork is a very charitable bird. Note how much

more frequently it visits the poor than the rich.

STORM

3893. People who like to stir up a storm are not likely to look for a rainbow afterwards.

STRAIGHT-AND-NARROW PATH

3894. More people would follow the straight and narrow path if there were an admission charge.

3895. To get some people to follow the straight and narrow path, stop giving them advice and start leading the way.

3896. The advantage of always following the straight and narrow path is you avoid all the traffic.

3897. A young girl's idea of the straight and narrow path is to hold her figure that way.

3898. It seems absurd to expect human beings to walk the straight and narrow path when they have so much trouble staying on a four-lane turnpike with four wheels under them.

3899. More people would follow the straight and narrow path if it weren't on an upgrade.

3900. When it comes to following the straight and narrow path, it helps if you can shoot in the 70's.

3901. Training a child to follow the straight and narrow path is easy for parents — all they have to do is lead the way.

3902. One way you could get more people to follow the straight and narrow path would be to build gas stations alongside of it.

3903. The main trouble with the modern generation is that it has made superhighways out of almost every path except the straight and narrow one.

3904. It is easy to get the neighborhood children to follow a straight and narrow path — all you need is a corner house with a lovely lawn in front of it.

STRAIGHT-FROM-THE SHOULDER

3905. Sometimes the fellow who says he's speaking to you straight from the shoulder doesn't have much resting on it.

STRESS

3906. A life with stress under control is a life in which the brakes are on only when needed.

STRAPLESS GOWN

3907. Strapless gown — a dress that has visible means of support.

3908. A woman who can wear a strapless gown knows she's not sticking her neck out.

3909. A young woman's idea of getting over the hump is to succeed finally in feeling comfortable in a strapless gown.

STRENGTH

3910. The reason some girls insist on a double-ring ceremony is they feel it strengthens their hand.

3911. All a girl needs to regain her strength is the appearance of a better prospect than the one she's going with.

STRONG ARM

3912. The most valuable thing a man can have up his sleeve is a good strong arm.

STUBBED TOES

3913. In any organization, the man on the go is one who is careful never to stub his toe.

3914. As long as you do stub your toe now and then you have a chance of stumbling onto something great and important.

3915. Stubbing your toe now and then is a low price to pay for learning how to pick up your feet.

STUBBORNNESS

3916. Stubbornness can be a tremendous virtue when it becomes happily wedded to an honest conviction or a principle.

3917. Stubbornness is a virtue only when it is used to resist temptation.

STUDENT

3918. An enterprising college student is one who studies while he waits for his date to get ready.

STUMBLING BLOCK

3919. Sometimes the biggest stumbling block in a man's career rests on his shoulders.

STUPIDITY

3920. Man is the most stupid creature because he alone has an intellect with which to propel stupidity.

3921. The trouble with stupidity among human beings is that it afflicts everybody in varying degrees without exceptions.

3922. A woman suspects that a man is stupid when he says he understands her; as soon as he tries to prove it, she's convinced.

STYLES

3923. The change in the style of women's clothing always is felt most in men's pockets.

SUBSTITUTE

3924. The best substitute for a rich father is a rich father-in-law.

3925. Nobody has yet found a better substitute for an empty brain than a closed mouth.

SUCCESS

3926. Success and obesity do have something in common — both can result from chewing up more than you should have bitten off.

3927. The secret of success in life lies not so much in keeping out of the rough as in knowing the best way to get out of it when you do.

3928. Success used to indicate superior ability, but now the people wonder what racket you're in.

3929. Some men I know were so determined to climb the ladder to success that they built their own ladders.

3930. Of all the thousands of formulas for success that have been offered, none is quite so ignored as deliberately losing your voice for a couple of weeks.

3931. The difference between success and failure usually depends on whether you read everything attentively or indifferently.

3932. The first step to success in any job is a determination that you will never fail in it.

3933. It is a wise man who appreciates that it is the men underneath him who are holding him up.

3934. Sleep is the best eraser in the world and work is God's best medicine; one's success in life depends on how well he balances the intake of both.

3935. One of the most powerful combinations for success that I can envision is that of crossing a Texan's ability to think big and a Vermonter's cautiousness to say little.

3936. A successful man is one who can't count the number of other successful people he helped to the top.

3937. Any man who is lavish with praise and a glutton for hard work can't help being successful.

3938. Nothing breeds success like a refusal to accept defeat.

3939. Nowadays the success of a citizen is determined by how much the government takes away from him in taxes.

3940. Success is never in greater danger of being lost than immediately after you think you have completely captured it.

3941. If you wish to use a ruler to measure success, calibrate it by the number of other persons who attribute their success to you.

3942. The one sure thing that makes any successful man lose

380

credibility with me is to hear him say it all happened by accident.

3943. Before a man starts climbing the ladder of success it helps to pick the right girl to stay on the ground and hold it steady for him.

3944. Any time that success comes to you too easily it may turn out to be short-lived.

3945. Some of the most successful people in the world are those who went looking for trouble — and found a way to solve it successfully.

3946. One of the surest ways to lose your bearings in your search for success is to blow a fuse.

3947. The surest way to reach the pinnacle of success is to build the stairway to the top by an accumulation of "little successes."

3948. Life is a battle between pleasing others and pleasing yourself; success is the result of doing the first better.

3949. Success in the business world is not unlike living to ripe old age — in both cases they depend on how well you adapt to your environment.

3950. The secret of successful 40 hour week is to put in at least 60.

3951. Success is about the only thing that even has a chance of transforming a vain egotist into a tolerant, and charitable recluse.

3952. The surest way to become the highest paid employee in any organization is to work as hard as you can to prove that you're already overpaid.

3953. I do not know a single exception but one where success has been achieved without working a 16-hour day for years — and that one exception is where you had a father or an uncle who worked the 16-hour day for you.

3954. An outstretched hand in friendship, a personality radiating love and warmth for the other fellow, is the magic key, the "Open Sesame" to ever-increasing success and happiness.

3955. Success depends on beginnings, so start now with what you are, where you are, and with what you can do in the next 60 seconds!

3956. Reason may triumph in the end, but enthusiasm will carry a project to success.

3957. The greatest obstacle that most people must overcome to climb the ladder of success is the lethargy that makes it so hard always to put your best foot forward.

3958. The surest way to succeed in life is to outlive all of your competitors.

3959. When a man arrives at the top in any field of great importance, how long he will remain there depends on how long it will take for success to go to his head.

3960. The most valuable attribute for success is an insatiable capacity for enduring humiliation.

3961. I find that every important event in my life that affects me today — came about by careful planning at least ten years in advance.

3962. You have reached the pinnacle of success as soon as you become uninterested in money, compliments, or publicity.

3963. If at first you don't succeed, you're one in about 4,000,000,000.

3964. It is impossible for any man to achieve success without enduring criticism and humiliation.

3965. Most people would succeed with great ambitions if they wouldn't let themselves get bogged down doing nothing.

3966. One of the first steps a modern man must take to climb the ladder to success is to turn off the television.

3967. Do everything in your power to increase the happiness and success of the other fellow — and you can't miss guaranteeing your own.

3968. The secret ingredient of success is a confident expectation of it — as long as this is kept to yourself.

3969. Many people who join in the hunt for success use up all their ammunition taking pot shots at others who have already outdistanced them.

3970. Success that goes to a man's head soon plants a tombstone over it.

3971. A record of human technological progress is replete with noble achievements that were considered by all, save one human being, to have been utterly impossible.

3972. There is no greater formula for success than deliberately seeking out the needs in other people's lives and then devotedly filling them.

3973. Anybody who can keep his eye on the ball is bound to be a success, especially if he likes golf.

3974. A person who was an itch for getting somewhere probably started out from scratch.

3975. Success requires that you play the game with all your might without showing any outward signs that you are using force.

3976. When a little success goes to a man's head it usually means that he has reached the top of his ladder.

3977. Anybody can become a success in America if he's

willing to work while everybody else is killing time.

3978. The reason that there is always room at the top is that so many people become satisfied long before they get there.

3979. The first thing to do to climb the ladder of success is forget that there's such a thing as office hours.

3980. Most men discover — sometimes too late — that as a man's success increases it becomes more difficult for him to keep his wife . . . or his money.

3981. The most successful people I know keep so busy trying to better themselves that they haven't any time left to try and better the other fellow.

3982. If at first you don't succeed, be prepared for trials and trials again.

3983. A successful man is one who makes enough money that it pays Uncle Sam to watch every penny of it for him.

3984. A successful man today is known by his mortgage-free deeds.

3985. A sure sign that a man is not a failure is the generosity with which he gives others credit . . . for his success.

3986. Nothing gives a man an edge over competition along the road to success more than getting jobs done ahead of deadlines.

3987. Nothing helps you to get up in the world like rolling out of bed at 6 o'clock every morning.

3988. Success that goes to a man's head usually pays a very short visit.

3989. You know a man has reached the pinnacle of success when he shows as much happiness over an honor bestowed on someone he helped as he would if he had received it himself.

3990. Success is just a matter of failures — overcoming them, that is!

3991. Most of the individuals I know who skyrocketed to the top of their ladder have prospered by the sudden misfortune of one of their associates.

3992. The irony of it all is that more people have been ruined by success than by failure.

3993. Getting to know and like people, and getting people to know and like you are the trump cards in the game of success.

3994. You must give of yourself to get for yourself.

3995. Reaching for success is not nearly so hard on you as having to take it in your stride.

3996. Nobody can make a man go places like a pretty wife who sets his goals for him.

3997. Some men achieve success by trial and terror.

3998. Nothing breeds success like a refusal to accept defeat.

3999. If success were gauged by the number of enemies you can make it would be the easiest thing in the world to reach.

4000. To be a success spend from 6 to 8 a.m. each day thinking and from 8 a.m. to 8 p.m. working.

4001. The fellow who burns the brightest flames of success has long since mastered the art of keeping cool.

4002. A man is a success when his wife thinks just as highly of him as his friends and associates.

4003. The secret of success is to do everything you're told to do, and twice as much more.

4004. Never attribute outstanding virtues or character to a person who outwardly is financially successful until you are sure that you have the same opinion of him as the Internal Revenue Service does.

4005. It is a scientific fact that energy, controlled by one's metabolism, deserves more credit for the success of the greatest men of all time than any other single factor.

4006. A good executive is one who can get people to succeed far beyond what they themselves thought they were capable of.

4007. A man on his way to the top is one who is still learning something from each mistake he makes.

4008. A successful man is one who has been married for 20 years and finally finds himself out of debt.

4009. A successful housewife is one who showed her husband how to be successful.

4010. A truly successful man is one who can get somewhere without people becoming suspicious that he is doing it illegally.

4011. All it takes to be successful today is a willingness to start an eight hour day immediately after you finish the first one.

4012. Any man can become successful if he's willing to stick at a thing for fifty years.

4013. At no time is self-control more difficult than in times of success.

4014. Behind every successful man you will find a woman — giving him a shot in the arm just when he needs it most.

4015. Coming down the ladder of success won't be nearly so bad if you say "hello" to those you pass on the way up.

4016. I have made a lot of speeches in my day, and I can't think of one where I stopped sooner than I expected to that wasn't a big success.

4017. One of the first things a person must do to climb the ladder of success is take his hands out of his pockets.

4018. Life is a bit like unwinding a piece of badly knotted string with success coming only to the few who persist to the bitter end.

4019. Most of the success in this world comes from doing things long before you get sense enough not to try them.

4020. Nothing increases a man's chances of finding success like setting out to look for it.

4021. One advantage of trying to do what everybody else thinks is impossible is that it improves your chances of success.

4022. One of the first steps a modern man must take to climb the ladder to success is to turn off the television.

4023. Some men rocket to the top because they are wife-propelled.

4024. Success is 99 percent beginning things and only one percent luck.

4025. Success consists in selling experience at a profit.

4026. Success in this life is the bull's eye, and in order to strike it you must be the bullet.

4027. Success defies the law of gravity; it means getting to the top of the ladder by staying on the level.

4028. Sympathize with everyone but yourself and you are certain to become a success.

4029. The best way to step into the job ahead of you is to step on it in the job you've got.

4030. The biggest block to many a man's success is his head.

4031. The fellow who always insists on getting what's coming to him frequently succeeds.

4032. The man who roars to success is one who is on fire with enthusiasm inside, but who appears calm on the outside.

4033. The most important reaction to any success is its aftertaste on your conscience.

4034. The people who help a man most to success frequently are the dunces who do everything they can to stop him.

4035. The secret of success is to keep raising the standards of those who work for you.

4036. There is always room at the top for the fellow who is willing to build his own ladder.

4037. You're well on your way to success as soon as you look upon every failure as an opportunity to success.

4038. When the modern youngster asks his father for his key to success he's really thinking of his car keys.

4039. If at first you don't succeed, you are about average.

SUCCESSFUL MAN

4040. A successful man is one who can get a woman to listen to reason, or anything else for that matter.

SUCCESSFUL WOMAN

4041. A successful woman is one who doesn't have to work as hard after marrying a man as she did trying to catch him in the first place.

SUFFERING

4042. When a woman says she has endured untold suffering, you're about to hear it.

4043. To a blade of grass the sun is as close as a man's kiss to a woman.

SUNDAY COLLECTION

4044. A man has religion in proportion to the ease with which he will part with a five dollar bill for the Sunday Collection.

SUNDAY DRIVERS

4045. The most dangerous Sunday drivers are those speeding to get to the golf course immediately after getting out of church.

4046. The trouble with many Sunday drivers is they don't drive any better during the week.

4047. The time has past when you can expect even Sunday drivers to show any courtesy.

SUPERIORITY

4048. An egotist is a person who suffers from an error of superiority.

SUPPORT

4049. A statistician is a man who can use figures to support himself in a calculated manner.

SURPRISE

4050. A man always can surprise his wife by coming home a

half-hour early with a bouquet of flowers — or without a
bouquet of flowers.

4051. The easiest way for a woman to surprise a man is to be
ready ahead of time.

SUSPENDERS

4052. A million years ago, Nature didn't know we were going
to wear suspenders, yet look how she built our shoulders.

SWEATER

4053. One time a sweater looks awful is when it is on a
stretching frame.

SWELLED HEAD

4054. Many men with drooping shoulders are only showing
the strain of supporting a swelled head.

SWIMMING SUIT

4055. A man reaches middle age when he can't wear the same
swimming suit two summers in a row.

SWITCH

4056. As soon as a man discovers the light in his life, he
willingly turns over control of the switch to her.

SYMPATHY

4057. Nothing is more conducive to mediocrity than self-
sympathy.

4058. Tact is the ability to light a fire under a person — without having to apply a torch.

4059. Tact is the ability to step on a man's toes without letting him feel your boot.

4060. One of the most tactful persons in the world must have been the fellow who first thought of putting the word "sales" before the word "tax."

4061. Tact is the ability to wish your relatives good-bye — and convince them that you're not happy to see them go.

4062. Tact is the ability to hammer home a point without hitting the other fellow's thumb.

4063. Tact is the ability to convince a man who's sure that he's never wrong that he is occasionally right.

4064. Tact is the ability to cut a pie into five pieces and let everybody else think you've given yourself the smallest piece.

4065. Tact is the ability to get a person to take advantage of an opportunity for you.

4066. When it comes to hammering home your point, you can't beat using a little tact.

4067. Tact is the ability to hammer home a point without hitting the other fellow's thumb.

4068. Tact is the ability to get the other fellow to solve your problem your way.

4069. Tact is the ability to get someone to do a thing without having to order him to.

4070. Tact is the ability to give the other person a shot in the arm without letting him feel the needle.

4071. Tact is the ability to step on a man's toes without scuffing the shine on his shoes.

4072. Tact is the ability of some women to block a man's advances without being deprived of his hospitality.

4073. Tact is the ability to change a porcupine into a possum.

4074. Tact is the ability to get a barber to listen to you.

4075. Tact is like air in an automobile tire; without it, driving through life will be rough going.

4076. Tact is the ability to spank a man's pride without letting him feel it.

4077. Tact is the ability to make a person see the lightning without letting him feel the bolt.

4078. Tact is what everybody wishes they had when they needed it the most.

4079. Tact is the ability to say yes or no equally agreeably.

4080. Tact is the ability to convince a woman that she ought to lose weight, without implying that she's too stout.

4081. Tact sometimes consists in being able to entertain people in a heavenly manner when you wish they were in another place.

4082. Tact is the ability not to describe others exactly as you see them.

4083. Tact is the ability to listen to your boss tell you a lot of things you already told him.

4084. Tact is the ability to say things without saying them.

4085. Tact is the ability to ask a person for a book you

loaned him and succeed in getting back the other half dozen he borrowed from you.

4086. Tact is the ability to agree with a person and still convince him he's wrong.

4087. Tact is the ability to get the fleece off the flock without a flinch.

4088. Tact is the ability to describe the other fellow as you can't see him.

4089. Tact is the ability to convince a man he is dead wrong — without making him your enemy.

4090. Tact is something that seldom fails where lack of tact never succeeds.

4091. Tact is the ability to rev up the other fellow without stripping your own gears.

4092. Tact is the ability to give a person a word of advice without infuriating him.

4093. Tact is the ability to provide a man with enough warmth to be able to take the cold water you're about to throw at him without feeling the shock.

4094. Tact is the ability to take the chill out of a person without letting him feel the heat you're putting on him.

TACTICS

4095. If medical men used the same tactics to earn their livelihood as politicians, there wouldn't be a healthy person in the country.

4096. The trouble with take-home pay today is that it turns out to be just about enough to get you there.

TALENT

4097. A really smart man is one who knows when to turn off the talent and turn on the tact.

4098. The greatest sin a person can commit is to possess a great talent and refuse to share it with his fellow man.

4099. Outstanding talent is seldom appreciated until it is recognized by persons outside of your home or immediate place of business.

TALK

4100. Human beings are such a wordy lot that most of what they say to each other goes unheard and unheeded.

4101. The trouble with some of the nice things people say to your face is they would never think of saying them behind your back.

4102. There is a fortune awaiting any man who can find something worthwhile that can be done with small talk.

4103. Talk is never cheaper than when it is at the other fellow's expense.

4104. A happily married man is one who would rather talk with his wife at breakfast than read the morning newspaper.

4105. The only way to talk about somebody is to speak as though you knew he was listening.

4106. Some people are never so happy as when they don't know what they're talking about.

4107. People should talk the way they eat and taste each mouthful of words before letting them go.

4108. A smart girl knows when to speak her lines, and also when to make her lines speak for her.

4109. To say the proper thing is easy enough; the hard part is to stop there.

4110. About the only time a man can't talk too much is when it comes to telling his loved ones how much he appreciates them.

4111. All you have to do to say the right thing at the right time is to speak softly, and seldom.

4112. The only fair way to talk about somebody is to imagine that he is listening to every word you say.

4113. Anytime you can get a woman to say just a few words, you should thank her for them.

4114. As a rule, the things that really count in this life are softly spoken.

4115. At no time do you feel better for not having said something than when you thought of saying something to belittle a person.

4116. The secret of good health lies not so much in eating half of what you do as in saying one-tenth of what you say.

4117. The two hardest things to do in the world are to stop people from talking and to start them thinking.

4118. There is a thin line that marks the difference between people who talk about themselves and people who talk to themselves.

4119. When a man's work speaks for itself, he's usually a man of few words.

4120. The best way to stop a woman in the middle of a sentence is offer her your seat on the bus.

4121. Anybody who thinks that talk is cheap doesn't have a wife who makes long distance calls to mother.

4122. When a single word makes a big difference in what you say it is usually a word you left out.

4123. When it comes to talking about people, take a tip from the tombstone and never say anything against a man when he's down.

4124. You can learn a lot about a man by how much he doesn't say.

4125. People who talk fast seldom say much that is worthwhile.

4126. People who say things off the top of their head frequently don't have much underneath it.

4127. People who are hardest to stand are those who do nothing but sit and talk.

4128. Silence is never more golden than when you have nothing to say.

4129. Some of the busiest people I've ever known could easily have gotten all their work done if they didn't talk so much.

4130. Sometimes a man who strikes you as having a lot on the ball is just able to pitch a good line.

4131. Sometimes the best way to make yourself heard is by letting the other fellow do the talking for you.

4132. Talk is never cheaper than when it is at the other fellow's expense.

4133. The average woman can talk circles around a man, even when he isn't listening to her.

4134. The best way to keep one's nose clean is to keep one's mouth shut.

4135. Even when some people weigh what they say about you, you still feel as though you've been shortchanged.

4136. How much you say in a man's favor frequently depends on how little you can say against him.

4137. If you think a woman's conversation is boring imagine what it would be like if she didn't have to stop and catch her breath now and then.

4138. If you wag your tongue, always make it sound friendly.

4139. In order to put in your two cent's worth nowadays, you've got to be a mighty fast talker.

4140. It seems like a mathematical contradiction, but it is true that the fellow who says the most is the one who speaks the least.

4141. Long before your child lets the cat out of the bag on you, the chances are you said something that made the cat jump into the bag.

4142. Many people waste a lot of time talking about themselves even though they would prefer you to do it.

4143. Money still talks, especially after taxes.

4144. Nothing adds sparkle to the other fellow's conversation like an unexpected compliment from him about you.

4145. Nothing will improve your chances of being understood like speaking in short, seldom sentences.

4146. Nothing will stop a woman from talking like a missing front tooth.

4147. One sure way to get a word in edgewise is to make it pointed enough.

4148. One of the healthiest habits a man can develop is the ability to keep his mouth shut nine times out of every ten that he gets the urge to open it.

4149. One man who can keep his mouth shut is more valuable than a man who can speak several languages with his mouth wide open.

4150. One of the virtues of silence is that people will think the world of you for it and you don't have to listen to a word they say.

4151. The value of a few well-chosen words depends on how little you dwell upon them.

4152. People who speak softly and seldom are listened to the most.

TALL TALES

4153. Women and fishermen tell tall tales about the big fish that got away from them.

TANTRUM

4154. A smart child knows how to throw a trantrum and when.

4155. One tried and sure way to get your wife out of a tantrum is to come home smelling strongly of a new kind of perfume.

TAPE RECORDER

4156. A parent who can't afford a tape recorder can always count on the children for play-backs.

TARDINESS

4157. People who arrive late for work usually are the first to have their desks all cleared away before quitting time.

TARGETS

4158. The target of too many people who aim to please is themselves.

4159. A person with a good aim is one who can hit the target the first time with a bottle of catsup.

4160. Some women who aim to please make attractive targets of themselves.

4161. When you make your mark in the world always remember that you've already made a target of yourself.

4162. The target of too many men who aim to please ... is often somebody else's pretty wife.

TAXES

4163. The man who devised the W-2 advance tax deduction system did more to rob Americans of one of their Constitutional freedoms than any other single person in American history.

4164. Two things can make a man happy — coming through his annual physical and his tax audit trouble-free.

4165. Distance makes the heart grow fonder of the income tax collector.

4166. There's nothing wrong with taxes that cutting them in half would not alleviate.

4167. All you have to do to ruin a perfect day is calculate how much of your salary will be withheld for taxes.

4168. With the state the world is in, any government could raise unlimited revenue simply by taxing sins.

4169. The man most admired by Internal Revenue Agents is the one from whom they can collect the most.

4170. The people who will tell you most convincingly to pay your taxes are serving time because they didn't.

4171. The phrase "to tax one's thinking" is becoming increasingly dangerous because one of these days the politicians will come up with a way to do it.

4172. Taxes are so high these days that even the Joneses aren't going places.

4173. Just as soon as a man starts blowing up his own success, an internal revenue agent is sure to arrive on the scene to pin his success down.

4174. If there is one statue that is begging for some sculptor to produce, it is a statue of limitations.

4175. An old timer is a person who believes that the best thing about the good old days was the low taxes.

4176. With taxes the way they are, most executives now receive less than 50 percent of their income for 100 percent of their talents.

4177. Taxes are the price we must pay for civilization, and on that basis our civilization would appear just about to have had it.

4178. There is only one subject in the newspapers that

receives more careful reading than sex crimes — and that is stories about income tax evasions.

4179. Computers are doing more to keep taxpayers honest than are their consciences.

4180. With taxes the way they are, even a computer would have difficulty in calculating what profit a man would make if he gained the whole world.

4181. There is only one thing in this world that is more certain than taxes — surtaxes.

4182. The ambition of the modern businessman, alas, has to be to increase his income until his taxes are higher than his take-home pay.

4183. One man you cannot convince that there is any such thing as petty cash is an internal revenue agent.

4184. A truly rich man is one who has paid all of his taxes.

4185. High taxes are the price we pay for letting the Government support the people.

4186. Nothing taxes your belief in free speech more than having to pay them.

4187. An honest taxpayer is one who has just had last year's tax return reviewed with him by an Internal Revenue agent.

4188. Nothing dulls a person's memory like an Internal Revenue agent asking questions.

4189. America is the only country in the world where the people who can think and the people who can't think pay about the same amount of taxes.

4190. Estimating your income tax would be a lot easier if it could be based on what income you expect to have left.

4191. Nothing makes paying your taxes seem fully justified like getting a refund.

4192. Nothing will hatch a nest egg like an Internal Revenue agent laying on you.

4193. Nowadays about the best a fellow can do with what he is able to salt away is pay his taxes with it.

4194. Nowadays it doesn't take much to wipe out a fortune — only one Internal Revenue Agent, for example.

4195. One thing that must be said about our tax laws is they're making it impossible to gain the whole world.

4196. Rolling in money is a painful exercise today because it is spiked with hidden taxes.

4197. Taxes are ruining the pleasures of living — nowadays the first thing the father of a new baby rejoices about is the fact that he has a new tax deduction.

4198. If envy and love each could be taxed, any government could bring in at least tenfold more money by taxing envy.

4199. There are two things in America that are growing bigger together — garbage cans and taxes.

4200. With the state the world is in, any government could raise unlimited revenue simply by taxing sins.

4201. Whoever said you can't take it with you must have been an Internal Revenue agent.

4202. At no time is it easier to keep your mouth shut than during an internal revenue audit of your tax return.

4203. You can't tell if opportunities are worthwhile today until you check them after taxes.

4204. The most heavily travelled pathways that lead to Washington are paved with taxes.

4205. Every time I pay my taxes I feel as though the government is on my payroll.

TAXPAYER

4206. An honest taxpayer is one who has just had last year's tax return reveiewed with him by an Internal Revenue Agent.

4207. A smart taxpayer is one who knows all the deductions.

4208. Judging from the size of Uncle Sam's bite, the taxpayer is the biggest fish of all.

4209. One thing the average taxpayer is sure to see these days is red!

4210. A tolerant taxpayer is a bachelor who votes for a new school bond issue.

4211. One of the hardest things to teach a taxpayer is that honesty is more important than the consequences.

4212. Events of recent years without a doubt will make our up and coming generation of Americans bigger taxpayers than we are!

4213. There are two types of conscientious taxpayers — those who are conscientious about paying their taxes and those who are equally conscientious about evading them.

TAXI DRIVER

4214. Nobody prays harder for rain than a taxi driver who also is the father of six children.

4215. An enterprising taxi driver is one who starts his meter running the instant you wave him down.

TEACHERS

4216. If the cost of babysitters continues to rise, it will be cheaper to raise teachers' salaries and lengthen the school hours.

TEACHING

4217. Do not be afraid of teaching others everything you know; but don't try to tell them all you know at one time.

TEAMWORK

4218. Teamwork is like the wheels on a train — they help to move the engine forward. But until a single man starts the whole thing with an idea, teamwork has little reason for existence.

TEARS

4219. A woman never knows how worthwhile a cry is until she adds up how much she got out of it.

4220. When a woman cries for nothing, it is a sure sign that she's really sick.

TEEN-AGERS

4221. All it takes for some teen-age girls to grow up quickly is a young man to fall in love with.

4222. Nothing helps to get the telephone answered on the first ring like having a teen-age daughter in the house.

4223. Middle age has set in when you become exhausted by your teen-ager telling you how she spent an evening.

1224. Many a teen-age crush crumbles a girl for life.

1225. Most of the criticism adults make about teen-agers stems from envy.

TEETH

1226. Nothing encourages a man to put his tongue in his cheek like finding a new cavity in a back tooth.

1227. A woman with pretty teeth always has plenty of smile power.

1228. One of the surest ways to lose your teeth is to insult a fellow who is much stronger than you are.

1229. The proper way to clean your teeth is exactly the way you do it just before leaving for a dental appointment.

TELEPHONE

1230. An optimist is a man who decides to stand outside a telephone booth to make a call after the woman in it will hang up.

1231. A man has not developed complete control over his emotions until he can step into a shower and say "to hell with it" when the phone starts ringing.

1232. The best proof that Americans talk too much is the size of the nation's telephone bill.

1233. All you have to do to get a telephone call is step into a bathtub.

1234. Nothing cuts into a modern housewife's working time like putting a comfortable chair beside the telephone.

1235. Anybody who thinks that talk is cheap doesn't have a wife who makes long distance calls to mother.

4236. One time I really hate to hear the telephone ring for my wife is when we're halfway through the dishes.

TELEVISION

4237. The very best thing you can do to get the most out of television is to work while you're looking at it.

4238. Nothing helps a modern housewife to get an average day's work done like the television set going on the blink.

4239. Television has many critics, but not among manufacturers of snack items or furniture.

4240. The success of television is ample proof that laziness is a disease of the majority.

4241. One of the advantages of the 25-inch television picture is that Junior can't completely obstruct the view with his head.

4242. Television is not only replacing movies and housework, it is also doing quite a job on furniture.

4243. Middle age has arrived when a man's idea of pitching into something is to draw up a chair beside a TV set.

4244. A man has reached middle age when all it takes to exhaust him is an evening of television.

4245. A man knows he is master of the house if he can turn off the television without being challenged.

4246. Willpower is the ability to turn on your thinking apparatus instead of the TV set.

4247. Blessed is the man or woman today who is more eager to open the covers of a good book than to turn the knob of a TV.

4248. Television's popularity has grown from the fact that it makes real life for the average viewer so much easier to take by comparison with what they see on TV.

4249. The trouble with many people today is that the only time they are lost for something to do is when their television is out of order.

4250. There's a fortune awaiting the man who can invent a pill that will cure televisionitis.

TEMPER

4251. Temper, when lost, can damage an individual with the same kind of devastation that a lighted match can destroy a dry forest.

4252. There's no quicker way of cooking your goose than by letting your temper boil over.

4253. The fellow whose temper goes off with a bang usually is a bluff.

4254. You may as well make up your mind to keep your temper because nobody else wants it.

4255. Few things will do more to fire up a person's temper than being proven dead wrong.

TEMPERAMENT

4256. You can tell a lot about a man's temperament by what he says when he hits his thumb with a hammer.

TEMPTATION

4257. When some people flee temptation first they make sure to tie a leash to it.

4258. Time was when temptation spoke in a whisper; nowadays, it parks out front and toots a horn.

4259. Anytime a man is working hard he never has to worry about hearing temptation's knock.

4260. A wink is a temptation in rompers.

4261. You can learn a lesson from temptations — their persistence usually overcomes!

4262. Give a temptation an inch and before you know it you're in trouble a yard long!

4263. A little temptation is a dangerous thing because its job is to introduce you to a bigger one.

4264. Stubbornness is a virtue only when it is used to resist temptation.

4265. Temptations, unlike opportunities, will always give you many second chances.

4266. When it comes to keeping an eye on temptation, everybody has 20/20 vision.

4267. A smart girl is one who can keep temptations and opportunities fighting each other until she's ready to break the draw.

4268. Temptations are like bargains. You never know how badly you're being stung until after you've fallen for them.

4269. Middle age is the time of life when it takes a smaller and smaller temptation to talk a man out of doing some more work.

4270. Temptation is a good thing because you can measure the state of your health frequently by the size of the pain you must endure to resist it.

4271. There is nothing wrong with temptations as long as you know the right ones to avoid.

4272. Nothing is more boring to a man like a temptation that isn't there to resist.

TEN COMMANDMENTS

4273. Christians all agree on the Ten Commandments, but that's about where their agreement ends.

4274. Too many people are preoccupied chasing after happiness, when if they would only live according to the Ten Commandments happiness would overtake them.

4275. Nothing makes the ten commandments harder to remember than war or alcohol.

TENNIS

4276. Some of the best ties between father and son are the result of a tennis game.

4277. Competition between father and son is extremely healthy especially when it is demonstrated on a tennis court.

TERMITES

4278. Experience is what makes a man check the basement for termites when he buys his second house.

TEST

4279. When a woman wants to test a man's strength, she gets sick for a day or two and watches how he does at running the house.

TEXANS

4280. In Texas, the weathermen go overboard with tornado,

thunder storm and flood warnings. Ninety percent of the time they are proven wrong and this makes their listeners feel good. And that's why weathermen are so popular in Texas.

TEXTBOOK

4281. There's no better way to become an expert on something you know nothing about than by writing a textbook on it.

THANKSGIVING

4282. Each time the November elections are over, its easy to understand why Thanksgiving Day always follows them.

THEATER

4283. When you take a cold to the theater, a lot of other people are going to catch your date.

THERMOSTAT

4284. The first touch of spring or winter is usually felt by the thermostat.

THINKING

4285. It must be a scientific truth, judging from all I hear, that a person cannot talk and think at the same time.

4286. Thinking must be one of the most difficult tasks known to man — just by the great efforts people will make to avoid it.

4287. The trouble with many people who are deep in a train of thought is they're usually carrying too much freight.

4288. The trouble with some people who stop to think is that they stay parked.

THIRST

4289. Nothing makes a child thirstier than two o'clock in the morning.

4290. All a parent has to do to make a child thirsty is fall asleep.

THOUGHT

4291. A good speaker is one who thinks twice before he speaks once.

THOUGHTFULNESS

4292. The world is filled with thoughtful persons if you count only those who think of themselves.

4293. A thoughtful wife is one who arranges the bedroom furniture so the night table is beside her husband with the alarm clock on it.

THRIFT

4294. The best exercise for encouraging thrift is running out of money.

4295. We appreciate praise and money from people who are thrifty with them.

THRILLS

4296. There are few thrills quite like picking a yellow ticket from under a windshield wiper and discovering that it is only an advertisement.

4297. To appreciate the thrill that comes from making both ends meet, most adults have to keep watching a baby until it succeeds in getting a foot in its mouth.

4298. It's the unexpected things in life that provide the biggest thrills — like a neighbor stopping you on the street to tell you what a wonderful little boy your son is.

4299. There are few thrills in this life that can come up to the one you get when you correct a mistake you're sure you could have gotten away with.

TICKET

4300. A careful driver is one who has just received a traffic ticket.

TIME

4301. Time heals all things, including overenthusiasm for sex.

4302. All too often the only thing time does to the human head is to make it whiter and smoother.

4303. Nothing makes time more valuable than knowing the best thing to do with it.

4304. Nothing makes time more valuable than reaching the age of 70 in vigorous physical and mental health.

4305. A man with time on his hands is either serving it or waiting for his wife.

4306. The easiest way to find more time to do all the things you want to do is to turn off the television.

4307. A young man's future is about to be decided when his girlfriend starts showing up on time.

4308. An attractive girl can find a man in a matter of

minutes, but it usually takes her the rest of her life to make a good husband out of him.

4309. At no time does the end of a day come faster than when the fish are biting.

4310. Nothing makes a woman shop sensibly like not having enough time to do it in.

4311. The longest interval of time is between a woman's promise that she will be ready in five minutes and the time she finally shows up.

4312. I recommend killing time to anyone, provided they do so by working it to death.

4313. The kind of woman who usually makes a good wife is the one who spends twice as much time cooking the meals as she does prettying up.

4314. The surest way to get a new lease on life is to work time to death.

4315. Some people believe in taking as much of your time as they need to prove you're wrong.

4316. The economy with which one uses time or money usually depends on how little of each one there is left.

4317. People who complain that they cannot find time usually do a tremendous job trying to kill it.

4318. Time is useless unless you use it.

4319. One of the characteristics of the 20th century is that the only persons who seem to have enough time to sit down and relax are those who are serving it.

4320. Some of the laziest people I know are the world's best clock watchers.

4321. Most of the social ills of the world could be made to

disappear if we could get people to reckon the cost of things in terms of time instead of dollars.

4322. Nothing makes time more valuable than knowing exactly what to do with it.

4323. Nothing makes you more impressed by the value of every minute than a taxi ride in New York City traffic.

4324. Nothing adds to your leisure time more than doing things — now!

4325. When it comes to stretching time you can't beat women in the 28-29 age bracket.

4326. Nothing makes time fly faster than parking your car beside a meter.

4327. The longest minute in the world is the one a traffic cop takes to write you a ticket.

4328. With all the time-saving devices that Americans have they have more trouble than anybody else to find time for all they want to do.

4329. The secret of getting the most mileage out of time is to work it the hardest when you know you've got the most of it behind you.

4330. The easiest way to find all of the time to do the things you want to do is to turn off the television.

4331. Nothing is more tiring for a conscientious man than trying to waste time.

4332. Time is a fleeting commodity, as anybody can discover by reserving some of it on a parking meter.

TIMING

4333. The secret of striking while the iron is hot is to do something about a good idea before it loses its steam.

TIREDNESS

4334.   A really tired woman is one who can't drum up enough energy to tell you she is.

TOLERANCE

4335.   Tolerance is the ability to listen to another person tell you one of your best jokes.

4336.   Tolerance consists in giving the other fellow every chance to prove that you're wrong — when you're certain that you're right.

4337.   Tolerance is the ability to be kind to dumb animals, especially when they're human beings.

4338.   Tolerance is the ability to listen to a person describe the same ailment you have.

4339.   Tolerance is the ability to listen to a fish story and let on that you believe it.

4340.   True tolerance consists in loving others for their virtues while you overlook their faults.

4341.   Tolerance consists in seeing things with your heart instead of with your eyes.

4342.   True tolerance consists in treating people you like and don't like with the same consideration.

4343.   Tolerance consists in giving the other fellow every chance to prove that you're wrong ... when you're certain that you're right.

4344.   True tolerance consists in realizing that you can explain the behavior of people you don't like by blaming it on their body chemistry.

4345. Tolerance is using your eyes and your ears in search of only what is good in others.

4346. True tolerance is the ability to love someone who obviously has a great dislike for you.

4347. If your tolerance towards the mistakes made by your fellowmen increases as your head grows smoother and whiter it means you have made many of the same mistakes.

4348. Tolerance consists in giving the other fellow every chance to prove that you're wrong — when you can prove that you're right.

4349. Tolerance consists in listening to a person who could not possibly do something to advance your own interests.

4350. True tolerance is the ability to let people be themselves without thinking anything worse or better of them for it.

4351. Tolerance is the ability to listen to a person describe the same ailment as you have.

TOMBSTONES

4352. The most enduring mark of many an executive is often a tombstone.

4353. I admire tombstones becuase they at least speak well of a man when he's down.

4354. When it comes to talking about people, take a tip from the tombstone and never say anything against a man when he's down.

4355. The only salesmen who can afford to sit around and wait for their customers are in the tombstone business.

4356. Tombstones aren't so democratic; after all, the rich fellows usually have more weighing on their chests than the poor fellows.

4357. Most of the world's indispensable persons are now resting under tombstones.

TOMORROW

4358. There's no surer way to insure a better tomorrow than by starting out now to make a better today.

4359. The best things to put off until tomorrow are the ones that will get you into trouble if you do them today.

TONGUE

4360. Most people know how to hold their tongue, but it is only the smart ones who do.

4361. Women have very long tongues by which many a man has been hanged.

4362. The best way to hold your tongue is frequently.

4363. The hardest part of using your tongue is not to lick yourself with it.

TONICS

4364. Of all the tonics devised by man none is as stimulating as a good day's work.

TOOL SHED

4365. Nothing raises your opinion of your immediate neighbor like a full tool-shed you can help yourself to.

4366. The most popular man in any neighborhood is the one who has the best equipped tool-shed.

TOP

4367. One place you can always be sure there's standing room only is at the top.

4368. The reason there's always room at the top is so many people become satisfied long before they get there.

4369. People who are top-heavy usually are easy to upset.

TORTURES

4370. Women will endure the tortures of the damned in silence to get thin, but for no other purpose.

TOYS

4371. How much a father spends for his son's toys isn't nearly as important as how much time he spends playing with them.

TRAFFIC

4372. The most annoying kind of Sunday driver is the one who is out trying to drive a hard bargain.

TRAFFIC COP

4373. A considerate traffic cop is one who will listen to your story from beginning to end before starting to write your ticket.

4374. The only time it pays to listen to someone who is trying to stop you from getting ahead is when the person happens to be a traffic cop.

4375. The longest minute in the world is the one a traffic cop takes to overtake you.

4376. You know a woman is in love with her husband if she smiles at him the way she does at a traffic cop.

4377. A considerate traffic cop is one who doesn't bother to take his gloves off before writing your ticket.

TRAFFIC LIGHTS

4378. Some persons go through life like traffic lights, dwelling for only a short time on caution.

TRAINING

4379. When it comes to training a child to follow the straight and narrow path, a parent ought to try using a ruler now and then.

4380. If you will train yourself never to believe bad news when you first hear it, you will discover that nine times out of ten somebody got the story all wrong.

TRANQUILIZERS

4381. When it comes to finding an effective tranquilizer it is hard to beat money.

4382. At no time is the sale of tranquilizers higher than at tax payment deadlines.

4383. Anyone who is calm these days must be taking tranquilizers.

TRACK RECORD

4384. You know a man is going places if what he says and his track record are equally creditable.

TRANSGRESSOR

4385. The reason the way of the transgressor is so hard is the traffic on it is so heavy.

TRAVEL

4386. Travel does more than broaden one's horizon — it also does a remarkable job of flattening your wallet.

4387. Nothing makes a man go places like a woman who likes to.

4388. At no time is the sight of home more endearing to you than after you've travelled a couple of thousand miles trying to get away from it.

4389. The trouble with many people who boast that they have arrived is how little time they stay before making the return trip.

4390. The really happy man is one who enjoys a plane trip even when his baggage is lost enroute.

TRAVELERS

4391. The best travellers I have known always have insisted on taking their own snapshots.

4392. The best travelers in life are those who can pack the most in a 24-hour day.

TREAT

4393. One of the best ways to treat yourself is to be good to somebody else.

4394. The most expensive treat you can give yourself is to tell the other fellow exactly what you think of him!

TRIAL

4395. Some men achieve success by trial and trial again.

TRICKS

4396. People who learn all the tricks of the trade usually aren't much good at it.

TRIP

4397. Nothing puts zest into planning a trip like the knowledge that it is going to be on an expense account.

TROUBLES

4398. When it comes to finding trouble, everybody has 20/20 vision.

4399. Some people manage to avoid walking into trouble by sitting down on the job.

4400. The trouble with some people who put their heads together is they don't bang them hard enough.

4401. All you have to do to keep your troubles alive is to nurse them.

4402. Troubles and weeds thrive on lack of attention.

4403. Whether or not you get yourself up to your neck in trouble depends on how you use what's above it.

4404. Those persons with the most troubles in this life say all they think and believe all they hear.

4405. People who like to stir up trouble usually do it with the chip on their shoulder.

4406. The trouble with many people who stick to their guns is they usually wind up behind bars.

4407. People who brood over their troubles are bound to hatch a lot of bad eggs.

4408. Most people find running a business is no trouble at all — as long as it is the other fellow's.

4409. The best things to put off until tomorrow are the ones that will get you into trouble if you do them today.

4410. One thing a person can always borrow without collateral is trouble.

4411. The trouble with many politicians today is that the only time they fall down on the job is immediately after they get elected.

4412. Nothing helps to keep your troubles alive like being a good nursemaid to them.

4413. One of the troubles with many modern marriages is the way husband and wife race each other — to get home from work.

4414. Ninety percent of the world's ills can be traced to the fact that our traditions and our laws — both civil and religious — are crude guideposts for behavior.

4415. Nothing helps to magnify your troubles like putting a spotlight on them.

4416. When it comes to sharing your troubles with others most people are philanthropists.

4417. There is no surer way of getting rid of your troubles than by letting on that you don't have any.

4418. Moaning over your troubles is silly. Few persons ever listen to you, and those who do are apt to like the sound.

4419. Persons who are always throwing light on their troubles would find that most of them would disappear if they were left in the dark.

4420. Nothing will make you forget all your troubles like finding yourself in urgent need of a rest room.

4421. Always remember that troubles have their own weaknesses, and if you ignore them it is surprising how many can get lost!

4422. The man who smiles when he observes someone else under fire probably does so because he lit the fuse.

TRUNK

4423. When a man respects a woman's bark, it is probably because she has a pretty trunk.

TRUST

4424. The more you trust people the less are the chances that their friendships will rust.

4425. The person I trust the least is one who is suspicious of everybody else.

4426. A woman who doesn't trust her husband to mail her letters usually trusts him in every other way.

4427. A man's trust in God diminishes in direct proportion to the growth of his power over people.

TRUTH

4428. Turning up the wick of truth is the surest way to dampen the sting of trouble.

4429. Any time the truth shocks you, the chances are it is well grounded.

4430. At no time does telling the truth make you feel better than right after filing your income tax return.

4431. Nothing is harder to see than the naked truth.

4432. Owning up to the truth is like taking medicine — it may not be pleasant at first, but you'll feel a lot better later.

4433. One of the hardest things to teach a child is that truth is more important than consequences.

4434. Any time the truth doesn't hurt it's a good idea to double-check it.

4435. I never have been able to understand why 50 percent of the religious people I know profess truths — and the other 50 percent profess different truths.

4436. A woman isn't afraid to tell the truth, but she is afraid that the truth will tell on her.

4437. Some persons are as truthful as a magnet — they can be twisted in whatever direction they are most attracted to.

4438. The truth hurts especially when you don't own up to it.

4439. Nothing is harder to straighten out than a distorted truth.

4440. To be truthful requires that you must say much that people will object to hearing or believing.

4441. The young people of America are more responsible than anyone else for exposing the naked truth.

4442. Truth is beauty and it is most clearly demonstrated either by the naked truth or a naked woman.

4443. A small town is a place where a man with a black eye has to give you the true explanation for it.

4444. Experience is what makes a man tell his wife the truth the second time.

4445. If you are more likely to tell the truth when you are talking about somebody else instead of yourself — you're just about average.

4446. An optimist is one who accepts something as true, a pessimist one who accepts the same thing as untrue, and a wise man is one who believes only half of it.

4447. Truth will win every argument if you will stick with it long enough.

4448. Nothing is more exhausting in life than trying to hide a lie.

4449. Nothing makes the truth hurt like abusing it.

4450. The only thing that gets hurt when you kick the truth in the teeth is your soul.

4451. Always tell the truth and many people will accuse you of distorting the facts.

4452. Truth, very often, turns out to be something you read or hear which gives you much pleasure if you believe it.

4453. Any time the truth doesn't hurt, it's a good idea to double-check it.

4454. Nothing puts spice into the truth like a pinch of lie.

TWENTIETH CENTURY

4455. History will record that in terms of the tens of millions of human beings involved, the savagery of times past was but a prelude to the barbarity of man to man in the so-called golden third quarter of the 20th century.

TWO-CAR GARAGE

4456. The two-car garage is what paved the way for three-car families and two all-day working parents!

TYPING

4457. An ideal stenographer is one who can type as fast as she can talk.

UNCLE SAM

4458. Judging from the size of Uncle Sam's bite, the taxpayer is the biggest fish of all.

4459. These days Uncle Sam doesn't try to make ends meet — he just tries to keep track of how far beyond his means the taxpayers are letting him go.

4460. Many modern Americans have forgotten that Uncle Sam owes most of his success to wearing overalls.

UNDERDOG

4461. Once you've helped an underdog it can be dangerous to turn your back on him.

UNDERSTANDING

4462. The best way to make yourself understood is to speak in short, infrequent sentences.

4463. An understanding man is one who will admit that you know more about the subject than he does.

UNDERTAKERS

4464. You know a man must have lived a good life if you notice at his funeral that the undertaker is in tears.

UNEXPECTED

4465. The unexpected things in life are what provide some of the biggest thrills — like a neighbor stopping you and telling you what a perfect little gentleman your son is.

UNHAPPINESS

4466. A sure sign of unhappiness is the eagerness with which a person tries to share it with you.

UPPER CRUST

4467. Before a person can rise to the upper crust he's got to make plenty of dough.

UNSELFISHNESS

4468. The law of unselfishness does seem quite fair, for the more unselfish you are, the more satisfactions out of life you are sure to get.

UPSETS

4469. Occasional upsets are good for everybody because it usually takes a champion to settle them.

USEFULNESS

4470. Sometimes to make yourself useful you must jockey into a position where you look like the best bet to fill an opening.

4471. The best way to figure out how far you should go on a vacation is to consult your bank balance.

4472. Nothing tends to flatten your fiscal stature like a vacation.

4473. There's nothing like a vacation with the entire family to make you appreciate that taking life easy can be hard work.

4474. Start saving now for next year's vacation and you'll probably have enough to pay for half of one.

4475. About the only thing worse than returning from a vacation broke is running into friends who didn't even know where you were spending all your money.

4476. The trouble with most people who go on a vacation is they spend it on the outskirts of their budget.

4477. It is easy to tell when your vacation is coming to an end — all you have to do is look at what's left in your wallet.

4478. There's nothing like a seashore vacation — especially the mildew, the mosquitoes and the sand in your bed.

4479. A vacation is one thing you always come back from with less money and less hair.

4480. A vacation away from work is followed usually by two weeks vacation at work.

4481. When it comes to getting a good rest, there is nothing more tiring to some people than a vacation.

4482. Some businessmen find that the only way they can relax on vacation is to take their secretary with them.

4483. Wouldn't it be nice if by a paid vacation, your company meant you could take it on an expense account?

4484. Most persons don't really enjoy their vacations until they start boasting about it to their friends.

4485. Nothing makes a vacation look better than hindsight.

VALUE

4486. A man's true cash value is how much he is worth if he were suddenly asked by God to check in.

4487. People who criticize their employer are under-estimating his value to them.

4488. Nothing makes something more valuable to you than throwing it away a day before you discover how badly you need it.

4489. One of the most valuable things you can save for old age is plenty of laughter.

4490. Praise can be especially valuable to you — when you shower it on your enemies.

4491. Nothing increases the value of a few well-chosen words like saying them briefly.

4492. The most valuable thing a man can have up his sleeve is a good strong arm.

4493. The dollar is still worth as much as ever when you find a man who works like the devil to earn a buck.

VERSATILITY

4494. To see versatility manifested in the most remarkable way you must study how a mother of eight children manages to make ends meet.

4495. A man never discovers how versatile he is with a pencil until he sits down to make out his income tax return.

VICES

4496. I find persons with vices far more interesting and considerate than persons who try to hide the fact that they have them.

4497. Everybody has vices — only different ones.

VICTORY

4498. There is little satisfaction in any victory that is achieved by always playing it safe.

4499. In retrospect, one always will discover that no victory is more fruitless than a victory motivated by revenge.

4500. Victory is at the end of a very long road — but it always is a straight road.

VIEWING

4501. One of the hardest things to understand is why they call a viewing a wake.

VIRTUE

4502. The noblest virtues are those that emerge from the ashes of sin.

4503. Virtue, at times, turns out to be any kind of behavior by the other person that reminds you of you.

4504. The number of virtues a child possesses increases as the distance of his house from yours.

VIRTUOSITY

4505. Beware the outwardly virtuous person — the chances are a worm is eating him inside.

VIRUSES

4506. Few things contribute more to the health of the body than a 24-hour intestinal bug that does a complete clean-out job.

VISION

4507. If we could see ourselves as others see us, one thing we'd need is a pair of rose-colored glasses.

4508. Good vision consists in seeing as far ahead as you can and, on getting there, never looking back.

4509. Usually a man's vision is at its weakest when he's in a proposing mood.

4510. People who do their duty as they see it seldom are credited with having 20/20 vision.

4511. One time you can be sure you have 20/20 vision is when you go looking for trouble.

4512. Nothing improves a person's vision like an opportunity to get into trouble.

4513. When it comes to spotting a blonde hair on a man's coat all wives have 20/20 vision.

4514. 20/20 vision is the ability to see the trivial at first sight.

4515. 20/20 vision is the ability to look at an obstacle and see a golden opportunity in it.

4516. People who see the handwriting on the wall seldom read it until it is too late.

4517. Today, 20/20 vision is the ability to see your way well enough to make both ends meet.

4518. A person is average only so long as he can see the other fellow's faults; he becomes above average when he can also see his own.

4519. All politicians claim to have 20/20 vision up to and including election day.

4520. Good vision consists of being able to see the trees and the forest.

4521. All women have perfect vision when it comes to spotting a man ten feet in front of them — or ten feet behind them.

4522. All of us have poor vision when it comes to spotting trouble at a distance.

4523. Nothing is harder for most people to see than the obvious.

VISITOR

4524. A welcome visitor is one you hate to see leave.

VISITORS

4525. Visitors who don't knock when they come to see you sometimes do after they go.

4526. The kind of visitors who make us unhappy are those who are here today and here tomorrow.

4527. Visitors always make us happy ... some when they come, others when they go.

4528. The kind of visitors who make us happy are those who are here today and gone tomorrow.

VOTERS

4529. Perhaps the best way to get people out to vote would be to propose a law which wouldn't let them.

WAITING

4530. An obedient husband is one who would not dare get upset while waiting for his wife.

4531. They also serve who stand, and wait on you.

4532. The trouble with some people who enjoy waiting is they're lazy.

4533. An optimist is a man who idles the car in front of the house while he waits for his wife.

4534. The latest thing in clothes generally is a woman you're waiting for.

WALKING

4535. Running out of gas is one of the few remaining reasons you can get an American to take a walk.

4536. The dog is one of the few remaining reasons why some Americans can be persuaded to go for a walk.

4537. Someday before the end of the 20th Century, human beings will discover that the greatest wonder drug of modern medicine is the lost art of walking.

WALL STREET

4538. Any physician can follow the ups and downs of Wall Street by using his stethoscope on his patients.

WARS

4539. The biggest farce of man's history has been the argument that wars are fought to save civilization.

4540. Hindsight can change the horrors of wars into the glories of wars.

4541. The only people who would have the courage to outlaw wars are those who lost their lives fighting them.

4542. The problems of the world can never be solved on the battlefields; the only possible location for their solution lies in the heads of men.

4543. The real culprit that proliferates wars is not power but poverty, without which not enough men could be found to do the fighting.

WASTE

4544. The most thoroughly wasted of all days is one on which you have not done somebody a good turn.

4545. Very often people who are scrupulous not to waste a scrap of paper are equally scrupulous not to speak a kind word.

4546. The most thoroughly wasted of all days is one on which you have not done somebody a good turn.

WASTEBASKETS

4547. The busiest men I know always have the fullest wastebaskets.

WATCH

4548. A punctual man is a fellow who doesn't own a watch.

WATER

4549. Time does change all things — now the cry is "Oh for water, water, everywhere — potable water, that is!"

WATERGATE

4550. Watergate is clear proof of the fact that when it comes to ingenuity the human mind is at its best trying to cover things up!

WEAKER SEX

4551. When it comes to letting her husband move the furniture around, all women will claim they are the weaker sex.

WEAKNESS

4552. In weakness there is strength, only when your weakness happens to be the girl you're in love with.

4553. No weakness need be a handicap to you unless you decide to live with it.

WEALTH

4554. The surest way to increase your wealth is to get another person to pay you for showing him how to increase his.

4555. The richest man in the world is the one to whom people owe the greatest number of debts of kindness.

4556. The richest man in the world is one who is married, has a loving wife, several children, and is completely out of debt.

4557. A rich man is one who refuses to give up the search for his golf ball, even after he finds a better one than he lost.

4558. A rich man is one who can plan two vacations a year . . . one with the children and one without them.

4559. At no time is controlling one's diet more important or more difficult than when the cost of food is of no consequence to your budget.

4560. A rich man lives on one side of the railroad tracks and gets his income from the people who live on the other side.

4561. You are wealthy when you have enough money to buy the things you've always wanted — but you don't.

4562. True wealth consists in being satisfied with what you've got — no matter how much of it you haven't.

4563. To become wealthy it is far more important to know best how to spend money than how to earn it.

4564. The richest people in the world are those who are making ends meet without breaking a law.

4565. A preoccupation with acquiring wealth far beyond that needed for maximum financial security is a mental disease.

4566. No man could possibly be wealthier than I am — I owe no debts, I have my health, I have enough money saved in case I lose my job — and internal revenue has given me a clean audit!

4567. One sure way to increase your wealth is to slash your wants.

4568. True wealth consists not in how much money you have but in how much you enjoy what you have.

4569. A man is rich in proportion to the number of invitations for publicity that he can turn down.

4570. Wealth is an asset much like knowledge — and those with the least of either are most irresponsible with them.

4571. Wealth can only be secure if those who have it make a determined effort to make others wealthy too.

4572. Wealth that is achieved almost overnight can usually be traced more to shady dealings than to brilliant flashes of genius.

4573. A truly rich man is one who can get his children to run into his arms when his hands are empty.

4574. Some of the richest people I've known always pretended they were poor.

4575. Wealth and old age are never overnight happenings, but you can be sure they've been long-time partners.

4576. Some of the poorest people in the world are well-to-do-people who are unhappy because they are not rich enough.

WEAR

4577. An easy job, like an easy chair, usually is the first to wear itself out.

WEATHER

4578. Every 4 years during the period between the nomination of presidential candidates in the summer and the elections in the fall, the United States endures its most severe wind storms all of which subside immediately after the new president is elected.

4579. A reliable weather forecaster is one whose microphone is close enough to a window so that he can decide whether to use the official forecast or make up one of his own.

4580. A contested man is one who never runs anything down except the weather.

WEATHERMAN

4581. One thing you have to admit about a weatherman's mistakes is that he doesn't leave a scientific stone unturned to make them.

WEDDING

4582. The reason some girls insist on a double-ring ceremony is they feel it strengthens their hand.

4583. There is no time in a young woman's life when she enjoys sweeping more than when she sweeps down the aisle.

4584. Nothing strengthens a double-ring marriage ceremony like 2 people who are madly in love with each other.

WEDDING RING

4585. When it comes to stopping a man's circulation, the best tourniquet of all is a wedding ring.

4586. A smart girl is one who doesn't believe that a man is single just because he isn't wearing a wedding band on his left index finger.

4587. The only time some married men will wear their wedding band is when they happen to be out with their wife.

4588. A happily married man is one who can feel his wedding ring tighten around his finger when he's alone with a pretty single woman.

4589. You can tell how you feel about a neighbor by what you do with weeds that are within your easy reach, but on his side of the fence.

4590. Nothing improves a weed's appearance like seeing it on the other side of your fence.

WEIGHT

4591. Any man who believes in pulling his own weight must keep so busy that he has no time for anything else.

4592. When a man starts throwing his weight around he's bound to knock himself off-balance.

4593. One of the surest ways for a man to control his weight is to buy a half-dozen expensive shirts with collars on the small size.

4594. The first sign that a man is throwing his weight around is that he starts losing his poise.

4595. No matter how broad a man's shoulders are they will buckle under the weight of a swelled head.

4596. The best way to throw your weight around is by dieting.

4597. It's a clever man who can throw his weight around without losing his balance.

4598. A man who is pulling his own weight never has any left over to throw around.

4599. Some women would be more successful at losing weight if they would stop chewing the fat.

4600. It is easy to spot the fellow who is pulling his own weight around by the way it requires his undivided attention.

WELCOME CHANGE

4601.   A housewife's idea of welcome change is anything she can salvage from a ten-dollar bill.

WELFARE

4602.   The fallacy of the welfare state is that it is intent on helping those whom even God refuses to.

WELL-ROUNDEDNESS

4603.   Most of the well-rounded people I know are either standing still or rolling down hill.

WENCH

4604.   Nothing will loosen the nut at the wheel quicker than a wench.

WET BLANKET

4605.   Anyone who goes through life being a wet blanket is bound to get cold treatment.

WHOLE SHOW

4606.   Frequently persons who like to be the whole show end up being the whole audience.

WIDOW

4607.   The saddest trend in the world today is the steep climb in the curve that shows the increase in the number of wealthy widows.

4608. The world is filled with widows who owe more to aggressive life insurance salesmen than they do to their deceased husbands.

4609. A widow is a woman with a burned-out husband — dead or alive!

WIDOWHOOD

4610. When it comes to bringing the best out of a woman, it is hard to beat widowhood.

WIFE

4611. No self-respecting wife will show concern about her husband talking to another woman unless, of course, she is much prettier than she is.

4612. When your wife asks you to do a little chore around the house it may really mean she has much bigger plans in mind.

4613. A man really loves his wife, if he will let her break in his new car.

4614. There are two times you can be sure that your wife will be at your side — during a lightning storm, and when a mouse is loose in the room.

4615. The most important thing a woman can do for her husband is to love him, love him, love him!

4616. Usually it is better to let your wife handle the money because in the end it will amount to the same thing.

4617. The most stimulating person in any man's life is a wife who is madly in love with him.

4618. A contented wife is one who can't think of a better man she could have married.

4619. A woman will go to almost any extreme to put a man back on his feet if he's comfortable, and her husband.

4620. The most dangerous way to select a wife is by how well her clothes fit her.

4621. A wife smiles with her husband when he is at the top because she knows she helped to put him there.

4622. Sometimes the pipeline to a man's dough is his wife.

4623. There are two ways a man can make sure of getting his wife to listen to him: Talk about buying something for himself, or for her.

4624. A smart wife is one who knows how to retie a package that her husband has hidden from her.

4625. Few things prove to me more that my wife still loves me very much than to discover that she has sewed on a missing button or replaced a trouser pocket that had a hole in it before I got around to mentioning them to her.

4626. A happily married man is one whose personality remains unchanged — whether his wife is with him or not.

4627. No matter how big a dynamo a man may be, he still needs a good wife to provide the spark.

4628. A man learns the real value of cooperation when his wife starts helping him with the dinner dishes.

4629. A self-made man is frequently one who can stand up and take his hat off to his wife.

4630. A clever wife is one who gets a mink coat by letting her husband wear the pants.

4631. The best way to surprise your wife is frequently.

4632. Nothing does more to improve a man's disposition than a wife who is very healthy — and wealthy.

4633. Nobody can push a man into a high income bracket like a wife who needs the money.

4634. A successful housewife is one who showed her husband how to be successful.

4635. Few things are more conducive to a happy marriage than getting to like the things your wife cooks for you.

4636. Money and brains may provide a man with the fuels of life, but he still needs a good wife to provide the spark.

4637. You can tell a lot about a man's wife by where he lands after getting up from the dinner table — in the living room or in the kitchen.

4638. A man can be sure his wife is up to something when she tries to get around him.

4639. You know a man is still very much in love with his wife if he jumps to his feet when she walks into the room.

4640. A wife who knows when and how to praise her husband doesn't have to be a good cook.

4641. A man's greatest asset is a wife who is madly in love with him.

4642. The easiest way to find out what is on your wife's mind is to sit down in a comfortable chair and listen!

4643. The average woman will never listen in on the extension phone — unless, of course, she's not sure who her husband is talking to.

WIGS

4644. Women are hard to understand; they seldom go bald yet insist on wearing wigs.

WILD OATS

4645. Some persons sow their wild oats and then starve from lack of nourishment when they're forced to eat the crop.

WILL

4646. A woman enjoys cooperating with a man when he has a very strong will   as long as she is its sole beneficiary.

4647. A man who doesn't have a will of his own always can marry one.

4648. It is a difficult and painful task to make a will, because then, for the first time, you realize that you are living on leased securities, and that you cannot take anything but your character with you.

4649. One of the best ways to make sure that your own will is prepared properly is to serve as executor for somebody else who did not leave one.

4650. A will is one of the first things a relative thinks about on hearing that another relative has died.

WILLPOWER

4651. A smart girl is one who has enough willpower to resist a man's advances and enough willpower to block his retreat.

4652. Willpower is the ability to stick to a diet for two days in a row.

WINNERS

4653. Sometimes a woman never discovers what a poor winner she is until after she's baggged her man.

4654. To win you must want to.

4655. The winners in life are the losers who keep on trying.

WINTER

4656. Nothing leaves a man colder in winter than adding up the fuel bill.

WISDOM

4657. Wisdom is just common sense dressed up in Sunday clothes.

4658. Wisdom is manifested by a person in its highest form when he comes to you and asks for help!

4659. An adult may see human wisdom at work by observing a person enjoying his work.

4660. A wise man is one who knows that it pays him to speak well of others, or not to speak about them at all.

4661. Just as many a fool passes for a wise man by keeping his mouth shut, so also many an evil man passes for a great benefactor by keeping his mouth open.

4662. True wisdom consists in expressing a boundless capacity for making the most — of today!

4663. An adult may see human wisdom manifested in its highest form by watching a child's boundless capacity for making the most of the next ten minutes.

4664. There is no greater wisdom a man can acquire than the ability to discard yesterdays and concentrate every ounce of mental and physical energy on making the most of today and preparing better for tomorrow.

4665. Divorce laws should be made by men who are married to witches, abortion laws by women who were butchered by quacks, and religious laws by sinners.

4666. Wisdom is the ability to spot and listen to that rare person who really knows what he's talking about.

4667. Wisdom is the ability to detect both the important and the urgent, and then knowing which to tackle first.

4668. Wisdom is the ability to act upon foresight with the advantage of hindsight.

4669. Where ignorance is folly, 'tis bliss to be wise.

4670. The only time a wise man thinks out loud is when he is sure that nobody is listening to him.

4671. Most wise old men owe their reputation for wisdom to their longevity.

4672. Few answers will make you appear wiser in the eyes of your fellowmen than "I do not know"!

4673. Nothing increases a man's reputation for wisdom like living to 80 or 90.

WISE MAN

4674. A very wise man frequently is someone who is an expert at concealing his ignorance.

4675. The difference between a wise man and a fool is in their hides — a fool can be skinned more than once.

4676. A wise man learns that defeat is only like a disappointing meal — and he develops a new appetite to relish a better one the next time.

WISHBONE

4677. The only part of the human anatomy that continues to grow after 21 is the wishbone.

WISHES

4678. Be conservative in your wishes or you will inherit bigger problems than you can cope with.

WIVES

4679. The easiest way to find out what's on your wife's mind is to sit yourself down in a comfortable chair.

4680. Some men embrace their wives as though they were afraid they may have to marry them again.

4681. The best wives generally are those who are not too pretty, not too thin, or not too fat.

4682. A smart wife is one who knows how to retie a package that her husband has hidden from her.

4683. As long as your wife tries to improve your table manners, your grammar, your posture, your attire, and your station in life, you know, at least, that she still loves you.

4684. All a man has to do to humor his boss is to offer to do the dishes for her.

4685. A wife doesn't mind her husband saying he can read her like a book as long as he doesn't put her on the shelf.

4686. The surest way for a wife to surprise her husband is to be ready ahead of time.

WOMAN

4687. A really sick woman is one who is too tired to talk.

4688. A beautiful woman among any number of men constitutes a majority.

4689. You can tell what a woman thinks of her husband by how proudly she Mrs. him.

4690. A woman is young only once, but it's a very long once.

4691. A contented married woman is one who can't think of a better man she could have married.

4692. Sometimes a woman never discovers what a poor winner she is until after she's bagged her man.

4693. Sometimes the biggest obstacle in a man's life is a woman who likes to make up his mind for him.

4694. A successful woman is one who isn't as interested in knowing all the answers as she is in getting a man to ask the right questions.

4695. Some women take up painting only because they're trying to save face.

4696. In the final analysis, what a woman looks for in a man is fiscal fitness.

4697. Whether or not a woman will pay any attention to what her husband is saying depends on how pretty the woman is that he is talking to.

4698. A woman never knows her true capabilities until her husband loses his.

4699. A woman who is an expert cook seldom has much trouble getting her husband to eat out of her hand.

4700. When a woman gets dressed up to look her best, she looks for the best she can.

4701. Any woman who is worth her weight in gold is probably a big success at keeping it under control.

4702. A woman who is an expert cook never has to argue with her husband to get what she wants.

4703. Any time a woman dresses to please her husband you can be sure she's careful of how much she pays for them.

4704. A truly contented woman is one who asks for no greater calling in life than to mother the children of the man she loves.

4705. When a woman becomes the light in a man's life, she automatically gets to control the switch, too.

4706. The first thing a woman should do to make a successful husband out of a man is to admire him.

4707. When a man respects a woman's bark, it is probably because she has a pretty trunk.

4708. Two things a woman always underestimates are her age, and the time it will take her to get ready.

4709. When a woman gets dressed up to stalk a man she usually props her feet on high heels.

4710. Nobody is harder on a woman's age than another woman guessing it.

4711. The hardest part of a woman's day is the half hour before her husband is due home from work.

WOMAN DRIVER

4712. A satisfied woman driver is one who has just succeeded in parking safely in a spot that a group of onlookers thought was too small.

4713. Sometimes when a woman driver gets off to a quick start, it's by accident.

4714. A careful woman driver is one who can carry on a conversation with both hands on the wheel.

4715. The safest time to pass a woman driver is when she's parked.

4716. When it comes to making a grade, a woman driver doesn't believe in letting anything stand in her way.

4717. All a woman needs to pass any grade is a car under her.

4718. A happily married man is one who holds the car door open for his wife so she can get into the driver's seat.

4719. The only time a woman's intuition can get her into trouble is when she is trying to decide whether to make a right turn or a left turn.

4720. About the only time a woman driver pays any attention to curves is when she's getting dressed.

4721. Sometimes a driver with a pretty dimple in her cheek can put an ugly dent in your fender.

WOMEN

4722. Nothing can stop a woman in the middle of a sentence like the arrival of another woman with two men.

4723. Women are consistent creatures, that is, consistently unpredictable.

4724. The easiest way for a woman to lose her husband is to insist that he follow her directions along the highway.

4725. From the way some women dress, it is obvious they cannot be trusted with secrets.

4726. A woman's idea of a good cry is one that gets the intended result.

4727. When it comes to sizing up a man, what most women weigh most heavily are his fiscal assets.

4728. It is with women as with chemicals; some of the most explosive ones are quite innocent-looking.

4729. Two things women always are trying to rearrange are their furniture and their weight.

4730. When it comes to getting into an evening gown some women don't go far enough!

4731. Women will slave to keep shipshape as long as they know they are see-worthy.

4732. Women always help their husbands get ahead; some by inspiring their husbands to earn more, others by spending more than their husband's earn.

4733. No woman will doubt a man's word when he's telling her that she's beautiful.

4734. The trouble with the bulk of most women is where it usually shows.

4735. A smart woman knows that men are willing to pay much more than a penny for her thoughts.

4736. Nothing adds poise to an attractive woman like a successful husband standing beside her.

4737. You can always interest a woman in taking a chance as long as it is a slim one.

4738. Any time you can get a woman to say just a few words, you should thank her for them.

4739. A woman reaches middle age as soon as she will wear shoes that fit her.

4740. When a woman can read a man like an open book — she means cover up to cover up.

4741. Most women have inquiring minds that become sharper right after they get married.

4742. A smart woman with a nose for business knows what perfume to use.

4743. One time you can accuse a woman of overdoing it is when she dresses to kill.

4744. One advantage of putting women in the back seat is you'll never run out of gas.

4745. One thing some women go through faster than men is a red light.

4746. Women are creatures of extremes — you can make them deliriously happy by putting something new on their head or on their feet.

4747. A contented woman is one who can't think of a better man that she could have married.

4748. When a woman doesn't outlive a man today, it is usually by accident.

4749. A woman's arithmetic is never better than when she's using her intuition to get your number.

4750. Women love to be bullied — provided it is done in a gentlemanly way.

4751. When a group of women start putting 2 and 2 together you can be sure that a couple of divorces are in the making.

4752. From the looks of things you would think designers' of women's clothes were in the show business.

4753. Nothing arouses a woman's curiosity like a neatly tied package that her husband thinks he has hidden from her.

4754. A courageous woman nowadays is one who dresses modestly.

4756. Some married women who waited for the right man to come along will tell you they didn't wait long enough.

4757. Too often nowadays the most irresistible women you meet are married.

4758. Women, like nature, to be commanded, must be obeyed.

4759. A calculating woman is one who figures out exactly how late she's going to be for a date.

4760. There are two kinds of women in the world — some hold their skirt when they run for a bus, the others grab their hat.

4761. Too often nowadays the irresistible women you meet are behind the wheel of a car.

4762. A woman never realizes how badly she needs a new car until her husband gets an unexpected promotion.

4763. Most women enjoy being bullied provided it is done in a gentlemanly manner.

4764. It usually costs a woman ten times as much to take off a pound than it does to put one on.

4765. When it comes to waging war on men, some women are chemical warfare experts.

4766. Nothing will make a woman endure great pain in silence like an attractive pair of new shoes.

4767. How much better a woman feels after a good cry depends on what she got out of it.

WOMEN'S LIBERATION

4767. By the year 2000, it will become evident that the greatest social disaster of the 20th century for women was the women's liberation movement.

WORDS

4768. The only people who really choke on their words are those who refuse to eat them.

4769. Words are treated so often as trifles when in reality they can be more devastating than rifles.

4770. When a single word makes a big difference in what you say it is usually a word you left out.

4771. Words are like feathers; it takes a lot of either to add up to much.

4772. Always remember to use words in such a way that should you have to eat them they won't feel pointed.

WORK

4773. You can tell when modern man is really working hard — by the sweat under his arms!

4774. Nothing will drive a sick man to his job like knowing how much work his wife has lined up for him if he stays home.

4775. The surest way to get awake surrounded by work is to go to sleep without cleaning up the mess in the kitchen.

4776. Anyone who loves work never feels surrounded by it on waking up.

4777. The best eraser in the world is a good day's work.

4778. When it comes to work or taxes nothing is more tiring than trying to evade them.

4779. To enjoy work you've got to.

4780. Persons who are crusading for a four-day work-week already are not at all conscientious about working a five-day week.

4781.   Nowadays a patient man is often the boss waiting for his employees to show up for work.

4782.   There are two real advantages in doing exactly what you like doing most — you free yourself from personal slavery, and you are bound to be a success.

4783.   To enjoy work you must know what you want to do next; the next minute, the next hour, the next day, the next ten years.

4784.   There is a lesson for all in this — God gives us wheat, but we must bake the bread. He gives us cotton, but we must convert it into clothing. He gives us trees, but we must build our homes. He provides the raw materials and expects us to make the finished products with them.

4785.   Anybody who is willing to dedicate himself to work towards any goal 16 hours a day for 25 years cannot miss being successful.

4786.   Hard work consists of an accumulation of easy things that you didn't do when you should have.

4787.   The only kind of pride that has never harmed a person is pride in one's work.

4788.   We need a new generation of Americans who will carry their enthusiasm to get ahead of traffic over into their jobs.

4789.   People who work only for themselves eventually discover what a poor employer they are.

4790.   Nothing is work — if you can do it untiringly!

4791.   Whan a man's work speaks for itself, he's usually a man of few words.

4792.   These days nothing gives the boss a shot in the arm like sneaking up on his help and finding them hard at work.

4793. There's a good reason why some housewives wake up surrounded by work — they went to sleep surrounded by it.

4794. The trouble with many people who object to doing a full day's work is they're such conscientious objectors.

4795. You know a person loves his work if you catch him whistling at it on Friday afternoon — and Monday mornings.

4796. There is an increasing number of persons in this world who keep alive until they get to work.

4797. Nothing is harder work than trying to find ways of avoiding it.

4798. Nothing in this world will add stature to a man more than doing his work — whatever it may be — with great conscientiousness and enthusiasm.

4799. Some persons get enjoyment out of life by rolling up their sleeves and letting the other fellow do the work.

4800. Usually the man who gets to work ahead of everybody else is the boss.

4801. The trouble with some people who object to a full day's work is they're usually already on the payroll.

4802. When a man is enthusiastic about hard work he is either self-employed or paying to have it done.

4803. A hard working girl is one who is still trying to catch a man.

4804. A father of five children is deathly sick when he doesn't show up at work.

4805 Any easy job, like an easy chair, usually is the first to wear itself out.

4806. Next to getting enthusiastic about your job, the most

important step to get ahead is to become an enthusiast about your boss.

4807. Nothing will put more zip into what you are doing today than estimating how many working days you have left in your lifetime.

4808. Judging from the number of persons who sit and look at it, work must be the most fascinating thing in the world.

4809. To enjoy work and get more fun out of life, you've got to have enough wisdom to do a lot more of it than the average person.

4810. A good executive is one who can keep his mind on his work — no matter how pretty his secretary is.

4811. A smart husband gets out of having to do a lot of chores around the house by dropping a piece of prized china now and then.

4812. All it takes to be successful is a willingness to start an eight hour day immediately after you finish the first one.

4813. Nothing helps a modern housewife to get a day's work done like the television going on the blink.

4814. The hardest working students in the world are those who set out to avoid work.

4815. People who arrive late for work usually are the first to have their desk all cleared away before quitting time.

4816. A good executive is a man who believes in sharing the credit for the work somebody else does.

4817. The fellow who lives the farthest from his work usually is the first one to get there.

4818. The real hazard of a reclining position is that when you're in it there's no way you can put your shoulder to the wheel.

4819. All play and no work leads to bankruptcy.

4820. Even though a woman's work is never done, it doesn't bother most of them.

4821. If you make work your friend, you'll find that you can get along without any other friends if you have to.

4822. Nothing makes it easier to get a lot more fun out of your work than an independent income.

4823. Of all the tonics devised by man none is more stimulating than a good day's work.

4824. The best way to ask for a raise at the top of your voice is to let your work do the talking for you.

4825. People are stimulated by example — those under you won't work unless you do.

4826. Work is like food — as long as you like it the chances are that it won't hurt you.

4827. Nothing is hard work as long as you can afford to pay somebody to do it.

4828. Nothing encourages a man to quit work early like a boss who just did.

4829. Some of the best swimmers in the world are those who drown themselves in their work.

4830. The trouble with the 8-hour day is that so many people are using it today to do an hour's work.

WORLD

4831. One of the reasons the world is putting on such a poor show today is that little of what the major actors are doing is ever rehearsed.

4832. You can tell what a bad shape the world is in by how hard you must now search to find something or somebody who is really good in it.

4833. What this world really needs on a truly international scale is open-heart surgery.

WORM

4834. The early bird not only catches the worm, but also the parking space.

4835. The fellow who always tries to worm his way out of things eventually gets hooked.

WORRY

4836. Worry is a perfect incubator; it will guarantee you a full batch of troubles.

4837. Worry is something many persons do a lot of without ever finding out why.

4838. People who can't stop worrying have but one future, and it will be a short one.

4839. Sometimes a man's deeds can be a worry to him — especially if they're heavily mortgaged.

4840. People who worry the most about the future, usually do the least to prepare for it.

WORTH

4841. Many a man is worth his weight in gold, but only his beneficiary can collect it.

WRITTEN WORD

4842. The greatest force that the written word alone can exercise is its ability to inflame one's mind, one's heart, one's conscience into action — good or bad— without raising a voice, using physical coercion, or public embarrassment.

YOUNG GIRL

4843. A young girl is growing up when she wouldn't be seen dead in her dad's shirt.

4844. Nobody can do more for a young girl's complexion than a handsome young man who has fallen in love with her.

4845. A young girl becomes a lady as soon as she starts complaining that her feet are killing her.

YOUNG MEN

4846. Many young men don't believe in standing on their own two feet as long as they can ride on four wheels.

YOUNGER GENERATION

4847. You can spot those in our younger generation who are headed for big things — they always get their weekend homework done first thing Friday nights.

YOUR WAY

4848. If you insist in having your own way you should not be disappointed if you get it.

4849. The wrong way to make your way in the world is to insist on having it.

4850. You never really know how wonderful the youth of America really are until you turn off television and talk to them.

4851. When it comes to holding on to their youth, college girls wouldn't dare think of introducing him to anybody.

SUBJECT INDEX

A

Ability, 1, 166, 1157
Abnormal, 2
Absence, 3
Accidents, 4, 5, 3581, 4748
Achievements, 7, 1225
Acid-test, 8
Accordian player, 6
Acting, 9
Action, 10, 12, 13, 14, 15, 895, 978
Actors, 530
Addiction, 16
Addresses, 17
Admiration, 18, 19, 20, 1800
Admissions, 21, 22
Adolescence, 24
Adultery, 33
Adults, 26, 27, 28, 29, 32, 34, 35, 528, 4659
Advantages, 36-41, 541, 3341
Adversity, 42, 43, 44, 2241
Advice, 45-55, 1288
Affection, 55
Affluence, 3406
After-dinner speakers, 56
Age, 57-72
Aging, 73, 75-76
Agreement, 77, 78
Aim, 79, 337, 4158
Air conditioner, 3116
Airplane, 80
Air travel, 81
Alarm, 82, 83
Alarm clock, 84, 85, 139
Alcohol, 86, 87, 2011, 2058
Algebra, 575, 2399
Alimony, 613, 989
Allowance, 383
Amazement, 88
Ambition, 89-91, 1701
America, 93-107, 1707, 2674, 4189
Americans, 97, 108, 110-113, 114
Amour, 115
Anatomy, 116
Ancestry, 117
Anger, 119, 1983
Anniversary, 120
Announcement, 121
Annoyances, 122, 3789
Annual physical, 3433
Antifreeze, 123
Antique furniture, 124, 570
Antiques, 124
Apartments, 125, 140
Apex, 125
Appearance, 126, 127
Appetite, 127, 392, 1334
Applause, 128
Appliances, 129, 1866, 1935
Appreciate, 130-132
Appreciation, 133
April, 134
Architects, 335
Arguments, 5, 135-141, 582, 630, 3366, 3577, 3705
Arithmetic, 143-147, 257, 2710
Armpit, 3621
Arm's length, 148
Artists, 149
Assets, 150, 151, 152, 160
Assistants, 153
Astonishment, 154, 155
Astronaut, 156
Atherosclerosis, 157
Atom, 158, 1666
Attention, 159-167, 1868
Attitudes, 168, 169
Attractiveness, 170
Audience, 171, 172
Authority, 173-175
Auto insurance, 177
Autographs, 176
Automobile, 3419
Average, 178, 179, 4040, 4447
Awakening, 180

B

Babies, 181-183, 185, 186, 1364, 3065
Baby-sitter, 188
Bachelor, 189-195, 1045, 1756, 1757, 2668, 2821, 3016, 4210
Back seat, 1134
Backbone, 196
Backyard, 58, 66, 565
Bacteria, 269
Bad actor, 197
Bad cold, 198
Badge, 1748
Badness, 199, 200
Baggage, 1696, 4390
Baggage claim, 81
Balance, 201, 202, 590, 2468, 4597
Balance of payments, 203
Baldness, 204, 205, 1599, 1600, 3064
Ball game, 206
Banana peel, 1339
Bank account, 207, 3634
Bank balance, 1706
Banking, 208
Bankruptcy, 209
Barbers, 210, 211
Bargain, 212, 213, 214, 2311, 2660, 4268
Base of operations, 215
Bath, 2818
Bathing suit, 19, 216, 217, 218, 219, 2220
Bathrub, 220
Beach, 221
Bearings, 3946
Beatniks, 222
Beauticians, 223
Beauty, 224, 225, 226, 227, 228, 240
Bedroom closet, 167
Beginning, 230, 231
Behavior, 232, 233
Belief, 234
Belittle, 235
Bellyachers, 236
Beneficiary, 4646
Bermuda shorts, 127
Best foot, 237
Best of life, 238
Best seller, 239, 3711
Better treat, 254
Bicentennial (U.S.A.), 241
Big gun, 244
Bigness, 243
Bills, 245, 246, 247, 248, 249, 250, 953, 1312, 2252, 2741, 3412
Birth control, 251
Birthdays, 70, 252, 253, 749
Blackmail, 2002
Blame, 255, 3849
Blank check, 256, 3426
Blessings, 145, 257, 2398, 2424
Bliss, 1834
Blondes, 258, 259, 656, 4513
Blood pressure, 260
Blood thirsty, 2767
Bluffing, 3726
Board, 3295
Board of directors, 3481
Boasting, 261, 262, 263, 264
Body chemistry, 378
Boners, 265, 1347
Bonus, 2792. 3044
Book, 266, 267, 3526
Boot straps, 3765
Bore, 268, 269, 1962, 3157
Borrower, 270, 2659, 3042
Boss, 14, 270, 271-279, 3112, 3424, 3616, 4792, 4800, 4806
Bother, 279
Brains, 152, 286, 3689
Brakes, 3906
Braying, 3210
Bread, 287
Breakfast, 288-290, 1961
Breath, 291

470

471

472